Nathan MacDonald
Priestly Rule

Beihefte zur Zeitschrift für die alttestamentliche Wissenschaft

Edited by
John Barton, Ronald Hendel,
Reinhard G. Kratz and Markus Witte

Volume 476

Nathan MacDonald
Priestly Rule

Polemic and Biblical Interpretation in Ezekiel 44

DE GRUYTER

ISBN 978-3-11-041003-7
e-ISBN (PDF) 978-3-11-041186-7
e-ISBN (EPUB) 978-3-11-041201-7
ISSN 0934-2575

Library of Congress Cataloging-in-Publication Data
A CIP catalog record for this book has been applied for at the Library of Congress.

Bibliographic information published by the Deutsche Nationalbibliothek
The Deutsche Nationalbibliothek lists this publication in the Deutsche Nationalbibliografie;
detailed bibliographic data are available on the Internet at http://dnb.dnb.de.

© 2015 Walter de Gruyter GmbH, Berlin/Boston
Printing and binding: CPI books GmbH, Leck
♾ Printed on acid-free paper
Printed in Germany

www.degruyter.com

MIX
Papier aus verantwor-
tungsvollen Quellen
FSC® C083411

Contents

Preface

The following book is an extended technical essay devoted to the interpretation of Ezekiel 44. It began a number of years ago as a brief examination of the relationship between that chapter and Numbers 18, but it soon became apparent that the challenges of Ezekiel 44 required more attention than I had initially anticipated. Since the chapter has played such an important role in scholarly reconstructions of the history of Israel's priesthood, I hope the reader will indulge my granting it an extended and detailed analysis. I have tried as far as possible to avoid superfluous discussion or merely repeating arguments already made by others.

The book has benefited from an extended gestation, which is to say I have profited from the wisdom of many others. Earlier versions of the argument were presented at the Georg-August-Universität Göttingen, the Humboldt Universität zu Berlin, Universität Zürich, the University of St Andrews, and at the annual Society of Biblical Literature meetings in San Francisco and San Diego. I am grateful to those who probed my interpretation and offered various criticisms. At the risk of forgetting someone who made an important contribution to my thinking, I am grateful especially to Peter Altmann, Stephen Cook, Anselm Hagedorn, Anja Klein, Reinhard Kratz, Thomas Krüger, Noam Mizrahi, Thilo Rudnig, Harald Samuel, Konrad Schmid, Jean-Louis Ska, and Hermann Spieckermann. My research team in Göttingen provided detailed criticisms from the time that I began to work on this topic, notably Robert Barrett, Ken Brown, Izaak de Hulster, Lydia Lee, and Roberto Piani. Their challenges at the earliest stage of my research had a decisive effect on the structure of the argument. In returning to the UK, and Cambridge in particular, I have enjoyed the advice of Jim Aitken, Charlotte Hempel and Bill Tooman. Any deficiencies that remain are attributable to me alone.

I am grateful to the Alexander von Humboldt Stiftung and the Bundesministerium für Bildung und Forschung who financially supported the research of the Sofja-Kovalevskaja Research Project, *Early Jewish Monotheisms* at the Georg-August-Universität Göttingen where this book was originally conceived. I am also grateful to the editors of *Beihefte zur Zeitschrift für die Alttestamentliche Wissenschaft* for accepting this volume into their series.

Claire as always deserves more thanks than anyone else. She has encouraged me onwards and insisted on regular updates and a definitive timetable. Callum, Eilidh and Morven have generously allowed me to work on "Daddy's book" despite there having been interesting films to watch, important games to play and exciting books to read. Finally, the book is dedicated to my own father, who has waited patiently for his book: ὁ γὰρ κύριος ἐδόξασεν πατέρα ἐπὶ τέκνοις (Sir 3:2).

Introduction: Post-Exilic Polemic over the Priesthood

At the beginning of the sixth-century BCE the small city-state of Judah in the southern Levant was destroyed by Nebuchadrezzar II and absorbed into the Neo-Babylonian Empire. A series of catastrophic political miscalculations by the Judean leaders in the preceding years had seen significant numbers of the upper classes and skilled artisans exiled to Babylonia.[1] When the last Hebrew kingdom was brought to an end, a further group of survivors was deported. In biblical memory these deportations began the Babylonian Exile: the land was depopulated for seventy years, and only under the Persian king Cyrus did the Jews return to their homeland. In reality, many Judeans were never exiled, and the exiled group though influential was fairly small. Nor did the Babylonian exiles return as a single group. Indeed, some did not return at all, and those that did trickled back to the Persian province of Yehud over many decades.[2]

The small group of Jews that returned from Babylon encountered a different reality to the one their ancestors had known. There was no king and the temple of YHWH in Jerusalem was destroyed. Towns and cities were ruined, properties had been occupied by those who had remained in the land, and economic activity was on a much lower level as a result of the depopulation of the country. Those who returned sought to establish a community orientated around the family and the rebuilt temple. Judean descent ensured membership of the community, and bearing children safeguarded its survival. These norms emphasized the continuity of the community and secured both the past and the future. In this way the returnees sought to create a new reality that would erase the rupture of exile.

However effective this was as a survival strategy, it marginalized a significant part of the population of Persian Yehud. Those who had never been in Bab-

---

1 The first deportation occurred after the defeat of Jehoiakim in 597 BCE. For a history of the period see Rainer Albertz, *Israel in Exile: The History and Literature of the Sixth Century B.C.E.*, Studies in Biblical Literature 3 (Atlanta: Society of Biblical Literature, 2003), 45–138.

2 Since the 1990s it has been appreciated that "exile" is far from being a neutral designation of the period after the fall of Jerusalem. In particular, it assumes the perspective of those who wrote, edited and transmitted books like Jeremiah and Chronicles. True Israel consisted of those who had been deported to Babylon and returned to Yehud many years later during the Persian period. See Lester L. Grabbe, ed., *Leading Captivity Captive: "The Exile" as History and Ideology*, JSOTSup 278 (Sheffield: Sheffield Academic, 1998); Hans M. Barstad, *The Myth of the Empty Land: A Study in the History and Archaeology of Judah during the "Exilic" Period*, SO Fascicle Supplement 28 (Oslo: Scandinavian University Press, 1996).

ylonia and had lived in the Judean hillsides their entire lives found themselves outsiders in their own country. The returning group enjoyed the patronage of the Persian overlords and could mould the community norms to a considerable degree. Inevitably perhaps these different visions of the community and its membership collided over the newly rebuilt temple and who could participate in its cultic worship.

Evidence for this communal struggle surface in the biblical text as is apparent if we read the opening oracle of Trito-Isaiah together with Ezekiel's temple vision. Isaiah 56 addresses those who regard themselves as cut off from the community: the son of a foreigner[3] and the eunuch. For both of them issues of lineage left them without a place in a society where the family gave meaning and location. The son of a foreigner could not claim pure Judean ancestry; the eunuch could not father the next generation. In Trito-Isaiah's oracle both groups are granted an honoured place within the community.

> For thus says the LORD:
>
> To the eunuchs who keep my Sabbaths, who choose the things that please me and hold fast my covenant, I will give, in my house and within my walls, a monument and a name better than sons and daughters; I will give them an everlasting name that shall not be cut off.
>
> And the foreigners who join themselves to the LORD, to minister to him, to love the name of the LORD, and to be his servants, all who keep the Sabbath, and do not profane it, and hold fast my covenant – these I will bring to my holy mountain, and make them joyful in my house of prayer; their burnt offerings and their sacrifices will be accepted on my altar; for my house shall be called a house of prayer for all peoples (Isa 56:4–7; NRSV)

The prophet envisages the eunuchs having a memorial in the temple and the son of a foreigner will bring sacrifices and minister in the temple, with perhaps even priestly service in view.

Trito-Isaiah's hopes are the opposite of what Ezekiel had in view in his temple vision. Ezekiel unequivocally rejected the presence of anyone of foreign descent in the temple he envisaged.

> Thus says the Lord GOD: O house of Israel, let there be an end to all your abominations in admitting foreigners, uncircumcised in heart and flesh, to be in my sanctuary, profaning my temple when you offer to me my food, the fat and the blood. You have broken my covenant with all your abominations. And you have not kept charge of my sacred offerings; but you have appointed foreigners to act for you in keeping my charge in my sanctuary. Thus says

---

3 The Hebrew expression is בן־נכר. I have used a gender-specific translation since males, rather than females are in view.

the Lord GOD: No foreigner, uncircumcised in heart and flesh, of all the foreigners who are among the people of Israel, shall enter my sanctuary. (Ezek 44:6–9; NRSV).

The prophet accuses the Israelites of allowing the sons of foreigners to act as priests – guarding the sanctuary and offering sacrifices – and condemns it in the strongest possible terms. It is an abomination, a profanation, a breach of the covenant. Not only must the son of a foreigner not offer sacrifices, he may not even enter the sanctuary.

The two prophecies have a significant shared vocabulary. Both passages concern the son of a foreigner (בן נכר) and their access (בוא) to the temple, which YHWH calls "my house" (ביתי). The cultic service in the temple is expressed with the verb "to serve" (שרת). According to Isaiah 56 the son of a foreigner must avoid profaning (חלל) the Sabbath and hold fast to my covenant (בריתי), whilst in Ezekiel the admission of the sons of a foreigner is a profanation (חלל) of the sanctuary and a breaking of my covenant (בריתי). The lexical connections are so many and so precise that it cannot be doubted that both texts stand in some relation to each other. It would appear, as Fishbane remarks, that "we have hit upon a live post-exilic issue".[4] Remarkably, although opposite positions are ventured, both books present their stance as divinely authorized.

The story about how these two texts relate to one another is usually told a certain way. Ezekiel and the circles that transmitted his prophecies numbered amongst the upper class Judeans exiled to Babylonia. Ezekiel himself was a member of the powerful Zadokite family of priests that had prevailed in the Jerusalem Temple. The oracle is a piece of Zadokite propaganda that blames the exile and the destruction of the temple on other priestly groups. These Levitical families were accused of encouraging foreign participation in the temple, and may even have been foreigners themselves. Ezekiel's temple vision envisages a new temple shaped according to Zadokite ideals. The Levites were given a subordinate role in the temple hierarchy and forbidden from offering sacrifices. The collection of laws about priestly conduct that follows the oracle is an early fragment of Zadokite priestly tradition (Ezek 44:17–31). Trito-Isaiah's oracle is a polemical response to Zadokite pretensions written by someone with sympathies for the priestly families that had been marginalized. Ezekiel's narrow, xenophobic vision of a restored temple is countered by a more generous acceptance of outsiders.

My intention in this book is to demonstrate that this common understanding cannot be maintained. At its very simplest then this book is no more than a re-

---

4 Michael A. Fishbane, *Biblical Interpretation in Ancient Israel* (Oxford: Clarendon, 1985), 138.

newed examination of Ezekiel 44, which will demonstrate that Ezekiel 44 is a response to Isaiah 56, and not the reverse. But does such an argument demand an entire book? Is this not an example of scholarly self-indulgence on my part? An example of the hyper-specialization that afflicts modern biblical study where more and more is written about less and less? In fact, this book will touch upon a variety of issues, including the nature of scriptural interpretation in the Second Temple period, the relationship between texts and the world of Persian and Early Hellenistic Yehud, the origins of the division between Levites and priests, and the existence of the Zadokite priestly sept. To understand how this can be the case, it is necessary to offer a brief review of Ezekiel 44 in modern scholarship.

1 Ezekiel 44 in Modern Scholarship

Ezekiel 44 is the pivotal text in the Hebrew Bible for scholarly reconstructions of the history of the Israelite priesthood. It assumed this position as a result of the seminal exposition in the fourth chapter of Julius Wellhausen's *Prolegomena to the History of Israel*. According to Wellhausen the distinction between the priests and the Levites was not found earlier than Ezekiel. Although the priestly literature of the Pentateuch portrayed the origins of both groups of cultic functionaries in the Mosaic period and sharply distinguished them (esp. Numbers 1–4; 16–18), the history of monarchic Israel showed no evidence of this distinction. In some texts Levites take a central role in the cult (Judges 17–18), whilst in others Levites and priests are equated (Deuteronomy 18). According to Wellhausen there were numerous cultic sites in Israel and Judah prior to Josiah's reform in the late seventh-century BCE. Each site had a hereditary priesthood, and various priestly families were active throughout the Hebrew kingdoms. These priests were served by foreign captives, who Wellhausen identified as the *netinim* known from Ezra-Nehemiah and Chronicles. They were assigned various menial roles within the cult. The reform of worship during Josiah's reign centralized sacrificial worship in Jerusalem. At a stroke all the priests at the high places outside Jerusalem were made redundant (2Kgs 23:9). The writer of Deuteronomy anticipated the social problems that might result and sought to prevent them by granting the provincial priests, whom Deuteronomy called "Levitical priests", the right to participate in the Jerusalem cult (Deut 18:6–8). Deuteronomy's idealistic vision was never realized, probably thwarted by the political power of the Zadokites who were the incumbents in Jerusalem.

In Wellhausen's estimation the sharp distinction between priests and Levites finds its first literary expression in Ezekiel, though Ezekiel's priestly hierarchy merely reflected the reality that operated in late monarchic Judah. The Jerusalem Zadokites serve as priests, but the non-Jerusalem priests were excluded from cultic service, performing instead the menial roles of the *netinim*. These former priests were demoted to the status of Levites, and Ezekiel explained their subordination as a consequence of their cultic infractions. The Levites had profaned the sanctuary by permitting foreigners to enter it and offer sacrifices. As Wellhausen famously put it, "Ezekiel merely drapes the logic of facts with a mantle of morality".[5] Ezekiel's cultic innovation was only later projected back onto the Mosaic period by the post-exilic composers of the Priestly code. For them the distinction between Levites and priests was ordained at Mount Sinai. In the later book of Chronicles, Israel's history from Samuel and Kings was systematically rewritten to reflect, amongst other things, this canonical division between Levites and priests.

It would be difficult to overstate the importance of Wellhausen's reconstruction of the history of the Israelite priesthood, and consequently Ezekiel 44, for later scholars of the Old Testament.[6] Not only was Wellhausen's thesis widely accepted with subsequent scholars working out in more detail particular aspects of it, but even Wellhausen's critics have taken his account as their starting point in offering alternative reconstructions.[7] Criticisms of Wellhausen's hypothesis often focused around a number of debatable interpretative moves. The first of these was his equation of the priests of the high places in 2 Kings 23 with the Levites of Deuteronomy 18.[8] Similarly, questions have been raised about Wellhausen's equation of the high places known from 2 Kings 23 with the worship of idols (גלולים) known from Ezekiel 44. Nowhere in Ezekiel are the גלולים associated

---

5 Julius Wellhausen, *Prolegomena to the History of Israel with a Reprint of the Article Israel from the "Encyclopaedia Britannica"*, trans. John Sutherland Black and Allan Menzies (Edinburgh: Black, 1885), 124.

6 It is thus rather odd that Nurmela should claim concerning Ezekiel 44 that "in my judgement, previous research has not paid sufficient attention to this passage" (Risto Nurmela, *The Levites: Their Emergence as a Second-Class Priesthood*, SFSHJ 193 [Atlanta: Scholars Press, 1998], 177).

7 For accounts of the history of subsequent scholarship, see, *inter alia*, Julia M. O'Brien, *Priest and Levite in Malachi*, SBLDS 121 (Atlanta: Scholars Press, 1990), 1–23; Joachim Schaper, *Priester und Leviten im achämenidischen Juda: Studien zur Kult- und Sozialgeschichte Israels in persischer Zeit*, FAT 31 (Tübingen: Mohr Siebeck, 2000), 1–9.

8 See discussion in Ulrich Dahmen, *Leviten und Priester im Deuteronomium: Literarkritik und redaktionsgeschichtliche Studien*, BBB 110 (Bodenheim: Philo, 1996), 279–302; Schaper, *Priester und Leviten*, 79–95; Antonius H. J. Gunneweg, *Leviten und Priester: Hauptlinien der Traditionsbildung und Geschichte des israelitisch-jüdischen Kultpersonals*, FRLANT 89 (Göttingen: Vandenhoeck & Ruprecht, 1965), 118–26; J. Gordon McConville, "Priests and Levites in Ezekiel: A Crux in the Interpretation of Israel's History", TynBul 34 (1983): 3–31; Ernest Nicholson, "Once Again Josiah and the Priests of the High Places (II Reg 23,8a.9)", ZAW 124 (2012): 356–68.

with the high places.[9] Thirdly, a number of scholars have questioned the relative dating of P and Ezekiel. Haran, for example, argues that P predates Ezekiel and that Ezekiel was part of the priestly school. The distinction between Levites and priests could not have originated with Ezekiel, since the Priestly writer already knew it.[10]

Whilst Haran holds to the compositional integrity of the book of Ezekiel and Wellhausen understood Ezekiel 44 to belong to the *ipsissima verba* of the prophet, many recent scholars have reckoned with a more complex redactional history for the chapter, and viewed the instructions about priests and Levites to be from a later hand than the prophet Ezekiel himself. Gese made the decisive contribution in the late 1950s. Prior to his tradition-historical study of chapters 40–48, Ezek 44 had largely been attributed to the exilic prophet.[11] Gese argued that the original prophetic vision, to be found in chs. 40–42, was expanded principally in two discrete strata. A *nasi*-layer introduced a leader into the temple vision. Significantly, this leader was identified as a prince, נשׂיא, rather than as a king (44:1–3, 45:20–25 and 46:1–10, 12). The *nasi*-layer was later extended through material on the division of the land (48:1–29) and various secondary additions (e. g. 45:8b–9; 46:16–18). The Zadokite-layer concerned priestly rights and responsibilities, and was largely to be found in Ezekiel 44 (vv. 6–16, 28–30a). It too was extended through various additions (44:17–27, 31; 45:1–8) and a number of glosses elsewhere in chapters 40–48 (40:46b, 48:11; 43:19). Scholarship since Gese has largely followed him in recognizing 44:6–31 as an interruption to the tour of the guiding angel, with vv. 4–5 a redactional suture.[12] Many have also accepted his analysis that vv. 6–16, 28–30a are a compositional unity,[13] and vv. 17–27 are a later and dependent set of instructions that resulted from a pro-

---

9 Stephen L. Cook, "Innerbiblical Interpretation in Ezekiel 44 and the History of Israel's Priesthood", *JBL* 114 (1995): 195.

10 Menahem Haran, "The Law-Code of Ezekiel XL–XLVIII and Its Relation to the Priestly School", *HUCA* 50 (1979): 45–71; Menahem Haran, *Temples and Temple-Service in Ancient Israel* (Winona Lake, IN: Eisenbrauns, 1985); Menahem Haran, "Ezekiel, P, and the Priestly School", *VT* 58 (2008): 211–18.

11 For references see Hartmut Gese, *Der Verfassungsentwurf des Ezechiel*, BHT 25 (Tübingen: Mohr Siebeck, 1957), 112 n. 1.

12 Ibid., 52–57; Gunneweg, *Leviten und Priester*, 188; Walther Zimmerli, *Ezechiel*, BKAT XIII (Neukirchen-Vluyn: Neukirchener Verlag, 1969), 1113–17; Walther Eichrodt, *Ezekiel: A Commentary*, OTL (Philadelphia: Westminster, 1970), 562–63; Steven Shawn Tuell, *The Law of the Temple in Ezekiel 40–48*, HSM 49 (Atlanta: Scholars Press, 1992), 54–62; Jon Douglas Levenson, *Theology of the Program of Restoration of Ezekiel 40–48*, HSM 10 (Missoula, MT: Scholars Press, 1976), 131.

13 Zimmerli, *Ezechiel*, 1136; Gese, *Der Verfassungsentwurf*, 62.

cess of *Fortschreibung*.[14] Though there are also some who hold that vv. 17–31 are essentially a compositional unity.[15]

Assigning Ezekiel 44 to a time after the prophet Ezekiel flourished raises the possibility of a different historical contextualization than that proposed by Wellhausen. For Wellhausen, Ezekiel 44 marked the *end* of a historical process that was then codified in the priestly literature. For much recent scholarship, Ezekiel 44 marks rather the *beginning* of the struggles for political ascendancy in postmonarchic Judaism. Ezekiel attributes blame for the exile to the Levites and favours Zadokite leadership for the future. His programme elicits response and counter-response.

A seminal contribution to understanding Ezekiel 44 as the cradle of post-exilic conflict was made by Paul Hanson in his influential study *The Dawn of Apocalyptic*. Hanson's central thesis was that competing visions for the restoration of Yehud could be found in the Hebrew Bible, which reflected strife between different priestly groups in Persian Yehud. Returning Zadokites sought to establish a hierocratic government with the assistance of the Achaemenid government, but they were resisted in those efforts by the Levites who had remained in Palestine and advocated a more egalitarian theocratic vision. Hanson identifies Ezekiel 44 as "a Zadokite addition to the prophecy of Ezekiel",[16] during the period when the first groups of exiles were returning from Babylon.[17] The views of the Zadokites were reflected not only in Ezekiel, but also in the books of Haggai and Zechariah. The Levitical literary legacy is found especially in Isaiah 56–66 and Zechariah 9–14, which reflect the anguish and proto-apocalyptic fantasies of those who had been disenfranchised by the Zadokite seizure of power.

Central to Hanson's thesis is the identification of competing priestly groups in post-exilic Yehud and the association of them with different textual compositions. As we have seen, one of the important contributions of Hanson's book in comparison to Wellhausen's earlier work is to highlight Isaiah 56–66 as the inclusivist response to the Zadokite programme articulated in Ezekiel 40–48.[18] But Hanson's thesis is vulnerable to the criticism that his binary understanding of

---

14 Eichrodt, *Ezekiel*, 566; Zimmerli, *Ezechiel*, 1123, 1133–40; Gese, *Der Verfassungsentwurf*, 64.

15 Hans Ferdinand Fuhs, *Ezechiel*, 2nd ed., NEchtB 22 (Würzburg: Echter, 1986), 246; Tuell, *Law of the Temple*, 59–60.

16 Paul D. Hanson, *The Dawn of Apocalyptic* (Philadelphia: Fortress, 1975), 227.

17 The Zadokite editing of Ezekiel's temple vision, including Ezek 44:6–16, is to be dated between the last quarter of the sixth-century and the middle of the fifth-century BCE (Ibid., 263–69).

18 Hanson adopts Wellhausen's account of the priesthood's history during the Josianic reformation, but thinks that Numbers 18 reflects a late pre-exilic attempt by the Zadokites to lay exclusive claim to the priestly office (Ibid., 220–28).

Yehud society is too simplistic, and the trajectories of competing parties "risk being too speculative to be useful".[19]

Much recent work has been chastened by such criticisms and has tended to concentrate on establishing textual relationships before reconstructing the social and political movements that gave rise to the text. Michael Fishbane's groundbreaking book, *Biblical Interpretation in Ancient Israel*, marked the beginning of a new, disciplined focus upon intertextual relationships. Fishbane argued that Ezekiel 44 was an "exegetical oracle". It utilized Numbers 18, the instructions about priestly perquisites, and possibly Deuteronomy 23, which excludes foreigners from the Israelite assembly.[20] Fishbane's careful textual argumentation is weakened by simply assuming the direction of influence, and his failure to engage with alternative accounts of the interrelationship between these chapters, most notably Wellhausen's.

Many scholarly examinations of Ezekiel 44 since Fishbane have maintained this attention to the phenomenon of inner-biblical interpretation. The many different proposals for intertextual relationships point to the difficulty in determining the textual precursors to Ezekiel 44. But they also raise the problem of how intertextual allusion might complicate the issue of historical referentiality. Earlier scholarship often viewed the text as a mirror of its moment of composition. In contrast, Levenson warned about the challenges the formulaic language of Ezekiel 44 presented to any reconstruction of Israel's religious history. Such language "keeps us at a distance from its historical nucleus, if it has one".[21] Levenson's instinct is to seek for allusions in Israel's canonical history, rather than finding reflections of Ezekiel's immediate historical context. He admits that the original story that Ezekiel draws upon may have been lost, but notes a suggestive association of foreigners, priesthood and idolatry in the Baal Peor incident (Numbers 25).

In his arguments about the importance of Israel's narrative history for the Zadokite writer, Cook echoes Levenson's strictures. He is similarly wary of attempts to reconstruct Ezekiel's immediate historical context, arguing that in critical scholarship "Ezekiel 44 has been misconstrued as a mirror of history".[22] He views the reference to גלולים as an Ezekielian trope that should not be understood literally, and draws attention to a number of parallels with the story of Korah's rebellion in Numbers 16 – 18. According to Cook the Zadokite author writes

---

19 Joseph Blenkinsopp, *A History of Prophecy in Israel*, 2nd ed. (Philadelphia: Westminster, 1996), 243 – 44.

20 Fishbane, *Biblical Interpretation*, 138 – 43.

21 Levenson, *Program of Restoration*, 134.

22 Cook, "Innerbiblical Interpretation", 186.

in light of the narrative history of the canon, rather than Israelite history as scholars critically reconstruct it. He is constrained in his response to circumstances in Persian Yehud by an existing priestly narrative that he views as authoritative.

In contrast to Levenson and Cook, Tuell and Schaper are more confident in the ability of historical scholarship to reconstruct the conflicting parties of the Persian period, and see the insights of inner-biblical exegesis as a means of doing that. Both argue that Isaiah 56 is a polemical response to Ezekiel 44.[23] Tuell insists that attention to biblical interpretation can confirm Hanson's analysis that Levites resisted Zadokite claims. Schaper develops Fishbane's suggestion that both passages may be a response to Deuteronomy 23: "we are confronted with a *clash of interpretations* of one and the same reference text, interpretations that reflect a clash of *interests* in post-exilic Judaean society".[24]

The focus on inner-biblical interpretation is most especially characteristic of recent American scholarship. In continental Europe the detailed redaction-critical studies of Rudnig and Konkel continue in the tradition of Gese and Zimmerli.[25] Rudnig seeks to correct Gese's tendency to consider chapters 40 – 48 separately from the rest of the book of Ezekiel. His most important departure from other redaction-critical work on chapter 44 is his challenge to the unity of vv. 6 – 16, observing especially that in vv. 9 – 16 the accused and accusation is different from that in vv. 6 – 8. In his view vv. 6 – 7 preserve the original accusation against the exiles that accompanied Jehoachin: they had allowed foreigners to transgress the temple *temenos*. Only later was this accusation expanded in two stages into a programme to separate Levites and priests.[26] Unfortunately, Rudnig ignores the phenomenon of inner-biblical interpretation and the possibility that the re-use of authoritative texts in Ezekiel 44 might shed light on the redaction of

---

23 Steven Shawn Tuell, "The Priesthood of the 'Foreigner': Evidence of Competing Politics in Ezekiel 44:1 – 14 and Isaiah 56:1 – 8", in *Constituting the Community: Studies on the Polity of Ancient Israel*, ed. John T. Strong and Steven Shawn Tuell (Winona Lake, IN: Eisenbrauns, 2005), 183 – 204; Joachim Schaper, "Rereading the Law: Inner-Biblical Exegesis of Divine Oracles in Ezekiel 44 and Isaiah 56", in *Recht und Ethik im Alten Testament: Beiträge des Symposiums "Das Alte Testament und die Kultur der Moderne" anlässlich des 100. Geburtstag Gerhard von Rads (1901 – 1971), Heidelberg, 18 – 21 Oktober 2001*, ed. Bernard M. Levinson and Eckart Otto, Altes Testament und Moderne 13 (Münster: Lit, 2004), 125 – 44.
24 Schaper, "Rereading the Law", 137. Italics original.
25 Thilo Alexander Rudnig, *Heilig und Profan: Redaktionskritische Studien zu Ez 40 – 48*, BZAW 287 (Berlin: de Gruyter, 2000).
26 Ibid., 204 – 215, 280 – 304.

the chapter.[27] Konkel follows Gese in identifying an original temple vision and two levels of *Fortschreibung*, one concerned with the *nasi* and the other with the Zadokites. Konkel's primary concern is understanding the location of each layer of the text tradition historically. As part of this Konkel also utilizes inner-biblical interpretation, especially in his discussion of the second level of *Fortschreibung*, in which he argues that Ezekiel 44 is dependent upon priestly texts.[28]

2 History and Hermeneutics, Redaction and Reception

Whilst there has been widespread agreement since Wellhausen that Ezekiel 44 is *the* pivotal text for understanding the history of the Israelite priesthood, the ways in which its significance has been understood has shifted markedly. Recent work has shown that earlier scholarship was generally too hasty in its move from text to historical hypothesis. In this respect attention to inner-biblical interpretation has been a helpful corrective to earlier work. The period for which the text is perceived to be relevant has also shifted. Ezekiel 44 is no longer an obvious exilic text and fewer scholars claim it sheds light on the priesthood in the pre-exilic period; its relevance to post-exilic debates about community boundaries, purity and the place of foreigners has become more and more clear. In this respect attention to the redaction of Ezekiel has helped refocus our historical lens.

Despite the attempts by scholars such as Levenson and Cook to chasten the instinct to move quickly from text to history, it is still the case that easy appeals are made to Ezekiel 44 as though its historical contribution were transparent. Levenson and Cook do not deny that Ezekiel 44 arose within a particular historical context that it reflects in certain ways. Nor is it the case that we should not be interested in the history behind the text. Far from it! They merely remind us that late biblical writers' perception of their present was shaped by a textually-constructed past.

---

27 For a perceptive attempt to combine insights from redaction criticism and inner-biblical interpretation in the exegesis of Ezekiel see Klein's dissertation on Ezekiel 34–39 (Anja Klein, *Schriftauslegung im Ezechielbuch: Redaktionsgeschichtliche Untersuchungen zu Ez 34–39*, BZAW 391 [Berlin: de Gruyter, 2008]). Some of her insights are now accessible in an article published in English (Anja Klein, "Prophecy Continued: Reflections on Innerbiblical Exegesis in the Book of Ezekiel", *VT* 60 [2010]: 571–82).
28 Michael Dominik Konkel, *Architektonik des Heiligen: Studien zur Zweiten Tempelvision Ezechiels (Ez 40–48)*, BBB 129 (Berlin: Philo, 2001).

As we have seen, the current scholarly approaches to Ezekiel 44 are dominated by redaction criticism and the analysis of inner-biblical interpretation. Only occasionally are both methodological perspectives utilized, but both approaches have their merits and need to be related with one another adequately. Redaction critical analysis is fine-tuned to detect inconsistencies that point to textual reworking. But inconsistencies may result from textual allusion or redaction. In addition, our sketch of the history of research reveals that various questions remain unresolved. In the matter of inner-biblical interpretation, disagreements persist over the exact textual precursors to Ezekiel 44, and the direction of influence. In the matter of redaction history, disagreements persist about the integrity of Ezekiel 44 and the details of its redaction.

History and hermeneutics, redaction and reception: these are the axes about which this book will turn. But how should these be related? I have already indicated that this book is written from the conviction that the relationship of Ezekiel 44 to Isaiah 56 has been misconceived. It is only as the relevant texts are subject to careful redactional analysis alongside an unravelling of their inner-biblical relationships that we can proceed with confidence to issues of historical referentiality.

2.1 Methodological Issues in Examining Inner-Biblical Interpretation

Since the issues of inner-biblical interpretation, and the related question of the direction of textual dependence, will occupy us for good parts of this book, it is worthwhile considering some of the methodological issues around inner-biblical interpretation. The central and most challenging problem facing the interpreter of Ezekiel 44 is determining the textual relationships with other similar biblical texts. Only when this has been resolved in a satisfactory manner is it possible to address questions of religio-historical significance. Fortunately, the phenomenon of inner-biblical interpretation has received considerable scholarly attention since the publication of Fishbane's *Biblical Interpretation in Ancient Israel*.[29] There is no need to review recent scholarship in detail, since a couple of competent surveys now exist in German and English.[30] We need only make a number of

---

29 Fishbane, *Biblical Interpretation*.
30 Bernard M. Levinson, *Legal Revision and Religious Renewal in Ancient Israel* (Cambridge: Cambridge University Press, 2008); Konrad Schmid, "Innerbiblische Schriftauslegung: Aspekte der Forschungsgeschichte", in *Schriftauslegung in der Schrift: Festschrift für Odil Hannes Steck zu seinem 65. Geburtstag*, ed. Konrad Schmid, Reinhard Gregor Kratz, and Thomas Krüger, BZAW 300 (Berlin: de Gruyter, 2000), 1–22.

observations about methodological issues as they touch upon the question of how to detect textual relationships and direction of influence.

It is increasingly apparent that there was a remarkable level of textual consciousness amongst scribes in Second Temple Judaism, evidenced through inner-biblical citation, transformation and interpretation. The scribes' detailed knowledge of a small number of texts suggests a scribal curriculum and training where texts were committed to memory.[31] This process of textual interpretation is evidenced in the different recensions of biblical books, as we know them from the Qumran biblical scrolls and the early versions, particularly the Old Greek translations. It is also to be seen in Jewish compositions from this period such as the Temple Scroll, Jubilees and other examples of rewritten Scripture. It is also apparent in the close parallels between biblical texts such as Samuel–Kings and Chronicles.

Whilst the different recensions of biblical books provide evidence of inner-biblical interpretation, they also suggest that it is not possible to make a clear distinction between scribal copying and reworking. Even when texts were relatively stable, scribes continued to relate texts to other biblical texts as scrolls were copied.[32] In other words, in the Second Temple period biblical books were not preserved in a fixed form, but continued to develop. In Ezek 44:13, for example, many Greek manuscripts have τὰ ἄγια υἱῶν τοῦ Ισραηλ, "the holies of the sons of Israel", where the Hebrew text has קדשי, "my holy (offerings)". The longer Greek text appears to have been inspired by Lev 22:15.[33] Similarly in Ezek 44:8 Greek manuscripts lack the Masoretic Text's first clause, ולא שמרתם משמרת קדשי, "and you have not kept charge of my holy offerings". The longer Hebrew text may have been an attempt to clarify the second half of the verse with a text like Num 18:5.[34] The extant Hebrew and Greek textual traditions provide only limited access to the history of the growth of the text. The growth of biblical texts presents particular challenges to the assessment of which text utilized the other, since we cannot preclude the possibility that during scribal transmission

---

31 David M. Carr, *Writing on the Tablet of the Heart: Origins of Scripture and Literature* (Oxford: Oxford University Press, 2005); See also Karel van der Toorn, *Scribal Culture and the Making of the Hebrew Bible* (Cambridge, MA: Harvard University Press, 2007).

32 See Jacob Stromberg, "Observations on Inner-Scriptural Scribal Expansion in MT Ezekiel", *VT* 58 (2008): 68–86.

33 See Daniel M. O'Hare, *"Have You Seen, Son of Man?": A Study of the Translation and Vorlage of LXX Ezekiel 40–48* (Atlanta: Society of Biblical Literature, 2010), 81–84.

34 Rudnig regards v. 8a as a gloss (Rudnig, *Heilig und Profan*, 209), though Zimmerli thinks the translator overlooked the clause (Zimmerli, *Ezechiel*, 1119).

both texts were mutually informing or exhibited internal development. In some cases it might only be possible to speak of the *general direction of dependence*.[35]

How might we ascertain where inner-biblical interpretation has occurred, and how can we determine the general direction of dependence? The frequent lack of citation formulae in these biblical and non-biblical texts presents a challenge to those seeking to discern whether parallels are evidence of conscious reworking or are merely coincidental. Various criteria have been developed to assist in this recognition. The most important is the recognition of multiple lexical linkages between two texts. The significance of these linkages depends upon their frequency and distribution elsewhere, and by other factors such as similar context.[36] Where parallels between two text are so numerous and precise so as to require a literary relationship, an additional problem presents itself in assessing the direction of influence. Criteria can often be deployed to argue in either direction.[37] Recognizing the subjectivity of many traditional arguments for direction of influence, recent scholarship of inner-biblical interpretation has sought to establish more robust criteria.[38]

First, a source text may provide the conceptual framework for the dependent text such that aspects of the dependent text cannot be fully appreciated without knowledge of the source text. Disagreement might arise, however, about whether the conceptual framework is distinctive to the source text, or whether it reflects shared cultural norms that could have been appreciated by an ancient reader without the source text. Secondly, the dependent text may have incongruous material that stem from its borrowing from the source text. This may be evidenced through grammatical inconsistencies, or orphaned themes. An alternative possibility, however, is that such incoherence may be explicable by appeal to theories of redaction. Thirdly, the distinctive perspectives or language of the dependent text may be reflected in modifications to the source text. A distinct instance of

---

35 For an example of such circumspection, see Klein's analysis of inner-biblical interpretation in Ezekiel 34–39 (Klein, *Schriftauslegung*, 49).

36 See most recently Michael A. Lyons, *From Law to Prophecy: Ezekiel's Use of the Holiness Code*, LHBOTS 507 (New York: T&T Clark, 2009); Jeffery M. Leonard, "Identifying Inner-Biblical Allusions: Psalm 78 as a Test Case", *JBL* 127 (2008): 241–65.

37 See esp. David M. Carr, "Method in Determination of Direction of Dependence: An Empirical Test of Criteria Applied to Exodus 34,11–26 and Its Parallels", in *Gottes Volk am Sinai: Untersuchungen zu Ex 32–34 und Dtn 9–10*, ed. Matthias Köckert and Erhard Blum, Veröffentlichungen der Wissenschaftlichen Gesellschaft für Theologie 18 (Gütersloh: Gütersloher Verlagshaus, 2001), 112.

38 See Carr, "Method"; Lyons, *From Law to Prophecy*, 59–67; Leonard, "Identifying"; William A. Tooman, *Gog of Magog: Reuse of Scripture and Compositional Technique in Ezekiel 38–39*, FAT II/52 (Tübingen: Mohr Siebeck, 2011), 31–34.

modification is the addition of substantial pluses to the paralleled text.[39] Since scribes were typically expansive, the dependent text is usually longer. Nevertheless, there are cases where later writers condensed and summarized an earlier source. Fourthly, a dependent text may allude to a number of source texts, and these may be used to enrich one another. In other words, the author of a dependent text inclined to allusion may do so more than once. Fifthly, where a lexeme or phrase appears only at one point in a text and is distributed more widely in the other text, the latter text is ordinarily the source text. On the other hand, we should be alert to the possibility that a writer may signal his dependence on a source text through multiple use of a lexeme or phrase.[40]

It should be apparent that what we have outlined are not a series of rules for determining dependence, but "rough guides requiring judicious use".[41] Particular cases must be assessed on their own merits; they cannot be adjudicated simply by the application of rules.

2.2 Methodological Issues in Redaction-Criticism

Redaction-critical analysis has a much longer pedigree within Hebrew Bible scholarship. It has been widely applied, and widely criticized.[42] Again, I do not intend to provide a detailed review of scholarship, but to address a few significant issues relevant to our examination of Ezekiel 44.

We should observe, first, that redaction criticism has been troubled by being applied to a range of alterations to an existing text. We may contrast the small-scale glosses and corrections written by hands other than the copyist evidenced in the Qumran scrolls to the rewriting of Israel's history in 1–2 Chronicles. Whilst scholars use the same textual evidence to identify change, the intentions of the composers and the scope of their work are completely different. The need for a

---

39 This formulation is dependent on Carr, who rightly emphasizes that pluses must be substantial (Carr, "Method"). It is possible to think of various reasons why a source text may have an additional word or phrase in comparison to a dependent text. These include: the source text may have expanded during textual transmission, the dependent text may have suffered a loss due to haplography, or the dependent text may reflect a memory variant.

40 For discussion of this issue, see Tooman, *Gog of Magog*, 32.

41 Carr, "Method", 126.

42 The most extensive criticism in recent scholarship has come from John Van Seters: John Van Seters, *The Edited Bible: The Curious History of the "Editor" in Biblical Criticism* (Winona Lake, IN: Eisenbrauns, 2006).

differentiated vocabulary and its disciplined use has become increasingly clear.[43] At the very least we can distinguish, as Williamson does, between the two poles that we have identified. The title "redaction" is only merited for scribal activity that rewrites and reworks an entire text for a new ideological purpose. Small-scale changes may be distinguished into at least two different sorts: glosses and *Fortschreibung*. A gloss is a brief clarification of an obscure word or expression. *Fortschreibung* is the interpretive development of a text.[44]

Distinguishing between *Fortschreibung* and redaction allows us to recognize the tendency in some recent scholarship for redactional hypotheses to disintegrate into hypotheses about *Fortschreibung*.[45] Part of the reason may simply be because the bar is set much higher for proving the existence of a continuous redaction. There must be evidence not only of textual development, but also that instances of textual development are linked as part of a consistent redaction. The theoretical imbalance between different hypotheses is problematic, since late Second Temple texts provide evidence for both redaction and *Fortschreibung*.

It is not only redaction and *Fortschreibung* that offer competing hypotheses for the same textual data; it is also the case that inner-biblical interpretation can sometimes be used to explain the same data. This should not be surprising, since inner-biblical interpretation is itself a form of diachronic analysis that seeks to

---

43 See Ibid.; Hugh G. M. Williamson, "The Vindication of Redaction Criticism", in *Biblical Interpretation and Method: Essays in Honour of John Barton*, ed. Katherine J. Dell and Paul M. Joyce (Oxford: Oxford University Press, 2013), 26 – 36.

44 As is well known, *Fortschreibung* was coined by Zimmerli in relation to Ezekiel. "Relativ selten sind in einer solchen Einheit einfach zwei in sich eigenständige Redestücke zusammengefaßt (=gesammelt), wie etwa in 33 1–20 und 33 23–33. Viel charakteristischer ist für manche Stücke des Buches der eigentümliche Vorgang der "Fortschreibung" einer Einheit. So schildert das Grundwort von Ez 16 1–43...die böse Geschichte zwischen Jahwe und dem von ihm hoch zu Ehren gebrachten Findelkind. An diesen Komplex sind in 44–58 und 59–63 deutlich abhebbare Erweiterungen angesetzt, die nicht einfach als selbstständige Überlieferungseinheiten angesprochen werden können, also nicht einfach in einem Prozeß der "Sammlung" dazugekommen sind, sondern unverkennbar das im Grundwort angeschlagene Thema nach neuen Richtungen hin verfolgen. Darin zeichnet sich ein Prozeß der sukzessiven Anreicherung eines Kernelementes ab, das in neuen Ansätzenm, wohl in einem etwas späteren Zeitpunkt, weiter ausgesponnen wird" (Zimmerli, *Ezechiel*, 106*). We should observe that Zimmerli uses *Fortschreibung* to characterize the extension of prophetic oracles where the later interpretation is clearly marked by references to divine speech, e. g. "thus says YHWH". He distinguishes *Fortschreibung* from the collection of oracles.

45 Gertz's and Berner's different analyses of the exodus story, published within a decade of each other, may be compared (Christoph Berner, *Die Exoduserzählung: Das literarische Werden einer Ursprungslegende Israels*, FAT 73 [Tübingen: Mohr Siebeck, 2010]; Jan Christian Gertz, *Tradition und Redaktion in der Exoduserzählung: Untersuchungen zur Endredaktion des Pentateuch*, FRLANT 186 [Göttingen: Vandenhoeck & Ruprecht, 2000]).

identify the use of prior textual material. On the one hand, there exists the possibility of conflict between competing explanations.[46] An example of the problem, to which we will return, is Konkel's suggestion that v. 7bβ is an addition to Ezek 44:6–16. Does the unexpected appearance of "my covenant" point to *Fortschreibung* or an allusion to Gen 17:14 composed by the author of the other verses? On the other hand, it is possible to view inner-biblical interpretation and redaction as mutually informing and complementary. The instinct of scribal authors to harmonize inconsistent texts and to use other scriptural references to enrich a text are important insights for understanding the development of biblical literature.[47]

One of the most frequently heard complaints against literary-critical analyses concerns their hypothetical nature and their inability to achieve consensus. No two redactional-critical analyses agree, and the conclusions drawn can sometimes be contradictory. In addition, the multiplication of redaction-critical layers strains credulity. This criticism makes the multiplication of alternative theories, which is the hallmark of academic research, more of a vice than is justified, and overlooks the ability of some theories to command the assent of a number of scholars.

Comparing late Second Temple texts to precursors that can be securely dated earlier demonstrate that glosses, *Fortschreibung*, redaction, and other literary-critical developments are reasonable hypotheses for clarifying various textual features that would otherwise remain unexplained. Nevertheless, as Stephen Kaufman argued over thirty years ago in an incisive study, whilst the analysis of the Temple Scroll demonstrates that literary-critical hypotheses are feasible, we would not be able to reconstruct the Temple Scroll's sources if we did not have many of them preserved in the Hebrew Bible.[48] Whilst the evidence for literary-critical development whets the appetite, it is not sufficient to satiate the desire for a convincing solution.

What then is the value of literary-criticism? The proposal of literary-critical hypotheses is no different to the venturing of hypotheses in other areas of academic research. They have heuristic value; they are "good to think with". They provide a means of thinking about the texts that we have, how they may have come about, and what this means for how we interpret them. This means holding

---

46 Schaper rightly identifies the potential for inner-biblical interpretation and redaction criticism to be in conflict (Schaper, "Rereading the Law", 131).
47 Schmid, "Innerbiblische Schriftauslegung"; Reinhard Gregor Kratz, "Innerbiblische Exegese und Redaktionsgeschichte im Lichte empirischer Evidenz", in *Das Judentum im Zeitalter des Zweiten Tempels*, FAT 42 (Tübingen: Mohr Siebeck, 2004), 126–156.
48 S. Kaufman, "The Temple Scroll and Higher Criticism", *HUCA* 53 (1982): 29–43.

to redaction-critical hypotheses rather more tentatively than has sometimes been the case. It is also to recall, as proponents of final-form and canonical readings insist, that the task of the biblical interpreter is to understand and interpret the texts that we have. The value of redaction-critical analyses lies ultimately in their attentiveness to the text in our hands.

3 Overview and Prospect

The divine oracle in Ezekiel 44 is the central focus of this book. That oracle can be divided into two halves. The first half concerns the rights of admission into the sanctuary complex. Distinctions are made between the foreigners, who may not enter, the Levites, who act as guardians of the inner court, and the priests, who may enter the inner court, sacrifice and offer food to YHWH. A hierarchical view of the restored temple is given in which the sons of Zadok have a higher status and more important roles than the Levites (vv. 6–16). The verses that follow are a diverse collection of rules regulating the conduct of the priests (vv. 17–31). The title of this book, *Priestly Rule*, plays on the different concerns of the two halves of this crucial chapter. The sons of Zadok priests rule over the Levites and are themselves ruled by the instructions that follow.[49]

My study will examine both halves of this chapter in turn. Particular attention will be paid to the intertextual relationships that Ezekiel 44 has with other biblical texts. The first chapter of this book will examine the relationship between Ezekiel 44 and Isaiah 56. Against the consensus that Ezekiel 44 is the earlier text, I will demonstrate that this conclusion has been assumed on the basis of a dating of Trito-Isaiah and Ezekiel that takes no account of redactional activity. When this assumption is set aside, it is clear that the consensus must be rejected. I will demonstrate further that there is a close relationship with Ezekiel 14 and 18 that has been overlooked. As a result it would be correct to view Ezekiel 44 as an exegetical oracle that developed in two stages, and the nature of its sophisticated inner-biblical interpretation will be delineated in detail. The second chapter will be mostly concerned with the relationship of Ezekiel 44 to the pentateuchal rules governing the priests. I will demonstrate that here too we have similarly sophisticated inner-biblical interpretation. A significant part of the

---

49 My title should by no means be interpreted as a claim that the priests in P or in Ezekiel exercised civil rule. For incisive observations on this issue, see Deborah W. Rooke, *Zadok's Heirs: The Role and Development of the High Priesthood in Ancient Israel* (Oxford: Oxford University Press, 2000).

chapter will be given to explicate the relationship of the laws to other rules about priests in Numbers 18, and Leviticus 10 and 21.

Having completed the analysis of Ezekiel 44 I will consider the evidence for the chapter's impact upon other Second Temple texts. Is there evidence for the sons of Zadok assuming control over the temple? I will examine the references to Zadok and the sons of Zadok in Chronicles, before turning to the evidence from Qumran, Ben Sira and Josephus. The absence of references to the sons of Zadok prior to the Dead Sea Scrolls do not prove that Ezekiel 44 is a late, inner-biblical composition, though they are consistent with the thesis adopted.

In the conclusion I will discuss some of the historical consequences of my thesis. I will argue that the reference to the sons of Zadok in Ezekiel 44 was driven by scriptural instincts, rather than by the existence of a priestly sept bearing that name. This will align the argument with those who reject the existence of Zadokites in the Second Temple period. I will also conclude that Ezekiel 44 is a very late text and post-dates Numbers 18. As a result we should seek the earliest evidence of a distinction between Levites and priests in the Pentateuch, rather than the book of Ezekiel.

1 The Rule of Priests

At the end of his prophetic book, Ezekiel receives a final vision of temple and land. Whether this was intended as a utopian vision or a blueprint for the restored community is much debated.[50] The vision opens with a detailed description of a temple. An angelic figure leads Ezekiel into the heart of the temple and back out again, completing the tour just in time for the prophet to witness the return of YHWH's glory to the sanctuary (40:1–43:12). The angel then relays to the prophet the "Law of the Temple" (תרות הבית). The law opens like other Israelite law codes with instructions about the altar: its construction and consecration (43:13–27). This is followed by rulings concerning the conduct of the prince (44:1–3), the priests (44:6–31), the allocation of land for the priests and prince (45:1–8), the prince (45:9–17), and the festival calendar and offerings (45:18–46:24).

Outlining the contents of the Law of the Temple highlights the way in which the regulations about the priests and the allocation of land have intruded into the instructions about the prince (44:1–3; 45:9–17).[51] The intrusive material is introduced by vv. 4–5:

---

50 Thus, Eichrodt writes, "The temple makes its appearance as a heavenly reality created by Yahweh himself and transplanted to stand on earth...The entirely miraculous character of the dwelling place of God described in the following passage must therefore be kept in view in estimating its significance as a whole. The same is true of it as of the descriptions scattered throughout Isa. 40–55 of the miraculous journey home across the wilderness by the returning exiles, or the statements made about the new Jerusalem in Isa. 60. Already they all shine with the colours of the new age, and are images of the future blessedness which transcends all the limits of history" (Eichrodt, *Ezekiel*, 542; cf. Susan Niditch, "Ezekiel 40–48 in a Visionary Context", *CBQ* 48 [1986]: 208–24). Liss characterizes the vision as a "literary utopia" (Hannah Liss, "'Describe the Temple to the House of Israel': Preliminary Remarks on the Temple Vision in the Book of Ezekiel and Question of Fictionality in Priestly Literatures", in *Utopia and Dystopia in Prophetic Literature*, ed. Ehud Ben Zvi, Publications of the Finnish Exegetical Society 92 [Helsinki: Finnish Exegetical Society, 2006], 122–43). On the other hand, Clements writes, "Ezekiel 40–48 is not just a vision of a new and restored Israel but a practical 'renewal program' for national reorganization" (Ronald Ernest Clements, *Ezekiel*, Westminster Bible Companion [Louisville: Westminster John Knox, 1996], 178). Distinguishing different redactional layers opens up the possibility that different perspectives are preserved.

There is disagreement too about the extent to which Ezekiel 40–48 had an effect on the early returnees. Whatever the case, the vision made a marked impression on some groups in later Second Temple Judaism.

51 The apportioning of land to priests, Levites and the prince is clearly premature and anticipates the detailed discussion of the land in Ezekiel 47–48. Nor does it really fit into the Law of the *Temple*. Gese observed the close relationship of 45:1–8 to 48:1–29, and suggested that 45:1–8

> Then he brought me via the north gateway to the front of the temple. I looked and behold the glory of YHWH filled YHWH's Temple, and I fell upon my face. YHWH said to me, "Human, mark well, look carefully, and listen attentively to all that I will tell you concerning all the ordinances of YHWH's Temple and its laws. Mark well the entrances of the temple and all the exits of the sanctuary."

Most of the elements in vv. 4–5 are adaptations of material found elsewhere in Ezekiel's vision, especially 43:1–11.[52] The composer of these verses has clearly sought in his selection to highlight the significance of what follows, but the result is somewhat jarring. The description opens by returning Ezekiel to precisely the location where he stood when YHWH's glory appeared (43:5).[53] Since the east gate was shut permanently following the arrival of the glory, the prophet must make a detour and enter via the north gate.[54] The prophet has returned to the same location so that he can see YHWH's glory filling the temple for a second time. Since the return of YHWH's glory to the temple should be a single, climactic event, its repetition is narratively incongruous. The description of the return of the divine glory uses wording that is almost identical to that found in 43:5,[55] and Ezekiel's response is again to fall on his face (cf. 43:3). As at the first appearance, the angel addresses the prophet, but on this occasion, the angel's very first words from 40:4 are blended with the references to the Law of the Temple from 43:11–12.[56]

בן אדם ראה בעיניך ובאזניך שמע ושים לבך לכל אשר אני מראה אותך
Human, look carefully and listen attentively and mark well all that I will show you (40:4).

צורת הבית ותכונתו ומוצאיו ומובאיו וכל צורתו ואת כל חקתיו וכל צורתי צורתיו וכל תורתיו וכל תורתו הודע אותם
Make known to them the form of the temple, its structure, its exits and its entrances, and its entire form, and all its ordinances and its entire form and all its laws (43:11).

---

52 Gese discusses the various theories about the relationship between 43:1–11 and 44:4–5 and makes a convincing case for the dependence of 44:4–5 (Ibid., 53–57).

53 The next step in Ezekiel's tour of the temple is found in 46:19. The use of בוא there is problematic, since Ezekiel is in the inner court, and needs to exit (יצא) through an inner-gate to reach the outer court where the holy chambers of the priests are (40:44–46).

54 Zimmerli, *Ezechiel*, 1110.

55 43:5: והנה מלא כבוד־יהוה את־בית יהוה; 44:4: והנה מלא כבוד־יהוה הבית.

56 The reuse of 40:4 is an instance of Seidel's law with the terms ראה בעיניך ובאזניך שמע and שים לבך reversed.

was a reworking of the land division in light of the instructions about Levites and priests in 44:6–31 (Gese, *Der Verfassungsentwurf*, 103–07).

בן אדם שים לבך וראה בעיניך ובאזניך שמע את כל אשר אני מדבר אתך <u>לכל חקות</u> בית יהוה <u>ולכל תורתו</u>
<u>ושמת לבך למבוא</u> הבית בכל <u>מוצאי</u> המקדש

Human, mark well, look carefully, and listen attentively to all that I will tell you concerning all the ordinances of YHWH's Temple and its laws. Mark well the entrances of the temple and all the exits of the sanctuary (44:5).

By appropriating the opening speech of the angel, the composer of these verses has realigned the beginning of the Law of the Temple and relegated 43:13 – 44:3 to a subordinate status. The two major sub-divisions of Ezekiel's vision – the Vision of the Temple and the Law of the Temple – are distinguished by attributing them to different senses. In the opening of the temple vision the prophet was permitted to see (מראה) the new temple (40:4), but for the Law of the Temple he will be told (מדבר) about the ordinances (44:5). In 43:11 Ezekiel is tasked with revealing various details about the temple, "all its laws". In contrast, 44:5 draws attention to one of these: the entrances and exits of the sanctuary.[57] These will be the focus of 44:6 – 16, or more precisely these verses are concerned with *who* it is that may enter the sanctuary through those entrances and exits.

The title of the second section of Ezekiel's vision, "the Law of the Temple", together with the references to ordinances and laws in vv. 4 – 5, incline the reader to anticipate a series of regulations. In fact, what the reader encounters is a divine oracle, which consists of a reproach in vv. 6 – 8 and YHWH's word of judgement in vv. 9 – 16. The divine word of judgement is not simply a description of punishment, but unusually includes within it various stipulations about sanctuary access. The two parts of the divine oracle are introduced by the familiar prophetic introduction to divine speech, כה אמר אדני יהוה, "thus says Lord YHWH" (vv. 6, 9). Only from v. 17 onwards do we find an unadulterated list of stipulations that vv. 4 – 5 caused us to expect.

The expectations of the reader are further unsettled by an apparent disjunction between the two parts of the divine oracle. There are three difficulties. First, Israel is sharply reprimanded in the second person plural, but the word of judgement that follows is not directed against Israel. Instead, Israel is spoken of in the third person and it is the Levites who are judged.[58] Secondly, Israel's failure is described in quite different terms in vv. 6 – 8 as compared to vv. 10 – 16. Verse 7 accuses Israel of admitting foreigners to the sanctuary who profaned it, an action that is vehemently condemned in v. 9. But the rest of the word of judgement de-

---

57 The text of 44:5 presents some difficulties. With the versions למבוא should be read as למבואי (cf. 43:11). We should probably also correct בכל to read ובכל. The NRSV should not be followed in emending the text to read למובאי הבית בכל מוצא מקדש based on the similarity to 43:11.
58 Rudnig, *Heilig und Profan*, 205 – 06.

scribes a different sin: Israel's preference for idol worship (vv. 10, 12, 15). Are these to be envisaged as related or distinct infractions? Thirdly, we would expect the reproach to refer to past transgressions and the word of judgement to draw future consequences. In fact, the word of judgement moves repeatedly between past and future. The verses oscillate between past actions, typically expressed with *qatal* and *wayyiqtol* forms (vv. 10a, 12a, bα, 13bβ),[59] and the consequences that are to result, expressed with *weqatal* and *yiqtol* forms (vv. 10b–11, 12bβ–13bα, 14).[60]

Such an obvious textual wrinkle might ordinarily suggest recourse to a literary-critical solution. Surprisingly, perhaps, such solutions have rarely been ventured and the unity of Ezek 44:6–16 has almost universally been assumed.[61] Thus, in his extensive study of the temple vision, Konkel notes the near unanimity of scholarship on the issue and insists that only the appearance in v. 7bβ of a covenant – an idea otherwise unattested in Ezekiel's temple vision – is problematic. "Eine weitere Infragestellung der Einheit des Abschnitts empfiehlt sich auf dem Hintergrund der synchronen Analyse nicht. Der redundante, mit Parenthesen durchsetzte, echauffierte Stil des Abschnitts ahmt die mündliche Rede nach. Der Text folgt dabei aber durchaus einer klaren Logik."[62] The difficulties we have exposed raises questions about the supposed "clear logic", and Konkel's appeal to orality evades the issue rather than solving it.

Amongst recent interpreters, only Rudnig has felt the force of the difficulties we have described. According to Rudnig the original oracle in 44:6–7a, bβ was directed against the pretensions of the first exiles (the Jehoiachin-*golah*) who were accused of allowing foreigners within the *temenos*. It was later reworked in vv. 7bαγ, 8b as a protest against certain cult personnel. The programmatic distinction between priests and Levites is a later stage of development.[63] Rudnig notes the repetitious nature of vv. 9–16 and identifies vv. 9–10, 13–15 as the original continuation of the reproach in vv. 6–8. The expansions in vv. 11–12,

---

59 In v. 12 the אשר יען clause is followed by *weqatal* and *yiqtol* forms. In this case "bezeichnet das Imperfekt einen frequentativen Aspekt einer in der Vergangenheit begonnenen Handlung, welche dann aufhört, wenn eine bestimmte Absicht erreicht worden ist" (M. J. Mulder, "Die Partikel יען", in *Syntax and Meaning: Studies in Hebrew Syntax and Biblical Exegesis*, ed. C. J. Labuschagne et al., OTS 18 [Leiden: Brill, 1973], 64). Consequently it is not necessary to resort to emendation.

60 Konkel, *Architektonik*, 104.

61 Konkel, *Architektonik*, 99. Doubts have been raised about whether v. 5 was originally a speech by YHWH. Since YHWH appears in the third person in vv. 5–6a, it is easy to envisage the Tetragrammaton as a later addition to a speech originally attributed to the guiding angel.

62 Ibid., 111.

63 We might also compare Niditch's distinction between 44:6–9, which she attributes to the prophet Ezekiel, and 44:10–31, which stems from a later pro-Zadokite hand (Niditch, "Ezekiel 40–48").

16 further clarify the roles of the Levites and sons of Zadok by reworking some of the existing expressions.[64] Thus, Rudnig resolves many of the difficulties we have observed, but only be reducing the oracle to fragments.

If we are to make progress in understanding the oracle, it will be necessary to examine the separate parts of the oracle. Neither Konkel's synchronic perspective nor Rudnig's redactional analysis is sufficient for the task, though both are valuable in their different ways. The crucial ingredient in this study will be attention to possible inner-biblical interpretation. Since we have observed a discontinuity between the reproach and the judgement, we will examine the two parts of the oracle in turn. In each case we will begin with the main protagonists: the foreigners in vv. 6–8, and the Levites in vv. 9–16. Beginning with the identity and characterization of these two groups, I will argue that it is the inner-biblical allusions that have given the oracle its distinctive shape.

1.1 YHWH's Reproach of Israel

However complex the present form of the divine oracle is, the initial cause for YHWH's ire is the presence of foreigners in the temple. Perhaps unsurprisingly critical efforts have focussed on identifying the situation that provoked the oracle. Who were the unspecified foreigners that had been permitted into the temple? Can we relate the oracle to foreigners known elsewhere in the Old Testament or in other contemporary historical accounts? The primary source of information about the identity of the foreigners is the reproach in vv. 6–8, but it does not provide a simple characterization of them.

1.1.1 The Identity of the Foreigners in Ezekiel 44

YHWH's reproach of Israel comprises at least three distinguishable accusations, each of which concerns the way that foreigners have been given access to the cultic worship of YHWH.

> Enough of all your abominations, House of Israel,
>
> in your admitting (בהביאכם) foreigners – uncircumcised in heart and flesh – to be in my sanctuary (במקדשי), to profane it, my house (את־ביתי),

---

64 Rudnig, *Heilig und Profan*, 204–215, 280–304.

in your offering (בהקריבכם) my food,[65] fat and blood, and they[66] have broken my covenant in addition to all your abominations.

And you did not keep (שמרתם) the charge of my holy things, but you set them[67] as keepers of my charge in my sanctuary.[68]

For each of these charges in vv. 7–8 the verbal action is key to the accusation: הביא, "to admit", הקריב, "to offer", שמר, "to keep". Each is a cultic action that has been abused. The first two accusations begin with temporal clauses that are introduced with ב and the infinitive construct. They are juxtaposed with one another without a conjunction suggesting that they are contemporaneous, but distinguishable actions.[69] The first accusation is somewhat complicated by the final clause, לחללו את־ביתי, "to profane it, my house". Apparently, this clarifies the admission of trespassers into the "sanctuary", but elsewhere in Ezekiel's Vision of the Temple, מקדש, "sanctuary" and בית, "house" are not synonymous terms: מקדש refers to the temple building proper and בית to the whole sacred area (cf. 43:21). In addition, לחללו את־ביתי is tautologous. Consequently, it has often been suggested that את־ביתי is a gloss.[70] The second accusation presupposes the first, but goes beyond it. The foreigners were not only admitted to the sanctuary, but were present at the sacrifices. To these two serious charges is brought an additional one, which appears to be an exacerbation of the accusations in v. 7. Not only did the Israelites admit foreigners and allow them to be present when food was offered, but they even charged them with protecting the sanctuary.

There has been no lack of proposals for identifying these foreigners who entered the sanctuary, offered sacrifices and took charge of its security. Israel's history prior to the exile has been scoured for potential candidates. Within critical scholarship it was long claimed that the foreigners of Ezekiel 44 were the *netinim*, cultic servants mentioned in 1 Chronicles, Ezra and Nehemiah. These, it was argued, were descendants from the Gibeonites and other foreign captives who were forced to undertake menial tasks for the temple. Ezekiel 44 removes those tasks from the *netinim* and assigns them to the Levites. The main lines

---

65 For לחמי as "my food" see Godfrey R. Driver, "Ezekiel: Linguistic and Textual Problems", *Bib* 35 (1954): 309.

66 Reading with MT; the versions suggest a reading ותפרו.

67 ותשימון is often emended to read ותשימום (cf. Gen 45:8; Ps 18:44; 1Chr 26:10). Otherwise the sentence does not make good sense.

68 לכם is often emended. Greek omits and has διὰ τοῦτο prefixed to the following verse, which suggests it read לכן. For arguments to retain לכם, see Daniel Isaac Block, *The Book of Ezekiel*, NICOT (Grand Rapids: Eerdmans, 1997), 2:621.

69 Cf. Gen 19:29; 35:17; Exod 16:3; 23:16 etc.

70 The other alternative is to omit the suffix on חלל (with the versions).

of this interpretation were already articulated by Wellhausen in his *Prolegomena*,[71] and further developed in the twentieth century.[72] Significant elements of this interpretation have, with justification, been abandoned in recent years. Key elements of this hypothesis depend upon evidence known only from the Mishnah, some of which is in tension with the biblical texts. In particular, there is no ancient evidence that connects the *netinim* and the Gibeonites,[73] and proof that they were foreign is also lacking.[74] In addition, there is no evidence in Ezekiel 44 that the Levites were given roles previously held by the foreigners. Duguid argues that the foreigners are the Carites who guarded Joash in the temple during the coup against Athaliah (2 Kings 11:4, 19). Since we know almost nothing about the Carites, Duguid's proposal is pure speculation, and he too assumes the Levites took over roles previously held by foreign servants.[75] Galambusch argues that the broken covenant was the one that Zedekiah made with Nebuchadrezzar (cf. Ezek 17:19), and Ezekiel objects to it being broken by alliance with Egypt. She identifies the Egyptians with the בני נכר of Ezekiel 44, and speculates that the Egyptians may have accessed the sanctuary during Psammeticus II's tour of Palestine in 592 BCE. The principal difficulty with this proposal is that we lack any evidence of a visit by an Egyptian delegation to Jerusalem or its temple.[76]

As we have already seen, the difficulties with identifying suitable historical candidates has led some scholars to seek scriptural precedents, though these have proved no more convincing. Jon Levenson appeals to Numbers 25 and its association of foreigners, priesthood and idolatry.[77] But there is no evidence

---

71 Wellhausen, *Prolegomena*, 147 n. 3, 218 n. 1.

72 See, e.g., Menahem Haran, "the Gibeonites, the Nethinim and the Sons of Solomon's Servants", *VT* 11 (1961): 159–69. For a short history of interpretation see Joel Weinberg, "Netînîm und 'Söhne der Sklaven Salomos' im 6.–4. Hj. v. u. Z.", *ZAW* 87 (1975): 355–357.

73 Baruch A. Levine, "The Netînîm", *JBL* 82 (1963): 207–12; Baruch A. Levine, "Later Sources on the Netinim", in *Orient and Occident: Cyrus Gordon Festschrift*, ed. Harry A. Hoffner, AOAT 22 (Neukirchen-Vluyn: Neukirchener Verlag, 1973), 101–07.

74 J. Galambusch, "The Northern Voyage of Psammeticus II and Its Implications for Ezekiel 44.7–9", in *The Priests in the Prophets: The Portrayal of Priests, Prophets and Other Religious Specialists in the Latter Prophets*, ed. Lester L. Grabbe and Alice Ogden Bellis, JSOTSup 408 (London: T&T Clark, 2004), 67.

75 Duguid's argument rests simply on the appearance of פקדות in 2Kgs 11:18 and Ezek 44:11. See Iain M. Duguid, *Ezekiel and the Leaders of Israel*, VTSup 56 (Leiden: Brill, 1994), 75–77; Iain M. Duguid, "Putting Priests in Their Place: Ezekiel's Contribution to the History of the Old Testament Priesthood", in *Ezekiel's Hierarchical World: Wrestling with a Tiered Reality*, ed. Stephen L. Cook and Corrine L. Patton, SBL Symposium Series 31 (Leiden: Brill, 2004), 43–60.

76 Galambusch, "Northern Voyage".

77 Levenson, *Program of Restoration*, 129–58.

that the physical integrity of the Tabernacle came under threat, nor that the Midianites assumed priestly duties in it. Instead, the Midianites lure the Israelites to worship a regional manifestation of Baal, presumably at a shrine in the locality of (Beth-)Peor. Similarly unconvincing is Stephen Cook's suggestion that Ezekiel 44 is a response to the narrative history of Numbers 16–17. Cook observes some verbal links including the use of מרי (Ezek 44:6; Num 17:25) and רב־לכם (Ezek 44:6; Num 16:7), and he notes the similarity of Num 16:9 to Ezek 44:11. Thematically we have Levitical rebellion that focuses around cultic access and privileges.[78] I will argue that there is significant evidence for the influence of Number 18 on Ezekiel 44, but the evidence that Cook adduces for the narrative in Numbers 16–17 is considerably thinner. Not only are the verbal links restricted to a few expressions scattered across Numbers 16–17, but also Cook's main contention that the Korah narrative provides the narrative-historical context overlooks several significant differences. In particular, the Korah narrative is not concerned, as Ezekiel 44 is, with the access of *foreigners* to the sanctuary, but that of the Israelite laity. Consequently it is difficult to see how Numbers 16–18 could have generated the focus on foreigners integral to Ezekiel 44.

A significant deficiency in the arguments developed by Levenson and Cook is a lack of significant and convincing lexical links between the pentateuchal narratives and Ezekiel 44. The same is true of the suggestion by Fishbane and Schaper that Deut 23:2–9 is a possible legal precursor to Ezekiel 44. There is a shared concern with the granting of sanctuary access to non-Israelites, but the verbal similarities are limited to the use of הביא.[79] The text with the greatest number of shared lexemes is Isaiah 56, but scholarship has been unanimous that Isaiah 56 is dependent on Ezekiel 44. In the following pages, however, I want to suggest that a reassessment of this assumption is necessary.

1.1.2 Isaiah 56 and Its Relationship to Ezekiel 44

The concern in Ezekiel 44 with the admission of foreigners (בני נכר) and their association with priestly duties provide a significant resonance with Isaiah 56 such that some relationship must exist between the two passages as Fishbane, Schaper and Tuell have rightly observed. In order to rightly appraise the relationship between the two passages, it is necessary first of all to give attention to the distinctive perspective of Isaiah 56.

---

78 Cook, "Innerbiblical Interpretation".
79 Fishbane, *Biblical Interpretation*; Schaper, "Rereading the Law".

In Isaiah 56 a divine oracle is given to the foreigners and the eunuchs: the former fear exclusion from YHWH's people, whilst the latter lament their lack of offspring. Provided they keep the Sabbath and hold to the covenant, YHWH promises both a place in the temple community. The eunuch will have a memorial and name in the Temple, whilst the foreigner will be permitted to offer sacrifices.

There is considerable disagreement amongst interpreters, however, as to whether the oracle envisages the foreigners serving as priests. Isaiah 56 describes the foreigners as joining themselves (לוה) to YHWH (vv. 3, 6). The verb לוה is used on a number of occasions in the Old Testament of those who join a community. In particular it is used of foreigners joining themselves to Israel (Isa 14:1; Zech 2:15; Esth 9:27). לוה was also employed, however, as a folk etymology for the name Levi (לוי).[80] Most significantly for our purposes, in Numbers 18 the assignment of the Levites to various duties in the Tabernacle is justified through a play on the root לוה. The Levites are "joined" (לוה) to Aaron and his sons and, consequently, share in the responsibility for the Tabernacle (vv. 2, 4). The "joining" of the foreigners to YHWH in Isaiah 56 could be understood as a play on this same etymology. This seems more likely when we observe that the foreigners are not only able to "join themselves" to YHWH, but they are also to minister to him (לשרתו). The root שרת can be used as a technical term for priestly service, and it is employed in this sense repeatedly in Numbers 18 in relation to the cultic service of the priests and Levites.[81] Consequently, it has often been suggested that in Isaiah 56 the foreigners are portrayed doing priestly service.[82] There are, however, those who argue that priestly service is not in view. Not only is לוה used in Isa 14:1; Zech 2:15 and Esth 9:27 without

---

[80] Leah names her third son Levi, explaining "now this time my husband will be joined to me" (Gen 29:34).

[81] For details see KB 1662 and discussion in Claus Westermann, "שרת Šrt", *TLOT* 3: 1405–07; Karen Engelken, "שרת Šrt", *TDOT* 15: 503–14.

[82] So, e.g., Joseph Blenkinsopp, *Isaiah 40–55: A New Translation with Introduction and Commentary*, AB 19A (New York: Doubleday, 2002), 140; Paul D. Hanson, *Isaiah 40–66*, Interpretation (Louisville: John Knox, 1995), 193–96; Jacob Stromberg, *Isaiah after Exile: The Author of Third Isaiah as Reader and Redactor of the Book*, Oxford Theological Monographs (Oxford: Oxford University Press, 2011), 74–86; Ulrich Berges, *Das Buch Jesaja: Komposition und Endgestalt*, HBS 16 (Freiburg im Breisgau: Herder, 1998), 513; Klaus Koenen, *Ethik und Eschatologie im Tritojesajabuch*, WMANT 62 (Neukirchen-Vluyn: Neukirchener Verlag, 1990), 29; John D. W. Watts, *Isaiah 34–66*, WBC 25 (Waco, TX: Word Books, 1987), 249; Engelken, "שרת Šrt", 509; John Oswalt, *Isaiah 40–66*, NICOT (Grand Rapids: Eerdmans, 2009), 459–60.

any cultic overtones, but שרת can be employed of general devotion and service to an individual.[83]

With lengthy list of advocates for both positions it should not be a surprise that there is no simple and convincing solution to the problem. Various pieces of evidence can be mustered, though, unfortunately, these often point in different directions. First, if we interrogate Isa 56:6–7 closely, we can observe that the devotion of the foreigner is seen not only in "ministering" (שרת), but also in "loving the name of YHWH" (לאהבה את־שם יהוה) and becoming a "servant" (להיות לו לעבדים). In both cases these expressions denote a general devotion; they are not circumlocutions for priestly service.[84] If שרת were intended to have a cultic sense, the addition of these expressions of general devotion would appear to blunt what would be a radical, unprecedented departure from Israel's tradition.[85] In addition, ministering, loving and serving appear to be qualifications that are *prerequisites* for admission to YHWH's holy mountain. The order hardly seems consistent with such actions being understood as cultic service.[86] Secondly,

---

83 Benjamin D. Sommer, *A Prophet Reads Scripture: Allusion in Isaiah 40–66* (Stanford: Stanford University Press, 1998), 147; Jan Leunis Koole, *Isaiah III.1: Isaiah 40–48*, HCOT (Kampen: Kok Pharos, 1997), 20; Willem A. M. Beuken, *Jesaja*, vol. IIIA, POuT (Nijkerk: Callenbach, 1989), 30; Roger Norman Whybray, *Isaiah 40–66*, NCB Commentary (Grand Rapids: Eerdmans, 1975), 198; Saul M. Olyan, *Rites and Rank: Hierarchy in Biblical Representations of Cult* (Princeton: Princeton University Press, 2000), 164–65; Paul A. Smith, *Rhetoric and Redaction in Trito-Isaiah*, VTSup 62 (Leiden: Brill, 1995), 58; D. W. Van Winkle, "Isaiah LVI 1–8", *SBLSP* 36 (1997): 240–41.

84 In the case of "loving the name of YHWH" we have the merging of two expressions characteristic of Deuteronomistic writings: "loving YHWH" and "the name of YHWH". In Deut 10:12; 11:13 and Josh 22:5 לאהבה את־יהוה is followed by לעבדו / לעבד יהוה as part of Deuteronomistic exhortations to Israel to be faithful to YHWH. Although the root עבד can be used in relation to priestly service (e. g. Num 18), this is only true of the verb and the derived noun עבדה. Riesener concludes her study on the root עבד by observing "In der Priesterschrift und im chronistischen Geschichtswerk gewinnt dann עֲבֹדָה, das zuvor in religiösem Sinn fast völlig fehlt, große Bedeutung. Damit wird einerseits der 'Dienst' des Kultpersonals (bei P der leviten, im chronistischen Geschichtswerk verschiedener Kultbeamter), andererseits auch die 'Wartung' kultischer Geräte sowie der ganze 'Tempeldienst' oder 'Kult' bezeichnet. Auch עָבַד dient hier dazu, die (berufliche) Erfüllung kultischer Aufgaben zu beschreiben, während עָבַד niemals als Terminus für die Kultbeamten (wie Leviten oder Priester) begegnet (nur die Kult-'Sklaven' können als עֲבָדִים bezeichnet werden)" (Ingrid Riesener, *Der Stamm* עבד *im Alten Testament: Eine Wortuntersuchung unter Berücksichtigung neuerer sprachwissenschaftlicher Methoden*, BZAW 149 [Berlin: de Gruyter, 1979], 271).

85 Van Winkle describes the position of שרת as anticlimactic (Van Winkle, "Isaiah LVI 1–8", 241).

86 Sommer argues additionally that "the passage does not attribute priestly roles to the eunuchs or the foreigners (since they are not said to approach the altar). It merely stresses that their presence and their offerings are welcome on my holy mountain" (Sommer, *A Prophet*

the use of שרת in Isa 56:6 can be compared with its use elsewhere in Isaiah 56–66. There are three other occurrences. In 60:7 שרת is used of the offering of animals to YHWH; in 60:10 foreign kings minister to the Israelites; and in 61:6 the Israelites are proclaimed as "ministers of our God" (משרתי אלהינו) which occurs in parallel with "priests of YHWH" (כהני יהוה). In each case we have verbal parallels to Isa 56:1–8, but since שרת is used in cultic and non-cultic senses, they provide no definitive answer to the problem of the meaning of שרת in Isa 56:6. Thirdly, the pericope 66:18–21 has a number of verbal parallels with 56:1–8,[87] and refers explicitly to the appointment of Levitical priests "from them" (אקח מהם לכהנים ללוים).[88] But who are "they"? Unfortunately the interpretative issues are just as contested in 66:18–21 as they are in 56:1–8: it is uncertain whether "they" are the brother Israelites (כל-אחיכם; 66:20) or the survivors (פליטים) from the gentiles who bring the Israelites back to Jerusalem (66:19).[89]

In my view the evidence probably tilts towards understanding שרת as an expression of general devotion. As Sommer suggests, the author may be seeking to make a provocative analogy between the foreigners and the Israelite priests.[90] Whilst the passage can and has been read as a promise that foreigners will take up priestly roles, I am not convinced that this was the intent of the writer. But, whatever the intent of the writer of Isaiah 56, the earliest textual evidence suggests that the chapter was understood in antiquity as a promise that the foreigner would receive a priestly role within the temple. This is apparent in the LXX and 1QIsaᵃ where we have evidence of scribal transmitters who were uncomfortable with the idea of non-Israelites becoming priests and sought to emend the text accordingly.[91]

Reads Scripture, 147). I am not convinced that much weight can be placed on the *absence* of any reference to approaching the altar, which insists too strongly on finding the language of Num 18 and Ezek 44 in Isa 56.

87 In both texts YHWH gathers (קבץ *piel*) the dispersed (56:8; 66:18) and people are brought (בוא *hiphil*) to "my holy mountain" (הר קדשי; 56:7; 66:20). It is usually suggested that both passages were composed by a single scribal editor who sought to frame chapters 56–66. For discussion see, *inter alia*, Koenen, *Ethik*, 28–29; Stromberg, *Isaiah after Exile*, 40–68; Odil Hannes Steck, *Studien zu Tritojesaja*, BZAW 203 (Berlin: de Gruyter, 1991), 229–65.

88 1QIsaᵃ reads אקח ליא לכהנים ללוים (cf. LXX). LXX, Vulgate and the targumim appear to read a ו between priests and Levites. MT should be preferred as the *lectio difficilior*.

89 For a recent discussion with literature, see Stromberg, *Isaiah After Exile*, 135–41.

90 Sommer, *A Prophet Reads Scripture*, 147.

91 1QIsaᵃ omits שרת and portrays the foreigners blessing YHWH, rather than loving him. LXX translates שרת with δουλεύειν rather than the usual λειτουργέω. In addition לעבדים is translated as εἰς δούλους καὶ δούλας. Since women cannot serve as priests this excluded a cultic understanding of Isa 56:6. For discussion see D. W. Van Winkle, "An Inclusive Authoritative Text in Ex-

When Isaiah 56 is read, as it appears to have been in antiquity, as a promise to install foreign converts as priests there is an impressive overlap between Isaiah 56 and Ezekiel 44, with a number of close verbal parallels. The intention of the divine oracles, however, is the opposite of one another. Both passages concern foreigners (בני נכר; Isa 56:3; Ezek 44:7, 9) and their access to the temple, which is also described as "my house" (ביתי; Isa 56:7; 44:7). Whilst Isaiah 56 permits the foreigners into the temple, והביאותים אל־הר קדשי (v. 6), Ezekiel 44 sees it as a matter for condemnation and forbids it, לא יבוא אל־מקדשי (vv. 7, 9). Where Isaiah 56 is concerned that the foreigner not profane (חלל) the Sabbath, but hold fast to the covenant (מחזיקים בבריתי), Ezekiel sees the admission of foreigners as a profanation (חלל) of the sanctuary and a breaking of the covenant (ויפרו את־בריתי). For Ezekiel 44 the numerous verbal resonances with Isaiah 56 are almost entirely limited to the reproach in v. 7 and its negation in v. 9.[92]

We may now turn to the question of the direction of dependency. Recent treatments of the textual relationship are unanimous: Isaiah 56 is dependent on Ezekiel 44. Neither Schaper nor Fishbane justify their position on the direction of dependence. Both appear to have made this judgement based on a broad chronological ordering of Ezekiel and Trito-Isaiah. Since it is generally agreed that both Isa 56:1–8 and Ezek 44:6–16 are late additions to their respective books, it is difficult to see how the texts can be dated relative to one another apart from a careful comparison of the texts. Tuell has made such an attempt. He argues that "Isa 56:1–8 represents a deliberate, polemical response to Ezek 44:1–14".[93] He examines the vocabulary common to both passages and concludes, "because the language found in Isa 56 is characteristic of material from throughout Ezek 40–48, it is more likely that Third Isaiah responds to the Zadokite program spelled out in Ezekiel than that Ezek 44 responds to Isa 56".[94] The language that Tuell refers to is: שרת, which is used of Zadokite altar service throughout Ezekiel 40–48; the concern with separation (הבדיל); the theme of God's holy mountain; and the use of הביא for entry to the sanctuary.

---

clusive Communities", in *Writing and Reading the Scroll of Isaiah: Studies of an Interpretive Tradition*, ed. Craig C. Broyles and Craig A. Evans, VTSup 70 (Leiden: Brill, 1997).

92 The main exception would be שרת which is found throughout Ezek 44:6–16. לוה does not appear in Ezek 44, and עבד only features in 44:14.

93 Tuell, "Priesthood", 187. It should be observed that this is a rather broad use of the word "polemic". The eirenic stance of Isa 56 is clearly a response to some other text or situation, but the element of dispute and argument is absent. There is, perhaps, a danger that the material that follows in Isa 56:9–57:13 has coloured the assessment of Isa 56:1–8. Ezekiel 44, on the other hand, is well described as "polemic".

94 Ibid., 198.

None of Tuell's examples are particularly convincing. Not only is each word that Tuell cites widely used in the Persian period across a variety of literature – P, Ezra-Nehemiah, Chronicles, Ezekiel – but close examination of each individual example undermines Tuell's argument. First, Tuell observes that שרת is used across Ezekiel 40 – 48 and we may recall that it is a good rule of thumb that a lexeme appears at one point in the dependent text and is distributed more widely in the source text. As Tuell observes, however, שרת always occurs in Ezekiel 40 – 48 in relation to the altar service of the sons of Zadok. These uses are thought either to represent a redactional layer or a variety of later additions, *Fortschreibung*, influenced by Ezek 44:6 – 16.[95] As such they can bear no more weight than a single occurrence in assessing dependency. But, further evidence needs to be taken into account, for Trito-Isaiah also employs שרת elsewhere. Significantly, these occurrences in 60:7, 10 and 61:6 stand in close relationship to the use of שרת in Isaiah 56 for they involve foreigners (בני נכר; 60:10; 61:5) in some way. It is usually thought that Isaiah 60 – 62 represents the original core of Trito-Isaiah, around which the surrounding chapters developed. Consistent with that thesis, Tiemeyer has made a persuasive case that Isa 56:6 – 8 develops statements about foreigners and the priesthood in Isa 60:7, 10 and 61:6.[96] This suggests we see the appearance of שרת and בני נכר in Isaiah 56 as an internal development of Trito-Isaianic themes rather than resulting from the influence of Ezekiel 44.

Second, although the idea of separation is integral to Ezekiel's vision, the root הבדיל is only found in 42:20, where the purpose of the wall around the sanctuary is to separate the holy and the common. The use of הבדיל in Isaiah 56 is somewhat different. The foreigner complains of his separation from the people. This is far closer to how הבדיל is used in Ezra and Nehemiah where the people separate themselves from foreigners (e. g. Ezra 9:1; Neh 9:2).[97] There is, thus, no basis for thinking that Ezekiel 44 has influenced Isaiah 56 in its use of הבדיל.

---

95 For the former position see Gese, *Der Verfassungsentwurf*, 64–67; and for the latter see Rudnig, *Heilig und Profan*, 318–31; Zimmerli, *Ezechiel*, 1122–40.

96 Lena-Sofia Tiemeyer, *Priestly Rites and Prophetic Rage*, FAT II/19 (Tübingen: Mohr Siebeck, 2006), 274–81. Tiemeyer provides additional evidence that Isa 56 is a development of ideas found in Isa 60 – 62: the use of בני נכר (esp. 60:10; 61:5), the use of קבץ (60:7; cf. 56:8), and the expression יעלו על־רצון מזבחי (60:7; cf. 56:7).

97 As recognized by Herbert Donner, "Jesaja lvi 1–7: ein Abrogationsfall innerhalb des Kanons – Implikationen und Konsequenzen", in *Congress Volume: Salamanca 1983*, ed. John A. Emerton, VTSup 36 (Leiden: Brill, 1985), 81–95.

Third, the theme of God's holy mountain is common to both eschatological visions in Isaiah and Ezekiel, as Tuell concedes.[98] Ezekiel's vision opens with the prophet being set on "a very high mountain" (40:2). The mountain location receives no further mention in Ezekiel's temple vision with the exception of the beginning of the Law of the Temple: "This is the Law of the Temple: the entire territory on the top of the mountain all around will be most holy (זאת תורת הבית על ראש ההר כל גבלו סביב סביב קדש קדשים)" (43:12). Both texts are at some remove from Ezekiel 44, and consequently Tuell's argument is irrelevant for the specific issue of determining the relationship between Ezekiel 44 and Isaiah 56. Even if this were not the case, the distribution of the expression "my holy mountain" (הר קדשי) across Trito-Isaiah (56:7; 57:13; 65:11, 25; 66:20; cf. 11:9) would also tell against Tuell's position. The theme of God's holy mountain has roots in earlier Israelite tradition and this is sufficient for explaining its appearance in both Trito-Isaiah and Ezekiel's temple vision.

Fourth, הביא is used in two different ways in Ezekiel 40–48. It is used of the way in which the angelic guide conducts the prophet around the temple and it is also used of priestly access to the sanctuary. Only the latter is comparable to the use of הביא in Isaiah 56. As was the case with שרת, the appearance of this usage of הביא only occurs in relation to the priestly privilege of the sons of Zadok. These occurrences are usually thought to be from the same redactional layer or to be dependent on the use of הביא in Ezekiel 44. In addition, the use of הביא in relation to access is already found in Deut 23:2–9. For many interpreters of Isaiah 56 the use of הביא is evidence of the influence of Deuteronomy 23,[99] rather than Ezekiel 44.

I want to argue that, *contra* Tuell, Schaper and Fishbane, Ezekiel 44 has drawn upon Isaiah 56, and not the reverse. This argument is grounded in three observations. First, and most significantly, the oracle in Ezekiel 44 responds directly to the situation envisaged by Isaiah 56, but Isaiah 56 does not respond directly to the situation envisaged by Ezekiel 44. The scenario that provokes the divine rebuke in Ezekiel 44 is the admission of foreigners into the sanctuary, their presence at the sacrifices and their ordination to the priesthood. The divine judgement in vv. 9–16 is a clear rejection of this state of affairs. The foreigner is excluded from temple service that is handed over to Levites and priests. The scenario that provokes the divine ire is exactly that envisaged in Isaiah 56, *if* שרת and עבד are understood as priestly service. The faithful foreigner behaves

---

98 "However, because the holy mountain is also an important aspect of the thought world of Third Isaiah (Isa 57:13; 65:11, 25; 66:20), the use of such language need not derive from Ezekiel" (Tuell, "Priesthood", 196).
99 See also Schaper, "Rereading the Law".

like a priest, is admitted to the sanctuary and offers sacrifices (Isa 56:6–7). Thus, Ezekiel 44 can be seen as a direct response to one common understanding of the oracle in Isaiah 56. But the reverse is not the case. The scenario that the foreigner laments is that he will be excluded from YHWH's people. YHWH's word of judgement in Ezekiel 44 prohibits the foreigner from entering the sanctuary, but says nothing about excluding him from the people. Indeed, the foreigner is said to be in the midst of the people (בתוך בני ישראל; Ezek 44:9). Now, while it can be argued that exclusion from the sanctuary is effectively to bar the foreigner from YHWH's people, this is to take a number of steps beyond what Ezekiel 44 explicitly says. A more convincing case could be made that the foreigner's lament echoes Ezra 9–10 and Nehemiah 9–13, or reflects the events described in those texts.[100] The divine generosity to the foreigner in Isaiah 56 is a development of ideas expounded in Isaiah 60–62, which is usually recognized as the earlier core of Trito-Isaiah. The core chapters of Trito-Isaiah view the foreigners in a similar way to Deutero-Isaiah. They envisage the sons of the foreigner (בני נכר) serving the returnee Israelites and bringing animals to be offered at the temple.[101] The nations will recognize Israel's vindication and do obeisance. The participation in the Israelite community is not envisaged and only emerges in the final stages of Trito-Isaiah's development

Second, and closely related to the first point, it is difficult to see why the oracle of Isaiah 56 with all its ambiguity would be given as a response to the oracle of Ezekiel 44 with its clear implications that foreigners may not serve as priests. It is more logical to argue that the clear is a response to the ambiguous.

Third, as we have seen, the distribution of vocabulary suggests that terms like שרת and בני נכר are at home in Trito-Isaiah, rather than in Ezekiel 40–48. In particular, שרת and בני נכר occur in Isaiah 60–62, which is usually recognized as the original core of Trito-Isaiah, whilst the occurrences of שרת in Ezekiel 40–48 are only in texts usually thought to be dependent on 44:6–16. The distribution of בני נכר is even more compelling evidence of the dependence of Ezekiel

---

100 As we have already observed, the verb הבדיל is employed on numerous occasions in Ezra and Nehemiah to describe the separation of foreigners from the Israelites. Particularly notable is Neh 9:2 which describes the separation of the seed of Israel מכל בני נכר. The logic of this development is apparent in Fishbane's exposition of these texts. Fishbane begins with the exclusion of the foreigners in the time of Ezra and Nehemiah. He then observes that this position was contradicted by Trito-Isaiah who will have pious foreigners officiating at the sacrifices. But this possibility was rejected in Ezek 44:7 (Fishbane, *Biblical Interpretation*, 118–19). This exposition is remarkable for the fact that Fishbane orders the texts according to their natural relationship to one another, *despite the fact that he believes their order of composition to have been quite different* (see, e.g., Ibid., 142–43 n. 98).
101 See Tiemeyer, *Priestly Rites.*

44. The only occurrences of בני נכר in Ezekiel are found in 44:7, 9. Elsewhere Ezekiel uses זר for the foreigner.[102] The dependence of Ezekiel 44 on Isaiah 56 would
explain this departure from the typical usage in Ezekiel.

1.1.3 YHWH's Reproach

Having examined the relationship between Isaiah 56 and Ezekiel 44 we are now
in a position to re-examine the first part of the divine oracle. The oracle opens
with Israel being addressed as rebellious (v. 6). A number of common expressions from the book are used: כל[105] כה אמר אדני יהוה[105] מרי,[104] בית ישראל,[103]
תועבתיכם.[106] These are used to generate a distinctive Ezekielian tone, rather
than to establish a particular allusion. The central charge is declared at the out-
set: the Israelites have admitted foreigners into the sanctuary (בהביאכם בני־נכר).
As we have seen, Ezekiel 44 repudiates precisely the situation that Isaiah 56 appears to have permitted.

---

102 Block rightly thinks the choice of בני נכר is deliberate. He suggests that זר is unsuitable because elsewhere in Ezekiel the term refers to the nations as agents of judgement or under judgement themselves, rather than the cultic access of individuals. The use of בני נכר may allude to
Gen 17:12, 27 where the foreigner is expected to undergo circumcision in order to join the community (Block, *Ezekiel*, 622). The first suggestion is not especially compelling and the second
avoids Ezek 44:9's exclusion of *all* foreigners. For the influence of Isa 56 upon Ezek 44 at this
point, albeit undeveloped, see already Cook, "Innerbiblical Interpretation", 207–08.
103 See Ezek 3:1, 4, 5, 7, 17; 4:3, 4, 5; 5:4; 6:11; 8:6, 10, 11, 12; 9:9; 11:5, 15; 12:6, 9, 10, 24, 27; 13:5, 9;
14:4, 5, 6, 7, 11; 17:2; 18:6, 15, 25, 29, 30, 31; 20:13, 27, 30, 31, 39, 40, 44; 22:18; 24:21; 28:24, 25; 29:6, 16,
21; 33:7, 10, 11, 20; 34:30; 35:15; 36:10, 17, 21, 22, 32, 37; 37:11, 16; 39:12, 22, 23, 25, 29; 40:4; 43:7, 10;
44:12, 22; 45:6, 8, 17. There are 147 occurrences of בית ישראל in the Hebrew Bible, 83 of which are
found in the book of Ezekiel.
104 See Ezek 2:5, 6, 7, 8; 3:9, 26, 27; 12:2, 3, 9, 25; 17:12; 24:3. There are 24 occurrences of מרי in the
Hebrew Bible, 16 of which are found in the book of Ezekiel. מרי usually appears in Ezekiel as בית
מרי (except 2:6). This has frequently led to the suggestion that Ezek 44:6 be emended, a proposal
supported by the Greek's πρὸς τὸν οἶκον τὸν παραπικραίνοντα.
105 See Ezek 2:4; 3:11, 27; 5:5, 7, 8; 6:3, 11; 7:2, 5; 11:7, 16, 17; 12:10, 19, 23, 28; 13:3, 8, 13, 18, 20; 14:4,
6, 21; 15:6; 16:3, 36, 59; 17:3, 9, 19, 22; 20:3, 5, 27, 30, 39; 21:3, 29, 31, 33; 22:3, 19, 28; 23:22, 28, 32, 35,
46; 24:3, 6, 9, 21; 25:3, 6, 8, 12, 13, 15, 16; 26:3, 7, 15, 19; 27:3; 28:2, 6, 12, 22, 25; 29:3, 8, 13, 19; 30:2, 10,
13, 22; 31:10, 15; 32:3, 11, 25, 27; 34:2, 10, 11, 17, 20; 35:3, 14; 36:2, 3, 4, 5, 6, 7, 13, 22, 33, 37; 37:5, 9, 12,
19, 21; 38:3, 10, 14, 17; 39:1, 17, 25; 43:18; 44:9; 45:9, 18; 46:1, 16; 47:13. There are 134 occurrences of
כה אמר אדני יהוה in the Hebrew Bible, 122 of which are found in the book of Ezekiel.
106 See Ezek 5:9, 11; 6:9; 7:3, 8; 11:18; 12:16; 14:6; 16:22, 43, 51; 22:2; 33:29; 44:7. There are 16 occurrences of כל תועבה with a pronominal suffix in the Hebrew Bible, 15 of which are found in the
book of Ezekiel.

Despite the numerous similarities with Isaiah 56, it is apparent that the characterization of the foreigners in Ezekiel 44 goes significantly beyond that which can be derived from Isaiah 56. A close examination shows that these evidence dependence on other biblical texts.

First, the foreigner is characterized as having "uncircumcised heart and uncircumcised flesh", ערלי לב וערלי בשר. The language of uncircumcised flesh is reminiscent of the covenant with Abraham in Genesis 17, where circumcision defines those who are within the household of Abraham and participate in the covenant. Significantly, Abraham is required to circumcise those that have been born into his household as well as those that have been bought from a foreigner (בן־נכר; vv. 12, 27). Clearly Genesis 17 shares with Ezekiel 44 the supposition that to be a foreigner, בן־נכר, is to be uncircumcised. According to Genesis 17, the male who is not circumcised "breaks my covenant" (את בריתי הפר; v. 14), language that finds its close parallel in Ezek 44:7bβ. The problem with the foreigner is that lack of physical circumcision is also mirrored in a heart that is uncircumcised. Such language reflects the development of circumcision into a metaphor for internal commitment to the covenant found in some late biblical texts: Lev 26:41; Deut 10:16; 30:6; Jer 4:4; 9:25. The reference to circumcision in flesh and heart, and the breaking of the covenant should almost certainly be seen as further evidence that Ezekiel 44 is dependent on other texts. Verses 7 and 9 are the only places in Ezekiel's temple vision that we have reference made to circumcision or its lack, and verse 7 is the only time that reference is made to a covenant.

If we are right to sense here an allusion to Genesis 17, an interesting light is shed on the problematic appearance of ויפרו את בריתי, "and they broke my covenant", in the Masoretic text of Ezek 44:7bβ. The versions translate as though they had read ותפרו, "and you broke my covenant". The problem with which the early translators struggled is that the accusation is against the house of Israel. So why are the foreigners blamed for breaking the covenant? The text-critical argument for keeping the MT is that of *lectio difficilior*.[107] But we can now recognize an additional argument in favour of the MT. The source text of Genesis 17:14 charges the uncircumcised male with breaking the covenant, and the dependent text of Ezek 44:7 follows accordingly. In the new context of Ezekiel 44, however, accusing *the foreigner* of breaking the covenant does not result in a great deal of cogency in an oracle addressed to *the Israelites*, and the versions alter the text to produce a smoother logic.

---

[107] For different arguments for MT's reading, see Driver, "Ezekiel", 309; Galambusch, "Northern Voyage".

Second, in v. 7bα a different accusation is introduced: "in your offering my food, fat and blood", בהקריבכם את לחמי חלב ודם. Awabdy and Konkel have convincingly argued that 44:7bα is dependent on Lev 22:25.[108] The decisive evidence for an allusion is the appearance of "my food" (לחמי). The use of לחם for sacrifice is attested nowhere else in Ezekiel, but is common within P and H.[109] The expressions "food of his/your God" and "my food" are particularly prominent in the instructions concerning priests in Leviticus 21–22.[110] In Lev 22:25 reference is made to the foreigner, בן־נכר:

ומיד בן נכר לא תקריבו את לחם אלהיכם מכל אלה כי משחתם בהם מום בם לא ירצו לכם

And do not <u>offer</u> as <u>food to your God</u> any such animals that you have received from a <u>foreigner</u>, because their blemish is in them, deformity is in them. They will not be accepted on your behalf.

It would appear, therefore, that Lev 22:25 has inspired in Ezek 44:7bα an additional reason for outrage at the conduct of the house of Israel: the offerings of foreigners are defiling.[111]

This analysis suggests that the divine oracle in Ezekiel 44 was a response to the situation envisaged in Isaiah 56. The Israelites have admitted foreigners into the sanctuary and permitted them to serve as priests. This possibility is unequivocally rejected in Ezekiel. On what basis could the authors of Ezekiel 44 reject what is presented in Isaiah as nothing less than a *divine oracle*. Why shouldn't foreigners be admitted to the temple as Isaiah 56 insists? The allusions to the Pentateuch reveal the underlying logic. Foreigners are excluded on the basis of what existing torah says about the בן־נכר. The first accusation, drawing on Genesis 17, characterizes the בן־נכר as uncircumcised and a violator of the covenant. The second, drawing on Leviticus 22, has the Israelites offering polluted sacrifices whilst the בן־נכר is present.

It is difficult to ascertain whether all of these allusions to pentateuchal texts were part of the original strategy to resist the agenda of Isaiah 56, or whether the text was enriched with them at a later stage. In both cases, the accusations in-

---

108 Mark Awabdy, "YHWH Exegetes Torah: How Ezekiel 44:7–9 Bars Foreigners from the Sanctuary", *JBL* 131 (2012): 685–703; Konkel, *Architektonik*, 103. *Contra* Awabdy, I do not think it is possible to explain vv. 6–8 as inspired by Lev 22:25 only.
109 See Lev 3:11, 16 (P) and 21:6, 8, 17, 21–22; 22:25; cf. Num 28:2, 24.
110 Awabdy, "YHWH Exegetes Torah", 692.
111 Lev 22:25 insists that the offerings of a foreigner are regarded as deformed. It is unclear, though, whether the author of Ezek 44:7bα understood Lev 22:25 to refer to the deformity of the foreigner. "Because their blemish is in them, deformity is in them" is sufficiently gnomic to be patient of more than one understanding.

troduce elements that find no further reflection in Ezekiel 44: uncircumcision, the covenant and sacrifice as "my food". Both are potentially instances of successive stages of *Fortschreibung*. The first accusation does not sit easily with the original oracle's focus on *Israel's* failure. The differences between MT's ויפרו and versional renderings provide evidence that early interpreters did find the juxtaposition of Israel's fault and the foreigners' violation of the covenant problematic. On the other hand, the charge that the foreigners "broke my covenant" directly challenges the notion in Isaiah 56 that a foreigner could "hold fast my covenant", and consequently could be viewed as integral to Ezekiel's rebuttal of Trito-Isaiah. When we turn to the second accusation we encounter a number of indicators of possible *Fortschreibung*. First, suspicions are aroused by the appearance of an additional temporal clause introduced by ב and an infinitive construct. Second, the complaint about offerings introduces a new issue that is only loosely connected to the admission of foreigners. The accusation finds no exact parallel in Isaiah 56 where the root קרב is not attested. Third, the complaint could be viewed as an interruption of the connection between the foreigners' lack of circumcision and the violation of the covenant. Its appearance contributes to the discomfort with MT's ויפרו, since the accusation about sacrifices shifts the focus to the actions of the Israelites and away from the foreigners. In neither case can we be certain that we have an instance of *Fortschreibung*, for this is precisely the kind of instance where inner-biblical interpretation and *Fortschreibung* can claim to account for the same data. My own tentative view is that v. 7bα is an instance of *Fortschreibung* inspired by Lev 22:25, but that v. 7aβ (ערלי לב וערלי בשר), bβ was part of the original response to the divine oracle in Isaiah 56.

The difficulty of a further accusation being introduced that is distant from the original complaint about the admission of foreigners is also present in v. 8. There where we have two accusations that have close verbal similarities to statements about the responsibilities of the sons of Aaron in Numbers 18. First, Ezek 44:8 has a negative statement about the offerings, which is very similar to Num 18:8:

ולא שמרתם משמרת קדשי

You have not kept <u>charge</u> of my <u>sacred offerings</u> (Ezek 44:8a).

נתתי לך את משמרת תרומתי לכל קדשי בני ישראל

I am giving you <u>charge</u> of my offerings, all the <u>sacred offerings</u> of the Israelites (Num 18:8).

This is followed, second, by a positive statement about the sanctuary, which is close to Num 18:5:

ותשימון לשמרי משמרתי במקדשי לכם

You appointed them <u>to keep my charge in my sanctuary</u> (Ezek 44:8b).

ושמרתם את משמרת הקדש

You shall keep the charge of the sanctuary (Num 18:5).

These two accusations move beyond the problem of admitting foreigners to the sanctuary, and envisage the foreigner taking responsibility for the sanctuary and the offerings. They raise questions about the relationship between Numbers 18 and Ezekiel 44. To consider this issue fully, we must turn to the remainder of Ezekiel's oracle for there are numerous other connections in vv. 9–16 with Numbers 18.

1.2 The Word of Judgement

The word of reproach (vv. 6–8) criticizes the Israelites for allowing the foreigners into the temple. The identification of the foreigners has been the central concern in my examination of the first part of the divine oracle. When we turn to the second part of the divine oracle, the focus is instead on the Levites who are literally at the heart of the word of judgement. The word of judgement opens with the foreigners (v. 9) and closes with the sons of Zadok (vv. 15–16), but most of the judgement is concerned with the Levites (vv. 10–14). What, then, does the oracle say about the Levites?

1.2.1 The Levites of Ezekiel 44

The word of judgement provides a complex set of distinctions that distinguish the Levites from both foreigners and Zadokites. Initially the Levites are contrasted to the foreigner: "No foreigner shall enter my sanctuary, rather (כי אם) the Levites...". Whilst the foreigners were "in my sanctuary" (במקדשי) profaning it, the Levites are to minister "in my sanctuary". They also minister in "my house" (ביתי) where they act as gatekeepers. They do not offer the fat and blood, but they do slaughter the burnt offering and the sacrifices for the people. Thus, the description of the Levites' tasks in v. 11 corresponds in various ways to the cultic abuses described in v. 7.

The contrast between Levites and the sons of Zadok is found in vv. 12–15. An account is given of the Levites' failure, introduced by יען אשר, "because" (v. 12a), and its consequences, introduced by על־כן, "therefore" (v. 12b).[112] The accusation

---

112 The causal clause introduced by יען אשר can precede or follow the main clause, but it is

concerns the service of the Levites. They did cultic service for the Israelites, but are faulted for doing it before idols, and not before YHWH. Consequently, a contrast is drawn between the Levites and the faithful sons of Zadok. The Levites will not act as priests (v. 13), unlike the sons of Zadok who are identified as Levitical priests (v. 15). The Levites may not partake of the sacred offerings, קדשי, which are further parsed as "the most holy", קדשי הקדשים; but the priests are allowed to approach YHWH's table. Finally, they will have charge (שמר משמרת) of the house (v. 14), unlike the sons of Zadok who will have charge (שמר משמרת) of the sanctuary (v. 15).

Thus, a careful literary examination of the passage in its received form reveals a subtle rhetorical pattern, which steps from the foreigners (vv. 6–9) to the Levites (vv. 10–14) to the sons of Zadok (vv. 15–16), who then become the focus of the rest of the chapter. The passage can, consequently, be represented as two parallel panels, the first contrasting foreigners and Levites, the second Levites and Zadokites:

Panel 1: Foreigners and Levites	Panel 2: Levites and sons of Zadok
Actions of foreigners (vv. 6–8)	Because (יען אשר) of actions of Levites (v. 12)
Leads to exclusion of foreigners (v. 9)	*Leads to* exclusion from priestly role (vv. 13–14)
Rather (כי אם) Levites went away from me (v. 10)	But (ו) Zadokites were faithful (v. 15a)
Exercise of cultic role (v. 11)	Exercise of priestly role (vv. 15b–16)

Arranging the text into two parallel panels highlights additional features of this divine oracle. The cultic role of the Levites (v. 11b) can be contrasted insightfully with the priestly role of the sons of Zadok (vv. 15b–16). In v. 11b we encounter repeated use of the emphatic "they", המה, just as we do in vv. 15b–16. If we compare the statements about Levites and the sons of Zadok in vv. 11 and 15, we can observe that the cultic service of the Levites is viewed in relation to the Israelites (לעם; v. 11), whilst the cultic service of the sons of Zadok is viewed in relation to YHWH (לי; v. 15). This differentiated service is represented by responsibility for distinct parts of the sacrificial procedure. The Levites slaughter the burnt offering

---

more common for it to precede (Mulder, "Die Partikel יַעַן". Connecting it to the preceding clause confuses the structure of the passage, e. g. Rodney Duke, "Punishment or Restoration? Another Look at the Levites of Ezekiel 44.6–16", *JSOT* 40 (1988): 68. In contrast Cook and Fechter correctly divide vv. 10–14 into vv. 10–11 and 12–14 (Cook, "Innerbiblical Interpretation", 200; Friedrich Fechter, "Priesthood in Exile according to the Book of Ezekiel", in *Ezekiel's Hierarchical World: Wrestling with a Tiered Reality*, ed. Stephen L. Cook and Corrine L. Patton, Society of Biblical Literature Symposium Series 31 [Leiden: Brill, 2004], 32).

and the sacrifice on behalf of the people, whilst the priests offer the fat and the blood to YHWH.[113]

Despite the central role that the Levites play in vv. 9 – 16, their introduction is for the attentive reader sudden and unexpected. There is nothing in YHWH's reproach of the Israelites that prepares us for an accusation of the Levites. Their appearance is partially what gives rise to the sense that there is a significant disjunction between the two parts of the oracle. The reader expects Israel to be punished, but YHWH's ire is reserved for the Levites.

The lack of correspondence between accusation and judgement does not arise in v. 9, which echoes the description of the foreigner in v. 7 and insists that every foreigner must be excluded (לא יבוא) from the sanctuary. Nor is the accreditation of the sons of Zadok especially problematic. Verses 15 – 16 grants to the priests descended from Zadok all the functions that the foreigners had been given. Each line is introduced with an emphatic "they", המה. As Rudnig has observed, the overall effect is rather repetitious:[114]

> *They* will approach (יקרבו) me to serve me, and they will stand before me to offer (להקריב) to me fat and blood, says Lord YHWH.
> *They* will enter (יבאו) my sanctuary,
> and *they* will approach (יקרבו) my table to serve me, and they will keep (ושמרו) my charge.

Despite the apparent redundancy, the description of the roles to which the sons of Zadok are appointed provide a pleasing counterpoint to the cultic infractions of the foreigners. The three cultic actions that the Israelites abused by handing them to the foreigners – בוא, קרב and שמר – are assigned to the sons of Zadok. Thus, a clear contrast between the sons of the foreigners and the sons of Zadok is created.

The unexpected appearance of the Levites together with the uncontrived contrast between the foreigners and the sons of Zadok raises questions about

---

113 Since the distinctive roles of the Levites and the sons of Zadok are introduced in vv. 11b and 15b–16 by the emphatic המה, we might wonder about the status of the line, "and they shall be ministers in my sanctuary, overseeing the temple gates and serving in the temple", והיו במקדשי משרתים פקדות אל־שערי הבית ומשרתים את־הבית (v. 11a). The cultic service of the Levites is now viewed in relation to the entire temple complex, rather than the sacrifices of the Israelites. There are at least two different ways to assess v. 11a. It could be regarded as a gloss. The apparent superfluity concentrated around הבית could be compared to את־ביתי in v. 7, which is also often regarded as a gloss. On the other hand, v. 11a could be viewed as providing important parenthetical information that provides context to the distinctive roles of the Levites introduced by the emphatic המה.

114 Rudnig, *Heilig und Profan*, 287. Rudnig finds the contents of the original oracle in v. 15.

the status of vv. 10–14. The removal of these verses would result in a simple and coherent oracle. The oracle would open with Israel accused of allowing foreigners into the temple. A satisfactory conclusion would be reached with the sons of Zadok being granted all the cultic responsibilities and rights that have been abused by the Israelites and the foreigners. Further confirmation of such suspicions are confirmed when we observe that the disjunction between reproach and the word of judgement arises especially in YHWH's words about the Levites. It is in vv. 10–14 that we find a different group being judged. It is here too that most of the references to different infractions occur: Israel went astray after the גלולים. It is also especially in the verses that address the role of the Levites in the temple cult that we find the striking distribution of verbal forms oscillating between past actions and future consequences.

1.2.2 A *Torah* Concerning the Levites

The oscillation between past actions and consequences is the most distinctive and unusual literary feature of the divine oracle in Ezekiel 44. Beginning at v. 10 and disappearing after v. 15a, it is also almost entirely restricted to the verses that discuss the Levites. As a result this feature demands closer examination if we are to reach a better understanding of the critique of the Levites. What might we find were we to separate past actions from the consequences that result? The results are fascinating. If we remove the references to the past, it is apparent that what remains are a series of rulings, a *torah*, about the cultic service of the Levites:

(10)...ונשאו עונם (11) והיו במקדשי משרתים פקדות אל שערי הבית ומשרתים את הבית המה ישחטו את העלה ואת הזבח לעם והמה יעמדו לפניהם לשרתם (12) ...ונשאו עונם (13) ולא יגשו אלי לכהן לי ולגשת על כל קדשי אל קדשי הקדשים ונשאו כלמתם... (14) ונתתי אותם שמרי משמרת הבית לכל עבדתו ולכל אשר יעשה בו (15)...המה יקרבו אלי לשרתני

(10)...They [the Levites] will bear their sin. (11) They shall be ministers in my sanctuary, responsible for the gates of the temple and ministering in the temple. They will slaughter the burnt offering and the sacrifice for the people. They will stand before them and serve them. (12) ...They will bear their sin. (13) They will not come to me to act as priests for me. They will not come near to any of my sacred things, the most sacred things, and they will bear their shame...(14) I will appoint them to keep the charge of the temple, all its service and all that is done in it. (15)...They [the Levitical priests, the sons of Zadok] will come near to me to minister to me.

The isolated *torah* is very similar to Num 18:1–7, where there is a similar division of responsibilities between priests and Levites. In both passages the Levites are excluded from priestly duties and may not approach certain sancta. Nevertheless, they have responsibility for some of the sanctuary and its activities. The idea of responsibility is expressed the same way through the idiom "to bear sin", נשא עון (Num 18:1; Ezek 44:10, 12). Finally, there is a shared concern with the sanctuary's limits being penetrated by an unauthorized individual: the זר of Numbers 18 (vv. 4, 7) and the בן נכר of Ezekiel 44 (vv. 7, 9).

The similarity between the two passages even extends to their structure. In Ezekiel 44 a positive statement about the Levites' responsibility for the temple and slaughtering the sacrifice (v. 11) is followed by a negative statement about their exclusion from priestly roles and the sacrificial portions (v. 13). A summary statement about Levitical roles (v. 14) is followed by the duties of the sons of Zadok (vv. 15–16). In Num 18:3–7 the Levites are assigned responsibility for the whole tent (v. 3a), but may not approach sanctuary or altar (v. 3b). Their duties are summarized (v. 4) and then the duties of the sons of Aaron are prescribed (vv. 5–7). The similarity is particularly striking in the case of the summaries in Ezek 44:14 and Num 18:4 which are almost identical.[115]

As a result of these parallels, there can be no doubt that a close literary relationship exists between the two passages. Scholars have long appreciated this fact, but the question that has been much debated is the direction of dependence. Since Wellhausen many have followed him in arguing that Numbers 18 draws on Ezekiel 44, but there has also been no shortage of scholars who have argued that Ezekiel 44 is dependent on Numbers 18.[116] In order to address this question we will need to give careful attention to how the different roles of the priests and the Levites are described in each passage.

My analysis of Ezekiel 44 has already demonstrated that the differences between the Levites and the sons of Zadok are described in a variety of different ways. First, the Levites may not act as priests, but the sons of Zadok are described as Levitical priests. Second, the differences are described in terms of "keeping the charge" (שמר משמרת). The Levites have responsibility for the house (v. 14), whilst the priests have responsibility for the sanctuary (v. 15). Third, the different roles are presented according to the one to whom the service is directed. The Levites stand before the people and minister to them (לעם; v. 11); the priests

---

115 ונתתי אותם שמרי משמרת הבית לכל עבדתו ולכל אשר יעשה בו, "I will appoint them to keep the charge of the temple, all its service and all that is done in it" (Ezek 44:14); ונלוו עליך ושמרו את משמרת אהל מועד לכל עבדת האהל, "they are attached to you and they will keep the charge of the tent of meeting, all the service of the tent" (Num 18:4).

116 See, e. g., the alternative positions taken by Reinhard Achenbach, *Die Vollendung der Tora: Studien zur Redaktionsgeschichte des Numeribuches im Kontext von Hexateuch und Pentateuch*, BZABR 3 (Wiesbaden: Harrassowitz, 2003) and Konkel, *Architektonik*.

stand before YHWH and minister to him (לי; v. 15).[117] Fourth, this service is represented by responsibility for different parts of the sacrificial procedure. The Levites slaughter the burnt offering and the sacrifice on behalf of the people (v. 11), whilst the priests offer the fat and the blood to YHWH (v. 15). Fifth, the location in which the service takes place is described in different ways. The priests may enter the inner sanctuary (v. 16) and, whilst we might expect them to be outside the inner sanctuary, the Levites are said to be in the sanctuary, but stationed at the gates (v. 11).[118] Sixth, the cultic dues highlight the different roles that the Levites and priests have, though these are only described negatively for the Levites. The Levites may not partake of the sacred offerings (קדשי), which are further parsed as "the most holy" (קדשי הקדשים); but the priests are allowed to approach YHWH's table.

In Numbers 18 Aaron's sons and the rest of the tribe of Levi are distinguished, with different cultic duties (vv. 1–7) and dues (vv. 8–32) prescribed. The description of duties in Num 18:1–7 is primarily concerned with access to the sanctuary and is described as "keeping the charge" (שמר משמרת). According to Numbers 18 the priests are responsible for the sanctuary, the altar and the holy vessels (vv. 3, 5), whilst the Levites have responsibility for the wider tent complex (vv. 3, 4). The list of cultic dues granted to Aaron's sons is extensive and described as "the holy gifts of the Israelites" (קדשי בני־ישראל) and then further as "the most holy things" (קדשי הקדשים) (vv. 8–9). These are sacrificial dues, and only to be consumed by the priestly families. For their service the Levites receive the tithes of the Israelites.

A careful comparison of Numbers 18 and Ezekiel 44 does not suggest an exact correspondence. At some points we appear to have a similar conceptuality, but with different vocabulary. Thus, although the terms for the different divisions of the sanctuary complex differ – הקדש and האהל/אהל מועד in Numbers 18, but מקדשי and הבית in Ezekiel 44 – a similar division of sacred space is envisaged in both passages. The different terms reflect the different constructions presupposed – the wilderness tent versus a building – and are consistent with the wider context of both passages. Similarly both texts agree that the cultic officials are responsible for protecting the various parts of the sanctuary complex from tres-

---

117 Konkel, *Architektonik*, 106.
118 Alternatively, מקדש may be being used here of the whole sanctuary complex. Stevenson argues for this position, observing that מקדש can bear different meanings (Kalinda Rose Stevenson, *The Vision of Transformation: The Territorial Rhetoric of Ezekiel 40–48*, SBLDS 154 [Atlanta: Scholars Press, 1996], 63). Milgrom overstates the opposing case by insisting that מקדש can only mean the wider sanctuary complex (Jacob Milgrom, *Leviticus 1–16: A New Translation with Introduction and Commentary*, AB 3 [New York: Doubleday, 1991], 754–55).

passers. In Numbers 18 these trespassers are identified with the term זר, a favourite of P and texts influenced by P, rather than בני נכר, which is found in Ezekiel 44. At other points terminology and conceptuality appear to overlap. Thus, the juxtaposition of קדש and קדשי הקדשים in Num 18:8–9 is identical to the cultic dues that Ezek 44:13 implies are accorded to the priest.[119] Additionally, the responsibility for the wider complex is described as כל עבדה in both passages (Num 18:4; Ezek 44:14).[120]

More important for investigating the relationship between the two passages are places where Ezekiel 44 and Numbers 18 part company. The first of these is the focus in Ezekiel 44 on the beneficiary of the cultic service. As we have seen this is a significant way in which Ezekiel 44 distinguishes between the Levites and the sons of Zadok: the Levites minister to the people and the sons of Zadok minister to YHWH. Numbers 18 recounts only that the Levites minister to the Aaronic priests (Num 18:2). Elsewhere in Numbers the Levitical service for the people is clearly described. In Numbers 16–17 Moses rebukes Korah and accuses him of despising the fact that YHWH has set apart the Levites for standing and ministering to the community. The final clause in Ezek 44:11 is almost identical to Num 16:9.[121] In Num 3:7 the Levites are ordained in order to "perform duties for Aaron and the whole congregation in front of the tent". If we turn to the duties of the priests, the book of Numbers focuses on the protection of the sanctuary. It does not explicitly state that the priest will stand and minister to YHWH as Ezekiel 44 does. Such a statement is made of the tribe of Levi as a whole in Deut 10:8 and of the priest in Deut 17:12 (cf. 18:5, 7). Thus,

---

119 Ezekiel 44:13 appears to draw its phraseology from Lev 21:21–23, denying to the Levites what Leviticus 21 permits to the priests. It is at this point that Ezekiel 44 departs noticeably from Numbers 18. The appropriation of Lev 21:21–23 might have been inspired by the similarities between Num 18:3b and Lev 21:23aα. Whilst Num 18:3b reads אך אל־כלי הקדש ואל־המזבח לא יקרבו Lev 21:23aα has the similar אך אל־הפרכת לא יבא ואל־המזבח לא יגש. It is notable that the animating concern in Lev 21:23 is the profanation of the sanctuary (ולא יחלל את־מקדשי). Leviticus 21:21–23 legislates for the member of the priestly family who has a blemish. He is forbidden from serving as a priest near the curtain or at the altar (לא יגש להקריב), but he may partake of the sacred portions (לחם אלהיו מקדשי הקדשים ומן־הקדשים יאכל). In Ezek 44 these statements are transformed by prohibiting both activities to the Levite and by assimilating the commandments to divine speech.

120 Num 18:4 has לכל עבדת האהל, which is almost identical to Ezek 44:14, לכל עבדתו. For discussion see Jacob Milgrom, *Studies in Levitical Terminology: I The Encroacher and the Levite. The Term 'Aboda*, UCPNES 14 (Berkeley: University of California Press, 1970), 73–75.

121 והמה יעמדו לפניהם לשרתם, "they will stand before them and serve them" (Ezek 44:11); ולעמד לפני העדה לשרתם, "and to serve before the congregation and serve them" (Num 16:9).

the distinction that Ezekiel 44 makes between Levites and priests can be found in other pentateuchal texts, but not in Numbers 18.

A second and related area of departure is the attribution of different sacrificial responsibilities to the Levites and priests. According to Numbers 18 only the priests are to approach the altar (vv. 3, 5). In the sacrificial legislation of Leviticus the altar is the place where the blood of the sacrifices is sprinkled or poured out and the fat offered up (Leviticus 1–7). These activities are a priestly responsibility as Lev 7:33, the closest parallel to Ezek 44:15b, makes clear.[122] In the sacrificial system of Leviticus no role is granted to the Levites, rather Leviticus envisages the lay worshipper slaughtering the sacrifice that he has brought (e.g. Lev 1:5). Thus, the perspective on the sacrificial responsibility of the Levites in Ezekiel 44 has no parallel in the Pentateuch. Nor does it appear to have been the usual practice in the Second Temple period, where reports of sacrifice suggest that the one bringing the sacrifice slaughtered it.[123]

Finally, we may also observe that whilst both passages speak of the cultic functionaries "bearing their sin" (תשאו את־עון; Num 18:1, 23; Ezek 44:10, 12; cf. v. 13), the act of transgression appears to be different in each passage. In Numbers 18 the concern appears to be a stranger encroaching upon restricted areas of the sanctuary. In Ezekiel 44 "bearing their sin" appears in conjunction with idol worship (vv. 10, 12), but the initial presenting issue was the encroaching of the foreigner (vv. 7, 9).[124]

The existence of a close relationship between Numbers 18 and Ezekiel 44 is clear; the question of the direction of dependence is critical. In addressing the question of dependence it is crucial to observe that, whilst in various ways Ezekiel 44 appears to go beyond Numbers 18, the same could not be said *vice versa*. This is apparent in the case of the different beneficiaries of the cultic service. Ezekiel 44 reflects an interpretation of Numbers 18 in the light of Deuteronomy. The influence of the book of Deuteronomy is unambiguously present in Ezekiel 44, because v. 15 describes the sons of Zadok as "Levitical priests", a distinctive coinage of Deuteronomy. It is more difficult to argue that the direction of depend-

---

122 Duke rightly observes that "a cultic system, much like that described in P, is assumed in this text" (Duke, "Punishment or Restoration?", 63).

123 Zimmerli, *Ezechiel*, 1127. The Chronicler has the Levites sacrifice the Passover in Josiah's day (2 Chr 35:10–13; cf. v. 6). Yet, as Duke observes the description of Hezekiah's Passover seems to assume lay sacrifice (Duke, "Punishment or Restoration?", 78–79 n. 30).

124 It has rightly been observed that נשא עון can have two possible meanings, "to bear sin" and "to be responsible for (others') sins". Duke makes much of this in his attempt to argue that there is no punishment or degradation of the Levites in Ezek 44, only a restoration (Duke, "Punishment or Restoration?", 65–66). The rephrasing of the idiom in v. 13 seems less open to such ambiguity.

ence has occurred in the opposite direction. First, the texts that parallel Ezekiel 44 are scattered throughout the Pentateuch, and it is more natural to suppose that Ezekiel 44 has creatively drawn material and ideas from a variety of contexts than that Ezekiel 44 had a scattered influence throughout the Pentateuch. Second, if Numbers 18 reflects Ezekiel 44 it is difficult to explain why the distinctive emphasis on the Levites serving the people and the priests serving yhwh is absent. An equally convincing case is the expression "bear their sin". Ezekiel 44 appears to develop the expression beyond Numbers 18 by associating it with idolatry. There is no evidence of influence in the reverse direction, for idolatry is not a concern in Numbers 18.

An additional argument for the priority of Numbers 18 is the responsibility of the Levites for slaughtering the sacrificial animals. We cannot exclude the possibility that the writer of Ezekiel 44 was simply familiar with a different practice, but there are reasons to believe that the difference is a matter of textual interpretation. According to Num 18:2 the Levites are to assist Aaron and his sons "before the tent" (לפני אהל). In what might this service "before the tent" consist? Since the same location is named elsewhere in the Pentateuch as the place where the animals are slaughtered (cf. Lev 3:8, 13), it would not be unnatural for an attentive reader of Leviticus and Numbers to suppose that the Levites had some role in slaughtering the animals. As we have seen, this is the same location where the Levites are said to minister to Aaron *and* the whole congregation (Num 3:7). Slaughtering the sacrifice could be seen as an act that serves both. In Ezekiel's temple vision, then, the Levites would be stationed at the gates of the sanctuary not only to guard the temple from trespassers, but also to act for both priest and people in slaughtering the animals and transferring the carcasses from people to priest.

Our close examination of Ezekiel 44 and Numbers 18 suggests that there are good grounds for thinking that Ezekiel 44 is dependent on Numbers 18. Nevertheless, from Wellhausen onwards many scholars have held that Ezekiel 44 is the earlier text, and that Numbers 18 is dependent on it. Two reasons have been given for this alternative understanding. First, it is argued that the division between priests and Levites is proposed as a novelty in Ezekiel 44. This could not have been possible were there already a tradition that associated the origins of the Levite-priest distinction with the wilderness period. Second, it is thought significant that Ezekiel 44 makes no mention of the Aaronide ancestry of the priesthood and, instead, associates the priesthood with Zadok. If Numbers 18 were dependent on Ezekiel 44, the absence of Zadok would be entirely explicable, since Numbers 18 is located in the wilderness period centuries before Zadok lived.

It is not clear that either argument is decisive. The first argument understands the oracle to be establishing the difference between priests and Levites on the basis of events that were contemporary to the prophet Ezekiel or the writer of Ezekiel 44. Our examination suggests that at the heart of the oracle is a novel, but exegetically grounded, development of the relationships of priests and Levites: the priests minister to YHWH and the Levites minister to the people. The punishment of the Levites is in proportion to the crime. Not only did the Levites go far *from* YHWH, but they also ministered *for* the Israelites before the idols. The downgrading of the Levites is an affirmation of the Levitical choice. It presupposes a division between priests and Levites; it does not create it. Against the second argument, it may be that the choice of Zadok rather than Aaron reflects the fact that Ezekiel's vision envisages a new polity in the land. Whilst the vision draws upon the Mosaic period, it also uses the united monarchy as a model. If the controversial *nasi* of Ezekiel's vision were to be understood as a Davidide,[125] the sons of Zadok, David's priest, would make suitable counterparts in the cultic sphere. This is an issue to which we will return shortly.

1.2.3 The Sins of the Past

If we turn to consider the past actions in Ezek 44:10 – 15a, it is apparent that what has been isolated is more fragmentary:

(10) כי אם הלוים אשר רחקו מעלי בתעות ישראל אשר תעו מעלי אחרי גלוליהם...(12) יען אשר שרתו אותם
לפני גלוליהם והיו לבית ישראל למכשול עון על כן נשאתי ידי עליהם נאם אדני יהוה...(13)...ותועבותם אשר
עשו...(15) והכהנים הלוים בני צדוק אשר שמרו את משמרת מקדשי בתעות בני ישראל מעלי

(10) But the Levites who went far from me when Israel went astray in that they went astray from me after the idols...(12) Because they ministered to them before their idols and made the house of Israel stumble into iniquity. Therefore, I have lifted my hand concerning them, says YHWH...(13)...and the abominations that they did...(15) But the Levitical priests, the sons of Zadok that kept charge of my sanctuary when the sons of Israel went astray from me...

The isolation of the past actions highlights the distinctive way in which the infractions of the Levites and the Israelites are described. Significantly, the terms used are almost identical to those found in Ezekiel 14: it involved idolatry, גלולים (14:3 – 7; 44:10, 12), and "abomination", תועבה (14:6; 44:13), the Israelites "went

---

125 For two different perspectives on this question see Levenson, *Program of Restoration*, 55 – 107 and Tuell, *Law of the Temple*, 103 – 20.

astray", תעה (14:11; 44:10, 15), and "they stumbled into iniquity", משכול עון (14:3, 4, 7; 44:12).

Although גלולים and תועבה are found throughout Ezekiel and cannot be used as evidence for a relationship between 14:1–11 and 44:10–14,[126] a careful examination of the other lexemes can leave us in no doubt that there is a close literary relationship. First, it is only in these two chapters in Ezekiel that the verb תעה appears (14:11; 44:10, 15). Second, the expression "stumbling block of sin" (מכשול עון) is unique to Ezekiel, but rather infrequent. Outside of 14:3, 4, 7 and 44:12 it is only otherwise found in 7:19 and 18:30. Finally, in 14:9 YHWH promises to "stretch out my hand" (ונטיתי את־ידי עליו) against the enticed prophet (cf. v. 13). This expression of divine power and judgement is not found in Ezekiel 44. Rather, the unique expression נשאתי ידי עליהם occurs, which blends two different Hebrew idioms. First, נשא יד occurs on a number of occasions (especially in Ezekiel) in the context of taking an oath. The content of the oath usually follows.[127] Second, נטה יד על is used in the context of acts of judgement. It is used particularly in the story of the exodus and in the prophetic literature (especially Ezekiel) with

---

126 For גלולים, see Ezek 6:4–6, 9, 13; 8:10; 14:3–7; 16:36; 18:6, 12, 15; 20:7, 16, 18, 24, 31, 39; 22:3–4, 7, 30, 37, 39, 49; 30:13; 33:25; 36:18, 25; 37:23; 44:10, 12; for תועבה, see 5:9, 11; 6:9, 11; 7:3, 8; 9:4; 11:18; 12:16; 14:6; 16:22, 36, 43, 51; 18:13; 33:29; 44:6–7; cf: 7:4, 9, 20; 8:6, 9, 13, 15, 17; 11:21; 16:2, 47, 50, 58; 18:12, 24; 20:4; 22:2, 11, 36; 33:26; 36:31; 43:8; 44:13.

127 With this sense נשא יד can be followed by ל and the infinitive construct (Exod 6:8; Num 14:30; Ezek 20:6, 23, 28, 42; 47:14; Ps 106:26; Neh 9:15), לבלתי and the infinitive construct (Ezek 20:15), or a verb for speaking (Deut 32:40; Ezek 20:5). On one occasion the idiom is followed by the oath itself (Ezek 36:7). There have been some recent attempts to argue that נשא יד is not an oath gesture (Johan Lust, "For I Lift Up My Hand to Heaven and Swear: Deut 32:40", in *Studies in Deuteronomy: In Honour of C. J. Labuschagne on the Occasion of His 65ᵗʰ Birthday*, ed. F. García Martínez et al., VTSup 53 [Leiden: Brill, 1994], 155–64; Casey A. Strine, *Sworn Enemies: The Divine Oath, the Book of Ezekiel, and the Polemics of Exile* [BZAW 436. Berlin: de Gruyter, 2013]). Lust and Strine rightly point out that there are instances where understanding נשא יד as an oath gesture is clearly incorrect, e. g. Ps 10:12. But there are other occasions where נשא יד appears to be an oath gesture. In Deut 32:40 the two cola are best understood as oath gesture and oath formula. Even more clear is Ezek 36:7, where נשא יד is followed by an oath formula introduced by אם לא. Lust argues that "the manuscripts of Ez 36:7 originally read אל. A copyist, who understood the נשא-ידֿformula as an oath-gesture, interpreted this as an abbreviation of the introductory oath formula א' ל. The Septuagint read ἐπὶ which presupposes Hebrew אל." (Lust, "For I Lift", 161). Even if we accept Lust's hypothesis, Ezek 36:7 still provides unambiguous evidence that an early scribe understood the Hebrew expression נשא יד as an oath gesture. This undermines Lust's argument that other interpreters have read into the Hebrew idiom a modern understanding of the act of raising a hand. Strine's approach to Ezek 36:7 is even more problematic. He appears to accept Lust's conjecture, and ignores the contrary evidence of the Hebrew text without discussion (Strine, *Sworn Enemies*).

God as the subject.[128] The unique formulation in Ezek 44:12 blends together the oath and the act of judgement.[129]

If we ask the question of the direction of dependence, we should again judge that it is most likely that Ezekiel 44 is the dependent text. A variety of idioms and ideas from Ezek 14:1–11 make an impression upon Ezekiel 44, but there is no evidence that the distinctive ideas of Ezekiel 44, such as the admission of foreigners into the sanctuary or the division between priests and Levites, have made any impact upon Ezekiel 14. What was the appeal of Ezekiel 14 to the composer of 44:10–14? Ezekiel 14 describes the elders of Israel coming to the prophet in order to receive a divine message, but the prophet reproves them for harbouring idolatry in their hearts. Whilst it might have been the condemnation of Israel, its leaders and prophets that proved of interest, similar condemnation is found throughout the book of Ezekiel. It is more likely that it was the appearance of נשא עון that was so important. Both idolater and prophet "will bear their sin" (ונשאו עונם; 14:10). This expression occurs a number of times in the Hebrew Bible, but rarely outside the Pentateuch. In Ezekiel it is only found in 4:4–6, 14:10 and 44:10, 12,[130] and it is this idiom that brings together Numbers 18, Ezekiel 14 and Ezekiel 44.

1.2.4 Bearing Sin

We have demonstrated that Ezek 44:10–14 is a sophisticated example of inner-biblical interpretation in which two distinct texts have been interwoven: Numbers 18 and Ezekiel 14. The text of Ezekiel 44 moves artfully back and forth between both texts. The common element is the expression "bear the sin", and it is no surprise to discover that this expression and the variant "bear their shame" (נשאו כלמתם; Ezek 16:52, 54; 32:24–25, 30) are found at most points where Ezekiel 44 transitions from one source text to the other:

---

128 See Exod 7:5, 19; 8:1, 2; 9:22; 10:12, 21, 22; 14:16, 21, 26, 27; Isa 5:25; Jer 6:12; 15:6; 51:25; Ezek 6:14; 14:9, 13; 16:27; 25:7, 13, 16; Zeph 1:14; 2:13. When used in this sense נטיתי ידי is nearly always followed by על (for exceptions see Exod 8:13; Isa 31:3). Note also the related idiom "an outstretched arm".

129 Duke rightly draws attention to the uniqueness of the idiom, although his arguments that it is Israel, rather than the Levites that YHWH lifts his hand against is unconvincing (Duke, "Punishment or Restoration?", 69).

130 Cf. Ezek 18:19–20.

Num 18:1–7	"bear the sin/shame"	Ezek 14:1–11
		10a
	10b	
11		
		12a, bα
	12bβ	
13a		
	13bα	
		13bβ
14		
		15aα
15aβ		

The transitional role of the expression "bear the sin" sheds light on two issues. First, it explains why interpreters have not been able to decide on the precise meaning of the expression.[131] Does it mean to bear responsibility for the sanctuary,[132] or suffer the consequences of a sin committed?[133] The first meaning is congruent with Num 18:1, but the second with Ezekiel 14 and 16. The use of "bear their shame" (נשׂאו כלמתם) in v. 13bα suggests that the composers of Ezekiel 44 had primarily in view the Levites suffering the consequences of sin. Nevertheless, the ambiguity is genuine and should not be settled decisively in either direction. It stems from the strategy of textual re-use. Second, we are now in position to elucidate how the composers of Ezek 44:10–14 developed the response to the admission of foreigners to the sanctuary. As we have seen pentateuchal texts concerning the בני נכר had already been utilized in vv. 6–8 in order to resist Trito-Isaiah's oracle. In vv. 10–14 further grounds for resistance are drawn from the programme for priestly and Levitical responsibilities in Numbers 18, which charges the Levites and priests with protecting the sanctuary from incursions by the stranger. The insistence that the Levites and priests "bear the sin" provided an association with Ezekiel 14, where the prophet confronts the people with their sins. But this association meant that "bear the sin" was understood as a punishment for Levitical transgression, an idea that is absent from Numbers

---

131 For this problem, see Duke, "Punishment or Restoration?", 65–67; Jacob Milgrom, *Ezekiel's Hope: A Commentary on Ezekiel 38–48* (Eugene, OR: Wipf & Stock, 2012), 150–53.

132 For this use, see Milgrom, *Studies in Levitical Terminology*, 84. The Levites will "bear the sin" should the sanctuary suffer an unauthorized incursion.

133 For this use, see Baruch J. Schwartz, "The Bearing of Sin in Priestly Literature", in *Pomegranates and Golden Bells: Studies in Biblical, Jewish, and Near Eastern Ritual, Law, and Literature in Honor of Jacob Milgrom*, ed. David Pearson Wright, David Noel Freedman, and Avi Hurvitz (Winona Lake, IN: Eisenbrauns, 1995), 3–21.

18. The different functions of the Levites and the sons of Zadok was not simply an ordering of cultic responsibilities, but was divine punishment for Levitical sin.

1.2.5 The Sons of Zadok

Our examination of the word of judgement has raised the possibility that the instructions concerning the Levites, vv. 10 – 14, are intrusive, and that if removed a rather straightforward comparison of the sons of a foreigner and the sons of Zadok results. Yet, we have also observed that there are grounds for thinking that the word of reproach, vv. 6 – 8, has grown under the influence of other biblical texts, and we must pose the question of whether the same is true for vv. 15 – 16 which describe the roles of the sons of Zadok. This possibility may be correlated with Rudnig's observation that vv. 15 – 16 are rather repetitive.

If we are correct to see vv. 10 – 14 as an expansion of the oracle under the influence of Numbers 18 and Ezekiel 14, we have an initial clue that the extended qualification, אשר שמרו את משמרת מקדשי בתעות בני ישראל מעלי, in v. 15 and the final loosely attached clause, ושמרו את משמרתי, in v. 16 are the result of the same process of growth. Further evidence that the first of these literary-critical operations is justified is provided by the inelegant resumptive personal pronoun המה, which the extended qualification of the sons of Zadok requires. Even with this alteration, the problem of repetition remains. We have two titles: the sons of Zadok and the Levitical priests. We also have two very similar descriptions of their roles. On the one hand, "they will approach me to serve me, and they will stand before me to offer to me fat and blood" (v. 15), and on the other, "they will enter my sanctuary, and they will approach my table to serve me" (v. 16). The presence of the divine speech formula נאם אדני יהוה, "says lord YHWH", at the end of v. 15 appears somewhat prematurely, and provides additional evidence for textual growth.

The appearance of the divine speech formula at the end of v. 15 probably marks the original end of the oracle. The originality of v. 15 is suggested by the shorter "approach me", rather than the longer "approach my table" in v. 16.[134] The priestly roles described in v. 15 are reminiscent of the Deuteronomic characterization of the Levitical priests who are said to stand and minister

---

134 So also Rudnig, *Heilig und Profan*, 287.

(Deut 17:12; 18:5, 7).[135] This has been blended with a verb for making a sacrificial offering favoured by the priestly writings, קרב, and a priestly characterization of sacrifice: offering fat and blood (Lev 3:16–17; 7:33).

It will be observed, however, that the expression "to offer to me fat and blood" has appeared in Ezek 44:7, and I have argued that it was an exegetically-inspired instance of *Fortschreibung*. In v. 7 the additional element that indicated the appropriation of Lev 22:25 was the identification of the offerings as לחמי. The characterization of the offerings as "fat and blood" did not stem from Leviticus 22. It would appear, then, that Ezek 44:7bα arose from blending v. 15bα with Lev 22:25. Insisting that the sacrificial offerings are YHWH's food magnifies the foreigners' offence. What has been permitted by the Israelites transgresses on the personal dignity of YHWH: his dining room has been invaded. The same interpretive instinct is visible in v. 16, where we find the other clause in v. 15 being appropriated in a similar way: the sons of Zadok are permitted to approach "my *table*". Nowhere else in the Hebrew Bible is the altar or the table in the sanctuary identified as "my table". An identical interpretative strategy presumably reflects the same hand:

והמה יקרבו אל שלחני לשרתני ⇐ המה יקרבו אלי לשרתני

בהקריבכם את לחמי חלב ודם ⇐ להקריב לי חלב ודם

We may now turn to the final issue: the duplicate title in v. 15. Did the appointed priests of the oracle always bear the title of both Levitical priests and the sons of Zadok? Two considerations suggest that the original oracle referred to the Levitical priests and that the reference to the sons of Zadok was a later addition. First, what we have identified as the original description of the priestly role in v. 15 appears to allude to those texts in Deuteronomy that mention the "Levitical priests". Second, the need to define the occupants of the priestly office more precisely only arose with the addition of the Levites in vv. 10–14.

But why was the expression "the sons of Zadok" chosen, rather than "the sons of Aaron", especially if the editor who inserted the title had to hand a developed form of the Pentateuch that included not only P and H, but also texts from Numbers? One possibility is that there existed a Zadokite sept that traced its ancestry back to David's priest in Jerusalem. Ezekiel 44 was composed by a Zadokite or a Zadokite sympathizer who inserted the sept's exclusive claim to the Jerusalem priesthood. We cannot exclude this possibility, and it has proved

---

135 See also the dependent texts Num 3:6; 16:9; Deut 10:8; 1Kgs 8:11 // 2Chr 5:14; 2Chr 29:11. See also Ezek 44:11. For discussion, see Dahmen, *Leviten und Priester*, 31–48.

attractive to numerous interpreters over the last century, but a couple of considerations tell against it. First, outside of Ezekiel 40–48 there is no evidence in the Hebrew Bible for a Zadokite sept. Second, the dense scriptural allusions throughout Ezek 44:6–16 suggest that the oracle's composers are most likely to have had a biblical allusion in view.

In Ezekiel's vision of the new temple and the new land, the scriptural traditions about Sinai and Jerusalem are used to imagine a new, post-restoration polity. The divine oracle concerning the foreigners and the Levitical priests has been inserted into the section of the vision concerning with the "prince", נשיא (44:3; 46:1–12*). The identity of the נשיא is a matter of considerable disagreement within scholarship. Some scholars have observed that Ezekiel 40–48 speaks about Israel's kings, מלכים, only negatively, and the נשיא, "prince", appears to be a deliberate downgrading of the monarch. Other scholars, however, have observed that the title נשיא is used in Ezek 34:24 and 37:25 of the ideal Davidic ruler.[136] It is not necessary for me to adjudicate between these two readings in order to ascertain what the original intention of the composer of 44:3; 46:1–12* was. It is important only to observe that for the composer of the original oracle in Ezekiel 44 and its reviser, the title נשיא was a given which would have been understood in light of its use elsewhere in Ezekiel 33–37 and 40–48. Thus, the natural way for a later redactor to read Ezekiel 33–37 and 40–48 was that the future community would have a Davidide as its ruler. It would be natural for this Davidic prince to have a priest that corresponded to him, a descendent of Zadok, David's priest. Thus, the expression "the sons of Zadok" should be seen as an allusion to the figure in the scriptural history of David's reign, rather than as a reference to a priestly sept of the exilic or post-exilic period.

Before we leave this issue, we must address a further issue. If it is correct to argue that the sons of Zadok were inserted into Ezekiel 44 in order to provide a counterpoint to the Davidic prince, why do we not find simply Zadok to correspond to an individual prince? Two reasons can be given. First, the earlier version of the oracle made reference to the Levitical priests and not to a single priest. Secondly, the expression "the sons of Zadok" (בני צדוק) was coined to contrast with the "sons of a foreigner" (בני נכר). Thus, despite the insertion of vv. 10–14 an attempt was made to maintain the original oracle's stark contrast between the priests and the foreigners. The same effect was also achieved by the addition

---

136 Levenson, *Program of Restoration*, 55–107; Paul M. Joyce, "King and Messiah in Ezekiel", in *King and Messiah in Israel and the Ancient Near East: Proceedings of the Oxford Old Testament Seminar*, ed. John Day, JSOTSup 270 (Sheffield: Sheffield Academic, 1998), 323–37.

of v. 16aα, "they will enter my sanctuary", המה יבאו אל מקדשי, which provides a contrast to the exclusion of foreigners from the sanctuary (v. 9).

1.3 The Composition of Ezekiel 44:6–16

I am now in a position to offer my proposed reconstruction of the composition of the first part of the divine oracle, Ezek 44:6–16. The expansion of the original oracle has been indicated by indentation, with possible glosses marked by text in square brackets.

> [6]Thus says YHWH: Enough of all your abominations, House of Israel, [7]in your admitting foreigners uncircumcised in heart and flesh to be in my sanctuary to profane it, [my house]
> > in your offering my food, fat and blood
> and they have broken my covenant in addition to all your abominations.
> > [8]And you did not keep the charge of my holy things, but you set them as keepers of my charge in my sanctuary.
>
> [9]Thus says YHWH: No foreigner uncircumcised in heart and flesh shall enter my sanctuary [of all the foreigners that are in the midst of the Israelites.]
> > [10]But the Levites who went far from me when Israel went astray in that they went astray from me after the idols. They will bear their sin. [11]They shall be ministers in my sanctuary, responsible for the gates of the temple and ministering in the temple. They will slaughter the burnt offering and the sacrifice for the people. They will stand before them and serve them. [12]Because they ministered to them before their idols and made the house of Israel stumble into iniquity. Therefore, I have lifted my hand concerning them, says YHWH, they will bear their sin. [13]They will not come to me to act as priests for me. They will not come near to any of my sacred things, the most sacred things, and they will bear their shame and the abominations that they did. [14]I will appoint them to keep the charge of the temple, all its service and all that is done in it.
> [15]But the Levitical priests,
> > the sons of Zadok that kept charge of my sanctuary when the sons of Israel went astray from me. They
> will come near to me to minister to me and they will stand before me to offer to me fat and blood – declaration of Lord YHWH.
> > [16]They will enter my sanctuary, and they will approach my table to serve me, and they will keep my charge.

The original oracle has a relatively simple structure. It vehemently rejects the insistence in Isaiah 56 that foreigners be admitted to the sanctuary, permitting only Levitical priests into the sanctuary to offer sacrifices. The rejection is based upon pentateuchal perspectives on the בני נכר and the instructions about priests in

Leviticus and Deuteronomy. As a result the original oracle is dependent on prior biblical texts at almost every point.

The subsequent expansion of the oracle also shows dependence on biblical texts. These are mostly a different set of texts: Numbers 18 and Ezekiel 14. Under the influence of the book of Numbers a distinction between Levites and priests is introduced that was alien to the original oracle. This complicates the structure of the oracle considerably, such that it now moves from foreigners to Levites to the sons of Zadok.

Both the original oracle and the subsequent expansion exhibit a sophisticated form of biblical interpretation that draws upon more than one source text and assimilates them to the conceptuality and vocabulary of Ezekiel's temple vision. The oscillation between Numbers 18 and Ezekiel 14 in 44:10 – 14 is particularly intricate. The different textual precursors of the different stages of growth can be instructively compared to some contemporary models of the growth of the Pentateuch. In these models the priestly instructions in the book of Numbers are viewed as some of the final layers of the Pentateuch, whilst the Holiness Code is seen as dependent on P and D. It is interesting, then, that the original oracle responds to Isaiah 56 by drawing upon texts from Leviticus 1–7 and Deuteronomy, but the expansion is informed by texts from the Holiness Code and the book of Numbers. This may suggest that the original oracle was composed prior to the Holiness Code and the priestly instructions in the book of Numbers.

2 The Rules for Priests

The transition from divine oracle to the rules about priests results in a complete change of tone. The sharp polemic disappears, as does the laudatory commendation of the faithful sons of Zadok. What follows in vv. 17–31 is a colourful collection of diverse rules exclusively concerned with priestly affairs;[137] the Levites fade completely from view. The order of the rules for the priests appear to have almost no guiding logic with the exception of an important macro-structural marker in v. 27, נאם אדני יהוה, which separates the instructions about the conduct of the priests (vv. 17–27) from instructions about priestly perquisites (vv. 28–31). The brief description of the second half of Ezekiel 44 that I have offered raises at least two interpretive issues that demand attention. First, how are we to explain the transition from accusatory oracle to priestly regulations? Second, is it possible to account for the order of the rules in vv. 17–31? This chapter will argue that both questions can only be adequately addressed if attention is paid to a further interpretive issue: what intertextual relations does Ezekiel 44:17–31 have to other texts in the Hebrew Bible, and how are those relations to be rightly understood?

2.1 The Continuation of the Divine Oracle in the Priestly Rules

Recent critical scholarship has correctly recognized that within Ezekiel's temple visions the instructions in vv. 17–31 develop from the oracle about priestly access.[138] In their present form, however, the instructions move on to subjects far removed from the original oracle's concern with sanctuary access. Consequently, many scholars have surmised that the current form of the instructions cannot have been the original continuation of the oracle, but also that there must have been an original core of instructions, which was closely linked to vv. 6–16. This core of instructions was the seed from which the present form of the text grew in one or more stages.

At the beginning of the twentieth century, Herrmann suggested that the oracle had originally concluded with the instruction about priestly vestments (vv. 17,

---

137 For 44:20–31 as a "bunte Sammlung", see Johannes Herrmann, *Ezechielstudien*, BWAT 2 (Leipzig: Hinrichs, 1908), 54.
138 Rudnig, *Heilig und Profan*, 284.

19).[139] These instructions maintain the oracle's theme of entering the sanctuary, but shift the focus from *who* may enter to *how* they are to enter. Half a century later, Gese proposed instead that the original oracle (vv. 6b–8, 9–16) continued with the instructions about priestly perquisites in vv. 28–30a. The link between the section on priestly perquisites and the divine oracle was evidenced in two ways: YHWH speaks in the first person, as occurred in v. 16, and the second person address of Israel last found in vv. 6–8 is taken up again. Herrmann's insights were incorporated into Gese's model. According to Gese, at an early stage vv. 17, 19 were inserted between vv. 9–16 and 28–30a, which subsequently gave rise to the addition of further rules.[140]

Gese's proposal has been very influential, but there is at least one outstanding difficulty and two issues that remain insufficiently clarified. The difficulty is that whilst the direct address of Israel in vv. 28–30 could be viewed as a continuation of vv. 6–8, Israel is spoken of in the third person in vv. 9b, 10, 12 and 15a. Thus, Gese's proposal does not resolve the literary-critical problems, for we still have an unexplained transition from second person to third person to second person. Gese has done nothing more than shift the problem to elsewhere in the passage. Further, there are two issues that Gese has not clarified. First, why is there the sudden and unexplained introduction of priestly perquisites in the original oracle? Secondly, why were the instructions about the entrances (vv. 17, 19) inserted between the oracle and the section about priestly perquisites? Our analysis of inner-biblical interpretation in the divine oracle and the resulting literary-critical picture that resulted will show that Gese's proposal was correct in its essential details, and my analysis will prove helpful in resolving the problems that remain and clarifying the logic of those who composed Ezekiel 44.

One critical factor in resolving the outstanding problems with Gese's proposal is my argument from the previous chapter that the divine oracle in 44:6–16 developed in two distinct stages. In the first stage a polemical response was made to the idea that foreigners could act as priests in the temple. In the second stage the distinction between priests and Levites is introduced. These two stages can be correlated with the two proposals by Herrmann and Gese for the original core of the instructions in vv. 17–31. The idea of YHWH as the priest's share (v. 28) is the continuation of the original oracle, whilst the instructions about priestly vestments (vv. 17, 19) continue the expanded oracle.

---

139 See Herrmann, *Ezechielstudien*.
140 Gese, *Der Verfassungsentwurf*, 64.

2.1.1 The Priests and Their Inheritance

The original oracle counters the idea that foreigners might act as priests in the temple by appealing to pentateuchal texts. Negatively, the sons of foreigners are, according to Genesis, uncircumcised and their admission means breaking the covenant (v. 7). Positively, the sacrificial task has been assigned to the Levitical priests (v. 15) as prescribed in Deuteronomy 18. The account of the Levitical priests' role in Deuteronomy 18 not only describes the priestly service as "standing and ministering" (v. 5; cf. Ezek 44:15), but also allocates the Levitical priest a sacrificial portion on the grounds that "they have no inheritance amongst their brothers; YHWH is their inheritance" (18:2).

The rule that the priests receive no inheritance because YHWH is their inheritance is precisely how Ezek 44:28 introduces the instructions on priestly perquisites. The rule has a number of parallels in the Hexateuch (Num 18:20; Deut 10:9; 18:2; Josh 13:33), but the particular formulation is closest to Deut 18:2.

ולא היתה להם נחלה אני נחלתם ואחזה לא־תתנו להם בישראל אני אחזתם

and there will not be an inheritance for them; I am their inheritance. You shall given them no holding in Israel; I am their holding (Ezek 44:28).[141]

ונחלה לא־יהיה־לו בקרב אחיו יהוה הוא נחלתו

they have no inheritance amongst their brothers; YHWH is their inheritance (Deut 18:2).

The first half of Ezek 44:28 is virtually a citation of Deut 18:2 with only minor adjustments to fit the context of Ezekiel 44: the use of the plural for the priests and rephrasing as a divine speech. The second half repeats the same idea, but with the replacement of נחלה with אחזה. The reasons for this repetition are not difficult to ascertain for it represents an assimilation of Deuteronomy's aphorism to the terminology of Ezekiel's vision. In Ezekiel 45–48 נחלה is the broadest expression and is used of any allocation of the land. By contrast אחזה is mostly used of the Levites' portion, the holy city, and the prince's portion.[142]

---

141 The text has been emended in light of the reading of Papyrus 967 (καὶ οὐκ ἔσται αὐτοῖς εἰς κληρονομίαν) and the Vulgate (*non erit autem eis hereditas*), though neither attests נחלה without the preposition. MT reads היתה להם לנחלה, which is problematic in a number of ways. First, it is unclear what the feminine antecedent of היתה is. Second, in no other text is anything other than YHWH said to be the priests' inheritance. Third, it destroys any parallelism between the two halves of Ezek 44:28, and introduces an overly subtle distinction between נחלה and אחזה. The MT's reading is probably the result of an attempt to harmonize 44:28 with 45:1–8; 48:8–23, which it appears on first reading to contradict (Ibid., 62; Rudnig, *Heilig und Profan*, 283).

142 Ezek 45:5, 6, 7, 8; 46:17, 18; 48:20, 21, 22. The only exception is a single reference in 46:18 where it is used of the people's possession.

Whilst Gese was of the opinion that vv. 28–30a should be considered as a literary unit, there are reasons for doubting this. As we shall see, Ezek 44:29–30 draws upon a different set of textual precursors, and is better associated with the second stage in the development of the divine oracle. In addition, the rule about the priests' lack of inheritance would provide an elegant transition to an early form of 45:1–8.[143]

It will be apparent that my reconstruction of the textual history of Ezekiel 44 does not have the difficulty that Gese's original proposal had: the problem of the references to Israel shifting from second person to third person and back to second person. The third person references that troubled Gese's proposal are only found in those parts of the oracle that I have identified as belonging to the oracle's second stage.

2.1.2 The Priests and Their Vestments

Herrmann's proposal that the oracle originally ended with the instructions about vestments (vv. 17, 19) draws attention to the fact that the instructions about priestly attire is much more closely attached to the theme of the oracle than any of the remaining instructions in vv. 20–27.[144] It is the only instruction explicitly concerned with entry into the sanctuary, the issue that animates the original oracle. When the priests enter the inner court, including the gate or inside the temple, they must put on linen garments. When they go out into the outer court they are to strip off their vestments and leave them inside the sacred rooms of the inner court complex.

The requirement that the priests wear linen (פשתים) is similar to the description of priestly attire in the book of Exodus, but the material is identified there with synonyms: either שש (Exod 28:5, 39; 39:27–29) or בד (Exod 28:42; 39:28; Lev 16:4). Why does the composer of Ezekiel 44:17 prefer the term פשתים? A valuable clue is to be found in the clause: ולא־יעלה עליהם צמר, "they shall not put on wool".

---

143 Gese made a similar observation, but saw the crucial link to be תרומה (Gese, *Der Verfassungsentwurf*, 67–68). We may note that תרומה is used in a different sense in 44:30 and 45:1–17 as Allen observes: "The theme of the תרומה 'contribution', broached in 44:30 is developed. Now it is used in the sense of 'reservation', ε contribution of land to Yahweh" (Leslie C. Allen, *Ezekiel 20–48*, WBC 29 [Waco, TX: Word Books, 1990], 264). The different sense of תרומה could be an indicator of the artificiality of the link.

144 Rudnig objects "doch scheint die Bestimmung über den Kleiderwechsel zu konkret, um einen Text mit so grundsätzlicher Stoßrichtung wie 44,6–16* fortzusetzen" (Rudnig, *Heilig und Profan*, 281–82). In my view, this falls short of constituting an argument.

Both פשתים and צמר are found in Deut 22:11, where clothes of interwoven linen and wool are forbidden:לא תלבש שעטנז צמר ופשתים יחדו, "you shall not wear clothes of wool and linen together". The use of פשתים ensures that the priests in Ezekiel's new temple are presented as scrupulous in their obedience of Mosaic Torah: they do not wear garments from mixed fibres.[145] Interestingly, the precise formulation of Ezekiel's prohibition of garments from wool owes more to the parallel commandment in Lev 19:19:

ולא־יעלה עליהם צמר

They shall not put on wool (Ezek 44:17).

ובגד כלאים שעטנז לא יעלה עליך

You shall not put on a garment of mixed materials (Lev 19:19).

It is possible that the composer of these verses was familiar with both versions of the prohibition, but in his recollection blended the two. Alternatively, he my have known a version of the prohibition that does not correspond to either that known from Leviticus or Deuteronomy.

The requirement that the priests don linen garments before their service and remove them afterwards finds its closest parallel in the instructions for the Day of Atonement in Leviticus 16.

והיה בבואם אל שערי החצר הפנימית בגדי פשתים ילבשו...ובצאתם אל החצר החיצונה[146] אל העם יפשטו את בגדיהם אשר המה משרתם בם והניחו אותם בלשכת הקדש

When they enter the gates of the inner court, they shall put on linen garments...When they go out into the outer court to the people, they shall remove their garments in which they have been ministering. They will lay them in the holy rooms (Ezek 44:17a, 19a).

בזאת יבא אהרן אל הקדש בפר בן בקר לחטאת ואיל לעלה כתנת בד קדש ילבש...ובא אהרן אל אהל מועד ופשט את בגדי הבד אשר לבש בבאו אל הקדש והניחם שם

In this way Aaron shall enter the holy place: with a young bull as a purification offering and a ram for a burnt offering. He shall put on the holy linen tunic...Aaron shall enter the tent of meeting and he shall remove the garments of linen that he put on when he entered the holy place and he will lay them there (Lev 16:3–4aα, 23).[147]

---

145 The application of Deut 22:11 and Lev 19:19 to the priestly vestments is the opposite understanding of Josephus. He insists that the prohibition in Leviticus and Deuteronomy stems from the fact that mixed garments were reserved for the priests only (*Ant.* 4.208).

146 The second אל החצר החיצונה is usually deleted as a case of dittography.

147 On the basis of the use of לבש in 44:19 and the parallel to Leviticus 16, it is apparent that בגדי פשתים ילבשו in v. 17 means not "they shall wear linen garments" (NRSV), but "they shall put on linen garments".

On this most important occasion in the priestly calendar the sacred vestment that is worn during the purging of the shrine behind the curtain is put on at the beginning of the ritual act and left in the Tent of Meeting at the end.[148] The only other occasion in the Pentateuch when fresh vestments are worn and then taken off and left at the conclusion of the task is the daily cleaning of the altar of burnt offering (Lev 6:1–6). The vestments are worn only for the task of removing the ashes to the side of the altar. Different garments are worn for carrying the ashes outside the camp. Both the day of atonement and the cleaning of the altar have in common an encounter with an item of the greatest sanctity: the sacrificial remains on the altar of burnt offering and the inner sanctum.

The performance of priestly duties behind the curtain and at the altar are linked not only by a distinctive use of priestly vestments, but also by their appearance in Num 18:7: "you and your sons with you will perform your priestly duties in all the matters of the altar and behind the curtain". I want to propose that Ezek 44:17, 19 is an exegetical inference from Num 18:7, and marks a continuation of the sequential interpretation of Num 18:4–7 that we have seen characterizes the second stage of the composition of the oracle in Ezekiel 44. This proposal would allow us to reconstruct the exegetical logic of the composer in the following manner. In 44:15 the composer credits the sons of Zadok with keeping the charge of the sanctuary. The language he uses is almost identical to the description of the priestly duties in Num 18:5. The responsibility coupled with keeping the sanctuary in 18:5 is that of keeping the altar. This is taken up in Ezek 44:16 when the sons of Zadok are granted responsibility for YHWH's table, an alternative way of describing the altar. The final responsibilities attributed to Aaron and his sons are the "priestly duties (כהנתכם) in all the matters of the altar and behind the curtain" (Num 18:7). But, what, reasoned our writer, are these special priestly duties? The rituals relating to "behind the curtain" (מבית לפרכת), which are only found in Leviticus 16, and those relating to the altar of burnt offering have in common the distinctive requirement to put on the priestly vestments before the ritual action and remove them immediately afterwards. Our writer identified this requirement as the priestly duties of Num 18:7 and reformulated the instructions in Leviticus 16 to produce those in Ezek 44:17, 19.

To this point I have not considered v. 18 and I shall turn to it now. In v. 18 additional items of clothing are mentioned besides the linen garments of v. 17: "they shall have linen turbans on their heads, and linen undergarments on

---

148 Milgrom is correct to argue that the linen garments are left in the Tent because of their sanctity, not because they have become contaminated (Milgrom, *Leviticus 1–16*, 1048).

their loins. They shall not bind themselves with anything that causes sweat". The language is drawn from the pentateuchal descriptions of the priest's attire.[149] Whilst the descriptions in vv. 17–18 do not correspond to any precise verse, we have a fourfold division of the priestly vestments similar to that in Lev 16:4.

Ezekiel 44:17–18	Leviticus 16:4
בגדי פשתים ילבשו	כתנת בד קדש ילבש
פארי פשתים יהיו על ראשם	ומכנסי בד יהיו על בשרו
ומכנסי פשתים יהיו על מתניהם	ובאבנט בד יחגר
לא יחגרו ביזע	ובמצנפת בד יצנף

They shall put on linen garments	He shall put on a holy linen tunic
They shall have linen turbans on their heads,	and he shall have linen undergarments
and linen undergarments on their loins.	on his body
They shall not bind themselves with anything	and be bound with a linen sash
that causes sweat	and wear a linen turban

The entirety of v. 18 is often treated as a secondary addition because it introduces an alternative explanation of the linen garments.[150] Whilst v. 17 draws on the pentateuchal prohibitions of mixed garments, v. 18 is concerned that the garments will cause the priest to sweat.[151] In addition, v. 18 interrupts the parallel instructions for entering the inner court and leaving it.[152] It is doubtful whether either reason provides sufficient grounds for considering v. 18 a secondary addition.[153] If, as we have proposed, Ezek 44.18 reflects the same intertextual influence of Leviticus 16 just as do vv. 17, 19, there are further grounds for questioning excision. Nevertheless, it is not entirely possible to exclude the possibility of an exegetically inspired *Fortschreibung*.

---

149 For פאר see Exod 39:28. The priestly headdress is more often identified as מצנפת, see Exod 28:4, 37, 39; 29:6; 39:28, 31; Lev 8:9; 16:4. The מכנסים are mentioned in Exod 28:42; 39:28; Lev 6:10 and 16:4.

150 E.g. Gese, *Der Verfassungsentwurf*, 59.

151 It is unclear why the priest must avoid sweating whilst performing his duties. Alongside the view that sweat was judged to be impure, Zimmerli ventures the opinion that wool as an animal product should not be brought into the world of the cult (Zimmerli, *Ezechiel*, 1134).

152 Rudnig, *Heilig und Profan*, 282; Fechter, "Priesthood", 33; G.A. Cooke, *A Critical and Exegetical Commentary on the Book of Ezekiel*, ICC (Edinburgh: T&T Clark, 1936), 484.

153 See also Konkel, *Architektonik*, 130.

2.2 Priestly Conduct

As Herrmann recognized, the instruction about the priestly vestments relates closely to the preceding oracle for it concerns entering and leaving the inner court. The five instructions that follow are much more loosely related to the oracle and concern various aspects of priestly conduct (vv. 20–27). The five distinct instructions concern hair (v. 20), consumption of alcohol (v. 21), marital partners (v. 22), teaching and judicial role (vv. 23–24), and contact with dead bodies (vv. 25–27). Some relate specifically to cult service, such as the prohibition against drinking alcohol, whilst others are general, such as the instructions concerning marriage partners. In each case the instructions follow a regular pattern: object followed by a *yiqtol* verbal form or לא and a *yiqtol* verbal form. This pattern occurs in vv. 20a, 21a, 22a, 23, 25a, and we can label these as the instructions proper. In every case the instruction proper has been extended by additional clauses, which can take various forms. In v. 20b a positive commandment about hair is given with an infinitive absolute and *yiqtol* verbal form, and in v. 21b the prohibition of alcohol is specified as only necessary in the inner court. In vv. 22b and 25b a qualification of the initial instruction is introduced by כי־אם. In v. 24 an additional instruction is added concerning the priests' judicial role. It departs from the other instructions by the presence of the third masculine plural pronoun, המה, prior to the *yiqtol* verb. In vv. 26–27 temporal clauses introduce clarification about cleansing from corpse impurity. The order of the instructions reveals no obvious logic, although the instructions to bring a purification offering seven days after cleansing from corpse impurity (v. 27) returns to the theme of entering the inner court. It could be seen as creating an inclusio with the instructions about vestments in vv. 17–19.

Each of the instructions concerning priestly conduct has a parallel in the book of Leviticus, and sometimes more than one.[154] The similarities between the instructions in Leviticus and those in Ezekiel requires us to posit some literary relationship between them, but there has been considerable disagreement about how the relationship should be understood. Logically, there are three main alternatives, each of which has had its advocates. First, the instructions in Leviticus are dependent on those in Ezekiel. Second, the instructions in Ezekiel are dependent on those in Ezekiel. Third, both sets of instructions derive from a common literary ancestor.

The first position arises from Wellhausen's arguments that the distinction between priests and Levites was unknown prior to Ezekiel, and was only later

---

154 Gese, *Der Verfassungsentwurf*, 60.

projected into the Mosaic past by the Priestly writer. Many commentators have subsequently followed Wellhausen's lead. A particularly persuasive observation for many is the absence of a high priest in Ezekiel 44 in comparison to Leviticus 21.[155] In recent scholarship Achenbach has argued that Ezekiel 44 reflects a Zadokite priestly lore, and that Leviticus 10 is a later "sharpening" of it. The relationship of Ezekiel 44 to the Pentateuch, however, is rather complex. In Achenbach's view Ezekiel 44 is a response to two claims made within his *Hexateuchredaktion*: first, that non-Israelites may be integrated into the community; second, that all Levites may act as priests.[156] In a similar way Grünwaldt has argued that the instructions concerning the priests in Leviticus 21 are dependent on Ezekiel 44. Grünwaldt observes that the instructions in Leviticus 21 contain expressions that are characteristic of the Holiness Code, such as שאר, "flesh", and בתולה, "virgin". The parallel instructions in Ezekiel lack these expressions. Similarly, in Lev 21:2 we find the word-pair "mother-father", which appears to be an assimilation to a typical H expression. Ezekiel 44:25 has the usual order "father-mother". In these cases, the absence of these typical H expressions in Ezekiel suggests that H is the more recent stage of the instruction. The presence in Leviticus 21 of additional qualifications such as הבתולה הקרובה אליו, "a virgin that is close to him", point in the same direction on the principle that the shorter text is usually to be judged the oldest. Grünwaldt also observes that the diction of Ezekiel 44 has been bifurcated as a result of the introduction of a distinction between ordinary priests and the high priest, a distinction unknown in Ezekiel. He concludes, "die Analyse hat ergeben, daß dem Verf[asser] die Priesterbestimmungen Ez 44 vorlagen. Er hat diese dem Sinn nach übernommen, an seine eigene Sprache angepaßt und v[or] a [llem] differenziert zwischen Priester und dem Hohenpriester".[157]

---

155 John Skinner, *The Book of Ezekiel*, The Expositor's Bible (London: Hodder & Stoughton, 1909), 433–34; Alfred Bertholet, *Das Buch Hesekiel*, KHC 12 (Freiburg im Breisgau: Mohr Siebeck, 1897), 225–29; Alfred Bertholet, *Hesekiel*, HAT I/13 (Tübingen: Mohr Siebeck, 1936), 157–59; John William Wevers, *Ezekiel*, NCB Commentary (Grand Rapids: Eerdmans, 1982), 321.

156 "Die enge Verwandschaft der nun vorgetragenen Torot mit Ez 44,20–27, welche gegenüber dem Ezechieltext eine gewisse Verschärfung beinhalten, ist schon anderorts beobachtet worden" (Achenbach, *Die Vollendung der Tora*, 105). Achenbach's assessment of Lev 10 is followed by Nihan who observes that in various ways Lev 10 "goes *beyond* Ez 44" (Christophe Nihan, *From Priestly Torah to Pentateuch: A Study in the Composition of the Book of Leviticus*, FAT II/25 [Tübingen: Mohr Siebeck, 2007], 592; cf. 604, 606; italics original).

157 Klaus Grünwaldt, *Das Heiligkeitsgesetz Leviticus 17–26: Ursprüngliche Gestalt, Tradition und Theologie*, BZAW 271 (Berlin: de Gruyter, 1999), 267. See also Andreas Ruwe, *"Heiligkeitsgesetz" und "Priesterschrift": Literaturgeschichtliche und Rechtssystematische Untersuchungen zu Leviticus 17,1–26,2*, FAT 26 (Tübingen: Mohr Siebeck, 1999), 256 n. 38.

The second position has a number of advocates particularly in English-speaking scholarship and amongst Israeli scholars.[158] Hurvitz undertakes a linguistic examination of the Priestly source and the entire book of Ezekiel.[159] He argues that some of the differences between the instructions in Leviticus and Ezekiel are due to the diachronic development of Hebrew. Ezekiel avoids the classical term שכר, "strong drink" (Ezek 44:21; cf. Lev 10:9), the formula לדרתיכם, "throughout your generations" (Ezek 44:21, cf. Lev 10:9; Ezek 44:30, cf. Num 15:21), and the older term שאר, "flesh". Ezekiel fails to recognize that עם means "kin" in Leviticus 21, only being aware of the sense "people" (Ezek 44:22; cf. Lev 21:14; see also 21:1). Finally, the classical formula בין...בין is replaced with בין...ל (Ezek 44:23, cf. Lev 10:10).[160] Along the same lines Rooker argues that כסם (Ezek 44:20) is the Late Biblical Hebrew equivalent of the Classical Hebrew גזז.[161]

An alternative argument for the same position has been made on the basis of inner-biblical exegesis: Ezekiel 44 is an exegesis of the instructions in Leviticus. This view is already articulated by Fishbane, who claims that "in Ezek. 44 the prophet...makes explicit use of an ensemble of cultic laws".[162] In his commentary on Ezekiel, Allen describes a number of ways in which the prophet develops the commandments in Leviticus:

> The permission in v 22bβ is not found in Lev 21. V 24 takes v 23 further in several respects, beyond the Lev 10 parallel. The judicial responsibility of the priests may have been inspired by Deut 17:9; 21:5, where their cultic closeness to Yahweh is stressed. The reference to Sabbath holiness and to public services reflects Ezekielian concerns: see 22:26; 45:17; 46:9–11.

158 McConville, "Priests and Levites"; Moshe Greenberg, "The Design and Themes of Ezekiel's Program of Restoration", *Int* 38 (1984): 181–208; Baruch J. Schwartz, "A Priest Out of Place: Reconsidering Ezekiel's Role in the History of the Israelite Priesthood", in *Ezekiel's Hierarchical World: Wrestling with a Tiered Reality*, ed. Stephen L. Cook and Corrine L. Patton, SBL Symposium Series 31 (Leiden: Brill, 2004), 61–72; Risa Levitt Kohn, *A New Heart and a New Soul: Ezekiel, the Exile and the Torah*, JSOTSup 358 (London: Sheffield Academic, 2002); Ronald M. Hals, *Ezekiel*, FOTL 19 (Grand Rapids: Eerdmans, 1989); Levenson, *Program of Restoration*, 143.
159 Avi Hurvitz, *A Linguistic Study of the Relationship between the Priestly Source and the Book of Ezekiel: A New Approach to an Old Problem*, CahRB 20 (Paris: Gabalda, 1982).
160 Ibid., 67–74, 98–100, 116–18. See also Mark F. Rooker, *Biblical Hebrew in Transition: The Language of the Book of Ezekiel*, JSOTSup 90 (Sheffield: JSOT Press, 1990), esp. 117–19.
161 Rooker, *Biblical Hebrew in Transition*, 55.
162 Fishbane, *Biblical Interpretation*, 294. See also Terry J. Betts, *Ezekiel the Priest: A Custodian of Tôrâ*, StBibLit 74 (New York: Lang, 2005), 103–04: "Ezekiel's new *tôrâ* was deeply rooted in the old Mosaic *tôrâ*" (Ibid., 104), and Duguid, "Putting"; Block, *Ezekiel*, II: 640–44; Margaret S. Odell, *Ezekiel*, SHBC 16 (Macon, GA: Smyth & Helwys, 2005), 510–11; Bruce Vawter and Leslie J. Hoppe, *A New Heart: A Commentary on the Book of Ezekiel*, ITC (Grand Rapids: Eerdmans, 1991), 201.

The purificatory ritual of vv 26–27 has been added to v 25: so the switch to a singular subject suggests. It may be based on the lay regulation of Num 19:11–19, with extra demands in view of a priestly status. The emphatic references to the sanctuary (קֹדֶשׁ) in v 27 reveal the necessity for these demands, as well as carrying forward the overall motif of holiness.[163]

The most recent detailed study of Ezekiel 44 as an example of inner-biblical interpretation comes from Lyons, who examines the use of the Holiness Code in Ezekiel.[164] He argues that we have a couple of instances of conflation (21:1–3 and 11, and 21:7 and 14), where commandments for the ordinary priests and the elevated priest are combined in Ezekiel. The result is that whilst there is no high priest in Ezekiel, a stricter standard of holiness is maintained for the priests. "In some cases, the transformation of addressee is accompanied by a transformation of *scope:* less stringent laws for normal priests (Lev 21:5, 7) and more stringent laws for the more important priests (Lev 21:10, 14) are combined and applied to all priests by Ezekiel (Ezek 44:20, 22)."[165] One of the more revealing examples of inner-biblical exegesis is found in 44:25. The plural form in 44:25b shows evidence of the redactor's assimilation to the predominant form of address in Ezekiel 44. However, the slip into the singular in Ezek 44:25a betrays the writer's dependence on Lev 21:11.[166]

Konkel also argues that Ezekiel 44 is a re-interpretation of earlier laws, though only in the case of the prohibition of alcohol and the teaching duties are the wordings of the commandments very close.

> Ez 44,17–31 ist weit entfernt, lediglich "a potpourri of regulations concerning priests" zu sein. Der Anspruch des Textes dürfte weiter reichen. Auf fünfzehn Versen deckt der kurze Abschnitt fast die gesamte Gesetzgebung des Pentateuch ab, die sich explizit an die Priester richtet (vgl. allein Lev 22). Diese wird aufgegriffen und *streng perspektivisch* neu interpretiert bzw. aktualisiert.[167]

---

163 Allen, *Ezekiel 20–48*, 263–64.
164 Lyons, *From Law to Prophecy*. See also Michael A. Lyons, "Transformation of Law: Ezekiel's Use of the Holiness Code (Leviticus 17–26)", in *Transforming Visions: Transformations of Text, Tradition, and Theology in Ezekiel*, ed. William A. Tooman and Michael A. Lyons, Princeton Theological Monograph Series 127 (Eugene, OR: Pickwick, 2010), 1–32.
165 Lyons, *From Law to Prophecy*, 145; cf. 133. Milgrom likewise argues that Ezekiel deliberately recasts P's instructions in a stricter manner, but thinks Ezekiel drew on an older tradition (Milgrom, *Leviticus 1–16*, 453, followed by Thomas Renz, *The Rhetorical Function of the Book of Ezekiel*, VTSup 76 [Leiden: Brill, 1999], 125).
166 Lyons, *From Law to Prophecy*, 64.
167 Konkel, *Architektonik*, 332–33.

Konkel rejects Milgrom's insistence that the laws in Ezekiel stand in clear contradiction to the laws in P and H.

The third position, that both sets of instructions derive from a common literary ancestor, has recently been advocated by Tuell. He observes that it is not possible for the laws in Leviticus 21–22 to have been derived from Ezekiel 44.

> The text from the Holiness Code lacks any mention of the requirements that the priests teach תורה, abstain from wine (both of these provisions are in Lev 10:9–11), or serve as judges...In the Leviticus text, vestments are mentioned in connection with the high priest, who does not appear at all in the Law of the Temple; and the law relating to cutting the hair comes in the context of regulations restricting mourning practices – not, as in the Law of the Temple, as an injunction to good grooming. Finally Ezekiel 44 bears no hint of the lengthy list of disfigurements that can bar a priest from service, an important aspect of the Leviticus 21 text.[168]

On the other hand, the list of disfigurements is equally as problematic for the view that Ezekiel 44 derives from texts in Leviticus, for it is inexplicable why it should have been omitted from the Law of the Temple. The only permissible conclusion argues Tuell is that there was an anterior set of instructions that both Leviticus and Ezekiel drew upon.

These three main positions can be nuanced in a variety of different ways. Haran thinks of the instructions in Ezekiel and P as essentially independent. The Priestly code preserves the earliest version of the laws, and one that Haran regards as more authentic.[169] Gese and Rudnig observe the unordered and rather disparate nature of the instructions in 44:20–27, together with the occasional *Numeruswechsel*, as evidence of a process of late *Fortschreibung*. In some cases, perhaps, these additions came under the influence of the instructions of P and H.[170]

Having reviewed the different positions, I wish to make a number of critical observations. First, it is often the case that the relationship between the different priestly instructions is assumed, rather than demonstrated. This is not so much a failure of critical examination, but more an indication of the variety of broader considerations that provide a pre-understanding of the issue. These considerations include most especially the date and literary integrity of P, H and the book of Ezekiel, as well as the significance of differences such as the absence of the high priest in Ezekiel's vision. Second, some of the arguments treat the

---

168 Tuell, *Law of the Temple*, 141.
169 Haran, "Law-Code"; Haran, "Ezekiel".
170 Gese, *Der Verfassungsentwurf*, 59–62; Rudnig, *Heilig und Profan*, 282–84; cf. Zimmerli, *Ezechiel*, 1133–36.

priestly instructions as part of a larger comparison of priestly materials in the Pentateuch and the book of Ezekiel.[171] My examination of Ezekiel 44 alone demonstrates that this is a problematic starting point. We cannot assume that what is true for other passages in Ezekiel is likewise true of Ezekiel 44, since the compositional history of the book is complex. Third, the existence of such divergent opinions is itself an important *datum* requiring explanation.

Clearly, then, it is imperative to undertake a renewed examination of each of the instructions in Ezek 44:20–27 and their parallels elsewhere in the Hebrew Bible, especially in Leviticus. A compelling account of the relationship between the different instructions for priests in the Hebrew Bible must not only explain the texts in Ezekiel and Leviticus, *but also* the existence of divergent opinions on the relationship. The failure to do so would make my own argument little more than another instantiation of a position already taken. In the pages that follow I shall argue that the two texts, and the divergent scholarly interpretations, are best understood if we distinguish the instructions proper from the additional clauses that extend them. I will argue that Ezekiel 44 usually preserves an earlier text of the instructions proper than Leviticus. The additional clauses, however, show the influence of various other Pentateuchal texts. Consequently, we should view Ezekiel 44 as dependent on Pentateuchal precursors, but the text of Leviticus 10 and 21 with which the composer of Ezek 44:20–27 was familiar was typologically earlier than the text preserved in the Masoretic tradition. I will analyse each of the instructions independently before considering the cumulative picture.

---

171 This is particularly striking in Lyons, who carefully discusses the possibility of redactional layers in the Holiness Code, but treats Ezekiel as a compositional unity (Lyons, *From Law to Prophecy*).

2.2.1 The Instruction Concerning Hair

וראשם לא יגלחו ופרע לא ישלחו כסום יכסמו את
ראשיהם

They shall not shave their heads, and they
shall not let their locks grow out. They must
trim their head (Ezek 44:20).

ראשיכם אל תפרעו ובגדיכם לא תפרמו

Do not dishevel your hair, and do not tear your
vestments (Lev 10:6)

לא יקרחו[172] קרחה בראשם ופאת זקנם לא יגלחו
ובבשרם לא ישרטו שרטת קדשים יהיו לאלהיהם ולא
יחללו שם אלהיהם כי את אשי יהוה לחם אלהיהם הם
מקריבם והיו קדש

They shall not make bald spots upon their
heads. They shall not shave the corner of their
beards or make gashes. They will be holy to
their God and they shall not profane the name
of their God, because they offer YHWH's gifts,
the food of their god. They will be holy.
(Lev 21:5 – 6)

והכהן הגדול מאחיו אשר יוצק על ראשו שמן המשחה
ומלא את ידו ללבש את הבגדים את ראשו לא יפרע
ובגדיו לא יפרם

The priest who is more exalted than his
colleagues, on whose head the anointing
oil has been poured, and who has been
consecrated to wear the vestments. He shall
not dishevel his hair or tear his
vestment (Lev 21:10)

The first of the rules about priestly conduct in Ezekiel 44 concerns the priests'
care of their hair. There is no exact parallel in the book of Leviticus, but there
are a number of similarities with the rules concerning *mourning practices* in Leviticus 21. The difference is important, for Ezek 44.20 does not address mourning.

There are two significantly different rules on mourning practices in the book
of Leviticus. This feature distinguishes the rule on mourning practices from the
other rules where the obligations placed upon the elevated priest can be seen as
more stringent than those required of the common priests. The ruling for the
priests in Lev 21:5 prohibits certain mourning practices that involve disfiguring
hair, beard or skin. A very similar injunction is placed upon the Israelites in
19:27 – 28:

---

172 Reading the *qere*; cf. SP. The *ketiv* is an error resulting from the following noun.

לא תקפו פאת ראשכם ולא תשחית את פאת זקנך ושרט לנפש לא תתנו בבשרכם וכתבת קעקע לא תתנו בכם
אני יהוה

You shall not round off the edges of your head and you shall not destroy the edges of your beard. You shall not make any gashes for the dead in your flesh or put any tattoo marks upon you. I am YHWH.

The obligations placed upon the priests do not appear to differ in any substantive way from those placed upon the Israelites.

The prohibition of certain mourning practices occurs immediately after the restrictions placed on the priests regarding corpse defilement. The absolute exclusion of mourning (21:1) allows for some exceptions (21:2–4). Since mourning for close relatives is permitted, it appears that the composer of the Holiness Code thought it necessary to reiterate the rules concerning mourning practices that apply to all Israelites. In contrast, the order of the rules has been inverted for the elevated priests. There is a logic to this presentation too. Because the elevated priest wears sacred vestments, he cannot even undertake legitimate signs of mourning: wearing his hair loose or tearing his garments (21:10).[173] Consequently, he is prohibited from mourning for anyone (21:11).

Precisely what is prohibited of the high priest is unclear, and uncertainty about the meaning of "loosen the head", את ראשו לא יפרע, is already reflected in the versions. The LXX understands it to mean that the turban is not to be removed (cf. Exod 28), but Tg. Ps.-J. and Tg. Onq. interpret it to mean that the hair is not to be allowed to grow out neglected.[174] In both cases פרע is understood to mean "loosen", and the differences stem from how to understand the collocation "loosen *the head*". In either case, it is likely that the result of transgressing the prohibition is that the hair will hang down free.

The rule in Ezekiel 44 is significantly different from both rules in Leviticus 21, for it is a general rule about the manner in which priests keep their hair, and not a rule about mourning practices. The difference provides an important clue to the relationship between the rules. It is readily apparent how a focus on the instructions about hair resulted in a loss of reference to mourning. It is difficult to see how the rules about hair would have developed into rules about mourning. There is a further difference between the rules which also con-

---

173 The same prohibition is found after the death of Nadab and Abihu (Lev 10:6).
174 Tg. Neof. understands covering (כסה) of the head to be prohibited. This is probably a contextual interpretation. Goerwitz's appeal to the Sahidic to justify translating פרע as "shave" is not convincing (Richard L. Goerwitz, "What Does the Priestly Source Mean by פרע את הראש?", *JQR* 86 [1996]: 377–94), nor his argument that שלח in Ezek 44:20 means "tear out" (Richard L. Goerwitz, "Long Hair or Short Hair in Ezekiel 44:20?", *JAOS* 123 [2003]: 371–76).

tributes to understanding the direction of influence. The rule for the ordinary priest in Leviticus 21 prohibits shaving the hair, whilst the rule for the elevated priest prohibits letting the hair hang loose. The rule concerning hair in Ezekiel 44 requires that the priests neither shave their head nor let their hair hang loose. Consequently, there is much to be said for understanding Ezek 44:20 as a textual conflation of both the instructions found in Leviticus 21. The final clause of Ezek 44:20 secures a *via media* between the two prohibitions: "they must trim their heads", כסום יכסמו את ראשיהם. The priests are required to maintain careful grooming: neither letting their hair grow too long, nor shaving it back to the scalp.

The rule in Ezek 44:20 provides guidance concerning priestly conduct that applies inside and outside the sanctuary. The careful placement of the law at this point in Ezekiel 44 has not been fully appreciated. It follows the rules concerning vestments, and so maintains the same connection between hair, vestments and sanctuary service found in the rules for the elevated priest in Leviticus 21. But by moving to a general rule that applies outside the sanctuary, the composer of these verses in Ezekiel 44 transitions to the rules concerning priestly conduct that follow the rule about priestly entrance to the sanctuary (vv. 17–19). Whilst the connection to vestments and sanctuary service has been preserved, Ezekiel 44 has achieved this by severing the connection to mourning.

2.2.2 The Instruction Concerning Alcohol

יין ושכר אל תשת אתה ובניך אתך בבאכם אל אהל מועד   ויין לא ישתו כל כהן בבואם אל החצר הפנימית
ולא תמתו

You and your sons shall not drink wine or strong drink when you enter the tent of meeting that you may not die. (Lev 10:9a)

None of the priests shall drink wine when they enter the inner court. (Ezek 44:21)

The prohibitions against the consumption of alcohol in Ezekiel 44 and Leviticus 10 are very similar to one another. A number of the differences between the two passages simply reflect the broader context of each passage. Ezekiel 44 is addressed to the Israelites, and the priests are spoken of in the third person; in Leviticus 10 Aaron is addressed directly. Both passages also differ because of the architecture of the sanctuaries described in Leviticus and Ezekiel. Ezekiel refers to "the inner court" and Leviticus to "the tent of meeting".

A number of differences indicate that Ezek 44:21 preserves an earlier form of the instruction than Lev 10:9a. First, Lev 10:9a has the merism יין ושכר, whilst

Ezek 44:21 has only יין. Whilst it is possible to argue that שכר was omitted accidentally, it is more likely that Ezek 44:21 preserves the oldest form of the text,[175]
which in Leviticus has been assimilated to the typical pairing.[176] Such an addition to the text is a typical scribal alteration that could have taken place at any
point in the composition or transmission of Leviticus. In other words, it could
just as easily have occurred during the composition of Leviticus 10 or during
its scribal transmission.

There are a couple of differences, however, that could be seen as evidence
that Ezek 44:21 is dependent on an earlier form of Lev 10:9a. First, the command
in Ezek 44:21 takes the form of an imperfect preceded by לא, whilst Lev 10:9a has
a jussive and אל. It is easier to imagine a shift from אל to an absolute prohibition
with לא. If Leviticus 10 had Ezekiel 44 to hand, why did its composer not simply
reproduce its unambiguous imperative?[177] Second, Ezek 44:21 applies the instruction to "every priest", כל כהן, in Lev 10:9a, to Aaron and his sons. Since
each of the instructions in Ezek 44:17–27 pertains to all the priests, the precise
specification at only this point is notable. Strictly speaking, it is unnecessary,
and it could be evidence that Ezekiel 44 has transferred a part of the structure
of Lev 10:9a to Ezek 44:21 despite the fact it was not needed.

One further difference between the two instructions does not provide any decisive evidence for the priority of Leviticus 10 or Ezekiel 44. Leviticus 10:9a includes a justification of the prohibition "that you may not die", ולא תמתו. The
threat to the life of the officiating priests is a major concern in Leviticus 10,
and the same justification is found in vv. 6 and 7. It does not fit the context of
Ezekiel 44, and for that reason the composer of vv. 20–27 may simply have chos-
en to omit it.

---

175 Nihan, *Priestly Torah*, 591. Hurvitz's contention that שכר is classical Hebrew that fell out of
use in Late Biblical Hebrew is an argument from silence (Hurvitz, *Linguistic Study*). Whilst it is
true that שכר does not occur in Chronicles or Ezra-Nehemiah, neither does it occur in Genesis,
Jeremiah, Ezekiel, Hosea or Amos. Such distributions have little value when the word occurs
only 23 times in Biblical Hebrew. Probable late uses of the term include Isa 24:9 and 56:12.
176 See Gen 9:21; Num 6:3; Deut 14:26; 29:5 etc.
177 Milgrom's claim that "the negative participle 'al is inexplicable because this prohibition is
permanent" is unduly pessimistic (Milgrom, *Leviticus 1–16*, 611).

2.2.3 The Instruction Concerning Marital Partners

אשה זנה וחללה לא יקחו ואשה גרושה מאישה לא ־יקחו
כי קדש הוא לאלהיו וקדשתו כי את לחם אלהיך הוא
מקריב קדש יהיה לך כי קדוש אני יהוה מקדשכם
They shall not take a prostitute or a victim of
rape. They shall not take a woman divorced
from her husband, for he is holy to his God.
You shall treat him as holy because he offers
the food of your God. He will be holy to you for
I, YHWH, who sanctify you, am holy.
(Lev 21:7 – 8)

ואלמנה וגרושה לא יקחו להם לנשים כי אם בתולת מזרע
בית ישראל והאלמנה אשר תהיה אלמנה מכהן יקחו
They shall not take a widow or a divorcee as a
wife, but only a virgin from the seed of the
house of Israel or a widow who is the widow of
a priest. (Ezek 44:22)

והוא אשה בבתוליה יקח אלמנה וגרושה וחללה זנה את
אלה לא יקח כי אם בתולה מעמיו יקח אשה ולא יחלל
זרעו בעמיו כי אני יהוה מקדשו
He shall take a virgin. He shall not take as a
wife a widow, a divorcee, or a victim of rape,
but only a virgin of his kin. He shall not
profane his seed amongst his kin because I,
YHWH, sanctify him. (Lev 21:13 – 15)

The prohibition against alcohol consumption in the inner court is followed in
Ezekiel 44 by instructions concerning marital partners. As a result, the immediate focus is no longer on the priests' temple service. According to Ezek 44:22 the
priests may only marry Israelite virgins; consequently, they are forbidden to
marry widows or divorcees. There is only one exception: they may marry the
widow of a fellow priest. In the Holiness Code there are two different marriage
rules: one for the "priest exalted above his fellows" (Lev 21:13 – 15) and one for
the rest of the priesthood (21:7 – 8). Both rules conclude a sub-unit of instructions
and are followed by a concluding formula that refers to YHWH's sanctification of
the people.[178]

There are so many verbal parallels that some literary relationship must exist
between the rules in Leviticus 21 and the rule in Ezekiel 44.[179] A close inspection

---

178 The rule about the daughter who acts as a prostitute (v. 9) gives every sign of being a later
Fortschreibung. Its concern with priestly offspring naturally follows on from the rule about marriage partners. It has been inspired by 19:29, which prohibits the Israelites from allowing any of
their daughters to act as a prostitute. Without v. 9 the concluding formula, כי קדוש אני יהוה
מקדשכם (v. 8bβ), occurs at the correct point (cf. v. 15).
179 Note especially the distinctive term גרושה for a divorcee which is only found in Lev 21:7, 14;
22:13; Num 30:10 and Ezek 44:22. With the exception of Lev 21:7 גרושה is always paired with
אלמנה.

shows that Ezek 44:22 is most similar to Lev 21:13–15. It is not possible to explain the preserved form of either instruction simply by viewing one as dependent on the other, since both Ezek 44:22 and Lev 21:13–14 contain expressions that are not found in the other.[180] It is not immediately apparent why the reference to a prostitute or a victim of rape[181] would have been omitted from Ezek 44:22 were it to be dependent on Lev 21:13–15. Likewise, if the instructions in Leviticus 21 were dependent on Ezekiel 44, why would a scribe have removed the additional qualification that a widow of a priest was a permitted marital partner?

Our understanding of these texts is aided by Ehrlich's perceptive observation that there is a considerable overlap between the instructions for the exalted priest and the other priests in Leviticus 21, and there are no other instructions in Leviticus 21 for which this is the case. To this observation, we may add various difficulties in 21:14. The asyndetic וחללה זנה is unusual, and corrected in the versions,[182] and the compound *casus pendens* is resumed by the somewhat awkward expression, את אלה "these".[183] Ehrlich suggests an original reading אלמנה אשה יקח מעמיו בתולה אם כי יקח לא זרה, where זרה implies non-priestly descent. Not only does Ehrlich's proposal read Ezek 44:22 into Lev 22:14, it does not explain how the text reached its present form.

There is a more convincing solution at hand, if we use the overlap between Lev 22:14 and Ezek 44:22 as evidence of the earliest recoverable form of the in-

---

180 See Konkel, *Architektonik*, 119.

181 The translation of חללה is uncertain. There are a number of issues that contribute to the uncertainty. First, should חללה be distinguished from זנה? Bertholet speculates that זנה may be a gloss on חללה (Alfred Bertholet, *Leviticus*, KHC 3 [Tübingen: Mohr Siebeck, 1901], 75), though most other interpreters distinguish the two terms. Second, does חללה come from the root I חלל "to profane" or II חלל "to pierce"? (The suggestion that it relates to מחולות "dance", and by extension to cultic prostitution, can be safely rejected [M. Z. Levin, "חללה", *Beth Mikra* 29 (1984): 180–81]). Third, having determined the root, what nuance should be granted the particular form? For discussion see, *inter alia*, Jacob Milgrom, *Leviticus 17–22: A New Translation with Introduction and Commentary*, AB 3A (New York: Doubleday, 2000), 1806–08; Moshe A. Zipor, "Restrictions on Marriage for Priests (Lev 21:7, 13–14)", *Bib* 68 (1987): 259–67.

182 SP reads זנה, and LXX reads καὶ βεβηλωμένην. MT should be preferred as the *lectio difficilior*.

183 "An dieser Stelle liegt uns der Text unmöglich in seiner Ursprünglichkeit vor, den es ist undenkbar, dass der Gesetz es nötig fand, dem Hohenpriester die Heirat mit drei der Weibern zu verbieten, die nach V. 7 auch der gemeine Priester nicht heiraten darf. Ist doch kein anderes der den gemeinen Priester betreffenden Verbote bei dem Hohenpriester wiederholt. Auch ist im ersten Halbvers der Satzbau und besonders die asyndetische Anreihung von זנה ungewöhnlich und kaum hebraisch" (A.B. Ehrlich, *Randglossen zur Hebräischen Bibel: Textkritisches, sprachliches und sachliches. Zweiter Band: Leviticus, Numeri, Deuteronomium* [Leipzig: Hinrich, 1909], 75).

struction. It would suggest that the instruction originally lacked וחללה זנה את אלה. We may reasonably hypothesize that the reference to the prostitute and the victim of rape was added to Lev 22:14 under the influence of v. 7. A scribe may have thought to include them because of the appearance of גרושה in both verses. The terms זנה and וחללה were reversed in accordance with typical scribal practice (Seidel's law), but this was done rather carelessly and without transposing the *waw*. The addition of these two terms resulted in the lengthy *casus pendens*, אלמנה וגרושה וחללה זנה. Its grammatical unwieldiness was eased by the addition of the resumptive את אלה. The only problem that Ehrlich raises that my proposal leaves unresolved is the prohibition of the גרושה to the exalted priest, when marriage to a divorcee is already excluded by virtue of him being a priest. In light of the two somewhat repetitive clauses in Lev 21:7, it is reasonable to speculate whether there was a prior stage in which the prohibition of divorcees was introduced into v. 7aβ from v. 13. In other words, the original prohibition for the priests consisted of v. 7aα, b and forbade only the marrying of a prostitute or a rape victim.

If the proposed solution were correct, it would sharpen the distinction between the priests and the exalted priest. Priests were forbidden from marrying a prostitute or the victim of a rape. In other words, they could not marry someone where an illicit act of intercourse had taken place. They were free to marry a divorcee or a widow. In both cases sexual intercourse with another partner had occurred, but the intercourse was licit. But for the exalted priest, even marriage to a woman who had had licit intercourse with another man was prohibited. He was only permitted to marry a virgin from amongst his kinfolk.

To this point my analysis has made a case that וחללה זנה את אלה (Lev 21:14) is a result of scribal expansion, and that this expansion was internal to Leviticus 21. We have also seen that the similarities between Lev 21:13–15 and Ezek 44:22 suggest that אלמנה וגרושה לא יקח כי אם בתולה, "you shall not marry a widow or a divorcee, rather a virgin", reflects the earliest recoverable form of the instruction. How were the virgin's ancestral origins originally specified? Was the virgin to be taken "from his kin" (מעמיו) as in Lev 21:14,[184] or "from the seed of the house of Israel" (מזרע בית ישראל) as in Ezek 44:22? The reference to "kin" (עמים) in Lev 21:14 is consistent not only with other uses in Leviticus 21:

---

184 Both contextually and because of its plural form עם must mean the exalted priest's own kin, i.e. the daughter of a fellow priest, and not simply from the people of Israel. See Milgrom, *Leviticus 17–22*, 1819–20; Karl Elliger, *Leviticus*, HAT 1,4 (Tübingen: Mohr Siebeck, 1966), 282. For plural עם as close relations, see *HALOT* I.837.

vv. 1, 4, 15, but with the Holiness Code more generally.[185] Taken on its own, this could plausibly be explained in two different ways. Either the marriage instruction originally belonged to Leviticus 21, or the scribe altered the marriage commandment to suit its new context. If we turn to the expression מזרע בית ישראל in Ezek 44:22,[186] we encounter an unusual collocation, which is only otherwise attested in Jer 23:8, a text with no obvious relation to Ezek 44:22. The expression בית ישראל is characteristic of the book of Ezekiel.[187] By contrast, זרע is surprisingly rare, occurring on only five other occasions in Ezekiel.[188] In the Holiness Code זרע appears frequently with the meaning "offspring", especially in the instructions concerning the priests.[189] Most notably, of course, זרע occurs in the final clause of the instructions concerning the marriage of the exalted priest (v. 15). Thus, whilst בית ישראל in Ezek 44:22 reflects the idiom of the book of Ezekiel, זרע reflects the idiom of the Holiness Code's instructions concerning priests.[190] The data would suggest that the collocation מזרע בית ישראל be seen as evidence for the dependence of Ezek 44:22 on Lev 21:13–15.

It is apparent that the instruction in Ezek 44:22 permit the priests to select a marital partner from a much broader circle than is the case for the elevated priest of Leviticus 21: any Israelite woman, and not just a woman from their immediate tribe. It is possible that the difference arose from the use of עם in Lev 21:14. Whilst the Masoretic Text reads the plural of עם and means by this the priest's nearest kin, the early translations – the Septuagint, the Peshitta, and the Targumim – render with a singular. The singular reading is probably secondary – on the grounds of *lectio difficilior* – but it had already made its way into the Hebrew textual tradition as the Samaritan Pentateuch and 4QLev^e show. The most natural way to understand a singular עם is of the people of Israel as a whole. The interpretive tradition is likewise divided. Although the earliest unambiguous evidence from the late Second Temple period suggests that the high

---

185 See Lev 17:9; 19:8, 16; 23:29 (cf. Lev 17:4, 10; 18:29; 19:18; 20:3, 5, 6, 17, 18; 23:30). For the oscillation between singular and plural, see Milgrom, *Leviticus 17–22*, 1471–72.
186 LXX reads ἐκ τοῦ σπέρματος Ισραηλ. The expression זרע ישראל is found on a few occasions in the Hebrew Bible. The text-critical arguments for both readings are fairly evenly balanced, but do not affect the main line of argument developed here.
187 Of 147 occurrences in the Hebrew Bible, no less than 83 occur in Ezekiel.
188 Ezek 17:5 (x2), 13; 20:5; 43:19.
189 Lev 18:21; 20:2, 3, 4; 21:15, 17, 21; 22:3, 4, 13.
190 *Contra* Konkel who writes, "In dem Adversativsatz Ez 44,22bα wird in der für das Ezechielbuch typischen Weise gesagt, daß die Priester Jungfrauen 'aus der Samen des Hauses Israel' zur Frau nehmen sollen, wohingegen Lev 21,14b von einer Jungfrau 'aus seinem Volke' spricht" (Konkel, *Architektonik*, 120).

priest could only marry within their clan,[191] the rabbis held that the high priest could marry any Jewish virgin.[192] The textual diversity and divergent interpretive traditions are easily explained by appeal to typical textual developments if the original reading was מעמיו, "his kin". At an early stage מעמיו was misread or mis-interpreted as the more familiar מעמו, "his people". Ezekiel 44's מזרע בית ישראל appears to reflect this secondary reading. In contrast, we must allow for some unusual developments to have occurred for Ezekiel 44's מזרע בית ישראל to have given rise to this textual diversity. In particular, it is quite unclear how the reading מעמיו in Lev 21:14 would have developed.

Finally, we must consider the significant qualification in the instruction of Ezekiel 44: והאלמנה אשר תהיה אלמנה מכהן יקחו, "he may marry a widow who was the widow of a priest". As Konkel observes the concern is not the sanctity of the priest, but the sanctity of his offspring. If the widow was previously married to a priest, there can be no doubts as to the priestly status of her children.[193] Significantly, this additional qualification would appear to presuppose the justification of the marriage instructions in Leviticus 22, which is not stated in Ezekiel 44: "he may not profane his offspring amongst his kin". It is not entirely certain why Ezek 44:22 has the further qualification that a priest may marry the widow of a priest. A plausible answer is that the composer of Ezekiel 44 is mindful of the so-called Levirate marriage legislation in Deut 25:5–6. According to this law, a

---

191 See the discussions in Philo and Josephus. "Further, it made clear distinctions as to the birth of the intended wives. The high priest must not propose marriage save to one who is not only a virgin but a priestess descended from priests so that bride and bridegroom may be of one house and in a sense of the same blood and so, harmoniously united, shew a lifelong blending of temperament firmly established." (Philo, *Spec.* 1.110; translation according to Francis Henry Colson, *Philo VII*, LCL 320 [Cambridge, MA: Harvard University Press, 1958]). "Not only did our ancestors in the first instance set over this business men of the highest character, devoted to the service of God, but they took precautions to ensure that the priests' lineage should be kept unadulterated and pure. A member of the priestly order must, to beget a family, marry a woman of his own race, without regard to her wealth or other distinctions; but he must investigate her pedigree, obtaining the genealogy from the archives and producing a number of witnesses." (Josephus, *Ag. Ap.* 1.31; translation according to H. St J. Thackery, *Josephus I*, LCL 186 [Cambridge, MA: Harvard University Press, 1976]) The same position is represented in the Septuagint of Leviticus 21, despite the translator's consistent use of the singular and his inconsistent translation of עם with ἔθνος (v. 1), λαός (vv. 4, 15) and γένος (v. 14). The use of γένος in v. 14 clearly aligns the Septuagint with the position expressed in Philo and Josephus.
192 See also Ibn Ezra who understands 21:14 to forbid only converts and a virgin captured in war. Rashbam takes the heterodox position that the high priest's wife had to be from the same clan. For discussion see Martin I. Lockshin, *Rashbam's Commentary on Leviticus and Numbers: An Annotated Translation*, BJS 330 (Providence, RI: Brown Judaic Studies, 2001), 115 n. 2.
193 Konkel, *Architektonik*, 120.

widow who has not given her husband an heir to his estate should be given to the next eldest brother who has the responsibility of providing an heir for his brother. The legislation requires that marriage of a widow be permissible, and it is possible to imagine a scenario in which Leviticus 21 and Deuteronomy 25 would result in a situation that could not be resolved. The instructions in Ezekiel 44 avoid what would otherwise be a contradiction.

In conclusion, the rule proper in Ezek 44:22 preserves an earlier text than we find in Lev 21:13–14. The rules in Leviticus 21 have undergone significant internal development that we are in a position to reconstruct. In a couple of respects, however, the rule in Ezek 44:22 has developed beyond the rules in Leviticus 21. First, it reflects the secondary reading מעמו and, second, its scope has been modified under the influence of the Levirate marriage legislation of Deuteronomy 25.

2.2.4 The Instruction Concerning Teaching and Judicial Roles

חקת עולם לדרתיכם[196] להבדיל בין הקדש ובין החל ובין הטמא ובין הטהור ולהורת את בני ישראל את כל החקים אשר דבר יהוה אליהם ביד משה

ואת עמי יורו בין קדש לחל ובין טמא לטהור יודעם ועל ריב המה יעמדו לשפט[194] במשפטי ישפטוהו[195] ואת תורתי ואת חקתי בכל מועדי ישמרו ואת שבתותי יקדשו

They shall teach my people the difference between holy and common, and instruct them on the difference between unclean and clean. In a dispute they shall stand to judge. By my judgements they will judge it. They will keep my teaching and my statutes concerning all my festivals, and sanctify my Sabbaths. (Ezek 44:23–24)

This is a permanent rule for you generations: to distinguish between the holy and the common, and between the unclean and the clean, and to teach the sons of Israel all the statutes that YHWH spoke to them by the hand of Moses. (Lev 10:9b–11)

---

194 The *qere* reads יעמדו למשפט, "stand for judgement". There is no parallel elsewhere in the Hebrew Bible to עמד לשפט, and the portrayal of the priests standing to judge is surprising. Other texts portray judges sitting and the plaintive standing (e.g. Exod 18:13), though Isa 3:13 and Ps 82:1 offer possible counter-examples. The *qere* might be an assimilation to the idiom עמד למשפט which is attested in Num 35:12; Josh 20:6, but this would not be apt as it is again the plaintive that is standing. The *ketiv* is supported by LXX, Tg., and Syr. and should be preferred.

195 The *qere* ישפטוהו is supported by Tg. and LXX's double translation (but see O'Hare, *Son of Man*, 110 n. 114). The *ketiv* ושפטהו appears to be a scribal error.

196 חקת עולם לדרתיכם could be understood as the conclusion to v. 9b or the introduction to v. 10. Watts cites the parallel in Lev 16:34: והיתה זאת לכם לחקת עולם לכפר, "and this will be a permanent rule for you: to atone...". This requires that the *waw* before the following להבדיל be omitted (with LXX and Syr.) (James W. Watts, *Leviticus 1–10*, HCOT [Leuven: Peeters, 2013], 539; cf. John E. Hartley, *Leviticus*, WBC 4 [Dallas: Word Books, 1992], 127).

In Leviticus 10 Aaron and his sons are given a twofold task in instructing the Israelites. They are to instruct the people concerning ritual distinctions (v. 10) and
to teach the Mosaic law (v. 11). Ezekiel's instruction concerning the teaching and
judicial roles of the priests corresponds closely to the ruling found in Leviticus,
but the Ezekiel text differs at two points.[197] First, the judicial role of the priests in
Ezekiel 44 has no parallel in Leviticus 10. Second, Leviticus 10 has the expansive
requirement that the priests teach the entire pentateuchal law. Ezekiel 44 is more
precise: the priests are to safeguard the ritual calendar.[198]

The inclusion of the priest's judicial role in Ezekiel 44 very likely reflects dependence on Deut 17:8 – 13.[199] Deuteronomy describes the priest's judicial role in
a manner similar to the description of the priest's ritual role in Leviticus. In Leviticus 10 the priests distinguish between (בין...ל) ritual categories: the clean and
the unclean, the holy and the profane. In Deuteronomy 17 the priests are to distinguishing between (בין...ל) different kinds of injuries. The cases to be brought to
the priests are collectively described as matters of dispute (ריבת; 17:8). Making
such distinctions is to render a decision (למשפט; 17:8, 10). In a similar manner
Ezek 44:24 envisages priests making decisions (במשפטי) about disputes (ריב).

The insistence that the priests have responsibility for appointed festivals and
Sabbaths (v. 24b) appears to have its roots within Ezekiel's temple vision. The ex-

---

197 We may exclude from our consideration Ezek 22:26, which parallels Ezek 44:23 – 24 even
more closely than Lev 10:10 – 11: כהניה חמסו תורתי ויחללו קדשי בין קדש לחל לא הבדילו ובין הטמא
לטהור לא הודיעו ומשבתותי העלימו עיניהם ואחל בתוכם, "Its priests have violated my torah and have
profaned my holy things. They have not distinguished between the holy and the profane, and
they have not made known the difference between the clean and unclean. They have closed
their eyes to my Sabbaths so that I am profaned amongst them". It is most likely that Ezek
22:26 is dependent on Ezek 44:23 – 24, rather than the reverse. The condemnation of the priests
in 22:26 is the second in a series of judgements that also includes officials, princes, and prophets
(vv. 25 – 29). In v. 25 קשר נביאיה, "conspiracy of its prophets", is problematic in view of the reference to the prophets in v. 28. LXX reads ἧς οἱ ἀφηγούμενοι, "whose leaders", which could suggest an original reading אשר נשיאיה (Zimmerli, *Ezechiel*, 521). Fishbane has demonstrated that
these judgements are the expansion of an oracle known from Zeph 3:3 – 4 embellished with literary material taken from Ezekiel, including chapters 13, 19 and 22 (Fishbane, *Biblical Interpretation*, 461– 62). We should, therefore, regard v. 26 as the combination of Zeph 3:4a with textual
material from Ezekiel 44:23 – 24.
198 If we compare Leviticus 10 and the material that directly parallels it in Ezekiel 44 there is
little basis to argue for the priority of either text. Hurvitz's claim that בין...ל is the Late Biblical
Hebrew equivalent to the classical בין...בין is not compelling. There are examples of בין...ל in classical Hebrew, not least the portrayal of the priests' judicial role in Deut 17:8.
199 The relationship is recognized and deepened in LXX, which reads καὶ ἐπὶ κρίσιν αἵματος for
MT's ועל־ריב. This would appear to reflect בין־דם לדם in Deut 17:8. For discussion see O'Hare, *Son
of Man*, 110 – 13.

pression ואת־תורתי ואת־חקתי is similar to many other combinations of legal terminology in the Hebrew Bible, but it is closest to Ezek 44:5, which refers to "the ordinances of YHWH's temple and its laws" (cf. 43:11). Similarly, Ezek 45:17 mentions "all the appointed festivals" and "the Sabbaths" in the context of the
prince's responsibilities. Christophe Nihan rightly observes that the responsibility for the festivals and Sabbaths in Ezek 44:24 corresponds to the requirement in
Lev 10:11 that the priests teach the entire law of Moses. He is also correct that in
Leviticus 10 "the priests who were traditionally responsible for teaching the *cultic tôrâ* have now become teachers of the Torah in general".[200] But whilst he
rightly describes the direction of the religio-historical development of the priesthood, this cannot in itself determine the direction of inner-biblical interpretation. We have examples of biblical interpretation in Qumran, for example,
where general commands from the Bible are made more specific, and where specific commands are made more general. Nor is it clear that the festivals were traditionally part of the priests' cultic teaching. Even in a text as late as Leviticus 23,
Moses, rather than the priests, teaches the people about the Sabbath and the festivals. Just as significant, both requirements of the priests have been integrated
into the textual corpora of which they are part. Leviticus 10 is part of a large,
comprehensive body of Mosaic law, and the priests are made responsible for
teaching it. Ezekiel 44 is part of Ezekiel's temple law, which is concerned with
the temple and its workings, most especially the festivals that take place there
(45:18 – 46:15).

As well as analysing the areas where the rules in Ezek 44:23 – 24 and Lev
10:9 – 11 differ, we need also to consider whether the shared material is more
at home in Ezekiel or Leviticus. The vocabulary of clean (טהור) and unclean
(טמא) is very common in Leviticus, especially in the purity laws (Lev 11– 15),[201]
but rare in Ezekiel.[202] In contrast, the vocabulary of "common" (חל) is not
found elsewhere in Leviticus, but is used in Ezekiel's temple vision (42:20;
48:15), whilst the vocabulary of "holy" (קדש) is ubiquitous in both. The evidence
from shared material is not unanimous, but there is a slightly stronger case for
seeing Leviticus as the original context.

---

200 Nihan, *Priestly Torah*, 593.
201 For טהור see Lev 11:36, 47; 13:13, 17, 37, 39, 40, 41; 14:4, 57; 15:8; for טמא see Lev 11:4, 5, 6, 7, 8,
26, 27, 28, 29, 31, 35, 38, 47; 13:11, 15, 36, 44, 45, 46, 51, 55; 14:40, 41, 44, 45, 57; 15:2, 25, 26, 33.
202 For טהור see Ezek 22:26; 36:25; for טמא see Ezek 4:13; 22:5, 10, 26.

2.2.5 The Instruction Concerning Dead Bodies

ואל מת אדם לא יבוא לטמאה כי אם לאב ולאם ולבן
ולבת לאח ולאחות אשר לא היתה לאיש יטמאו[203] ואחרי
טהרתו שבעת ימים יספרו[204] לו וביום באו אל הקדש אל
החצר הפנימית לשרת בקדש יקריב חטאתו

He shall not go to a dead person to defile
himself, but only for father, mother, son,
brother, and unmarried sister they may defile
themselves. After his purification, they shall
count seven days for him. On the day that he
enters the holy place, into the inner court, to
minister in the holy place, he shall offer his
purification offering. (Ezek 44:25–27)

לנפש לא יטמא בעמיו כי אם לשארו הקרב אליו לאמו
ולאביו ולבנו ולבתו ולאחיו ולאחתו הבתולה הקרובה אליו
אשר לא היתה לאיש לה יטמא לא יטמא בעל בעמיו
להחלו

He shall not defile himself for a dead person
amongst his kin, except for those who are close
to him: his mother, or his father, or his brother,
or his daughter, or his son, or his daughter.
Also, for his virgin sister, who is close to him
and has not had a husband, for her he may
defile himself. He shall not defile himself as a
husband among his kin and so profane
himself. (Lev 21:1–4)

ועל כל נפשת מת לא יבא לאביו ולאמו לא יטמא ומן
המקדש לא יצא ולא יחלל את מקדש אלהיו כי נזר שמן
משחת אלהיו עליו אני יהוה

He shall not go where there is a dead body. He
shall not defile himself for father or mother.
He shall not go outside the sanctuary and so
not profane the sanctuary of his God, for the
consecration of the anointing oil of his God
is upon him. I am YHWH. (Lev 21:11–12)

The instructions about corpse impurity provide a final example where Ezekiel 44
has a single instruction, but Leviticus 21 has two instructions, one for the priest

---

203 There is significant literary unevenness in vv. 25–27. The MT has a singular verb in v. 25a
followed by a plural in v. 25b; vv. 26–27 have singular verbs and suffixes. The Septuagint, however, has plural verb in v. 25a followed by a singular in v. 25b; v. 26 is in the singular and v. 27 in
the plural. Zimmerli argues that יבוא in v. 25a should be read as יבאו. This is a simple case of
consonantal metathesis, which explains the Septuagint's reading (Zimmerli, *Ezechiel*, 1121). If
Zimmerli's proposal were followed the MT would have a plural from v. 17 to v. 25, and transitions
to the singular in vv. 26–27. Equally plausible is Konkel's argument that we accept MT's יבוא in v.
25a, but correct יטמאו in v. 25b to read יטמא. This would accord with the Septuagint's *Vorlage*,
whilst MT's reading is simply dittography that resulted from the following clause. The plural
text would then reach only as far as v. 24 with the singular found in vv. 25–27 (Konkel, *Architektonik*, 113).
204 Zimmerli argues that in v. 26 the Septuagint's ἐξαριθμήσει should be preferred to MT's יספרו
(Zimmerli, *Ezechiel*, 1121). Both MT and LXX agree that the suffixes in the rest of the verse are
singular. Consequently, it could be argued that MT's יספרו is the *lectio difficilior* and to be preferred. The plural would then be the priestly contemporaries who have the responsibility of ensur-
ing that the appropriate number of days for purification has passed (Konkel, *Architektonik*, 113).

elevated above his brothers and one for the ordinary priests. The rule for the elevated priest is more stringent. He may not contract corpse impurity, not even for his father and mother (Lev 21:11). The ordinary priest may contract corpse impurity in a tightly prescribed set of circumstances (vv. 2–3). Very close blood relatives are included, but the priest's wife and her relatives are excluded (v. 4).

In its main thrust Ezekiel's rule is similar to the rule for ordinary priests in Leviticus. Ezekiel's priests may only mourn for the same list of close relatives specified in Lev 21:2–3. The rule begins, however, with a locution that is found in the rule for the elevated priest: "he shall not go", לא יבוא. On this basis Lyons cites the rule concerning corpse impurity in Ezekiel 44 as a good example of *textual conflation*.[205] Whilst Lyons has identified an important feature of the rules in Leviticus and Ezekiel, he neglects data that points to Ezekiel preserving an earlier text of the instruction proper.

There are four ways in which the instruction in Lev 21:2–3 can be demonstrated to preserve a more developed text than that found in Ezek 44:25. First, the kin for whom defilement is permitted are described in Lev 21:2 as "the relatives that are close to him", לשארו הקרב אליו. This expression is absent from Ezek 44:25. The use of שאר with the meaning "relative" is characteristic of the incest laws in the Holiness Code.[206] Second, whilst Ezek 44:25 has the typical order אב followed by אם, Lev 21:2 has the reverse order. The unusual order is found elsewhere in the Holiness Code: 19:3, 20:19 and could represent an assimilation to a distinctive diction of the Holiness Code.[207] Third, the unmarried sister is further defined in Lev 21:3 as "a virgin, close to him", הבתולה הקרובה אליו, which Ezek 44:25 lacks. Fourth, Lev 21:3 reads לה after אשר לא היתה לאיש. In Ezek 44:25 the exception clause is a single sentence ending with the verb יטמאו. In Lev 21:2–3 inclusion of לה divides the exception clause into two sentences (indicated by the verse division). This rearrangement of the verse is necessitated by the additional textual elements in Lev 21:2–3, which would otherwise result in a rather unwieldy and lengthy sentence. In all four cases we have evidence that Ezek 44:25 preserves an earlier text of the rule proper than Lev 21:2–3,[208] and in

---

205 Lyons, *From Law to Prophecy*, 96–97.

206 Lev 18:6, 12, 13; 20:19; 25:49. The use of לשארו הקרב אליו in Num 27:11 is probably dependent on H.

207 For the order father-mother in H, see Lev 18:9; 20:9, 17; 21:11.

208 As correctly observed by Grünwaldt, *Heiligkeitsgesetz*, 264. The only case where there is uncertainty is the occurrence of אם followed by אב in Lev 21:2. An argument can be made that Lev 21:2 may preserve the earlier text on the grounds of *lectio difficilior*. The unusual order mother-father was corrected to the typical usage in its transference to Ezekiel 44. This assimilation to the usual order took place in the text-history of Leviticus as seen in LXX, SP, and Syr.

most cases that Lev 21:2–3 has been assimilated to diction found elsewhere in the Holiness Code.

Although the wording of the instruction concerning corpse impurity shows unambiguous evidence that Ezekiel 44 preserves an earlier text than Leviticus 21, the law in Ezekiel 44 has also been developed in ways that are not evidenced in Leviticus 21. In Leviticus 21 no prescriptions are made concerning purification from corpse impurity. In Ezekiel 44 the process by which purification takes place is presupposed, but a waiting period is prescribed. After purification the priest may enter the inner court after an additional seven days have passed. At that time he must offer a purification offering (vv. 26–27).

Within the Pentateuch a distinctive ritual for corpse impurity is prescribed in Numbers 19. It applies to all Israelites, and not just priests. The corpse impure Israelite is purified through the application of the ashes of the red cow on the third and seventh days. The corpse impure Israelite becomes clean on the evening of the seventh day. There are grounds, however, for thinking that this ritual specification is an innovation that post-dates the Holiness Code.[209] Quite what purification may have presupposed by the composer of Leviticus 21 for the corpse impure priests is unknown, but we might assume something like the washings and passage of time that we find in the purity regulations of Leviticus 12–15.

Ezekiel 44 does not prescribe how the initial purification was to take place either,[210] but it does appear to draw on the regulations for the individual suffering from a skin ailment (14:8–11), the *zab* (15:13–15), and the *zabah* (15:28–30), by requiring that a further seven days pass before the priest is completely clean and may approach the sanctuary. Indeed, it is possible that the composer of Eze-

---

209 See Reinhard Achenbach, "Verunreinigung durch die Berührung Toter: Zum Ursprung einer altisraelitischen Vorstellung", in *Tod und Jenseits im Alten Israel und in seiner Umwelt: Theologische, religionsgeschichtliche, archäologische und ikonographische Aspekte*, ed. Angelika Berlejung and Bernd Janowski, FAT 64 (Tübingen: Mohr Siebeck, 2009), 347–69; Nathan MacDonald, "The Hermeneutics and Genesis of the Red Cow Ritual", *HTR* 105 (2012): 351–71.

210 Konkel is rightly circumspect about a relationship to Numbers 19: "Num 19,11–22 zufolge verunreinigt der Kontakt mit einem Toten für eine Frist von sieben Tagen. Offensichtlich wird eine solche Frist auch hier vorausgesetzt" (Konkel, *Architektonik*, 124). Similarly Zimmerli: "nach Nu 19 hat sich der an einer Leiche Verunreinigte mit dem Reinigungswasser, dessen Herstellung 1–10 berichten, am 3. und 7. Tage nach der Verunreinigung zu reinigen. Es ist nicht deutlich, ob Ez 44 dieses oder ein analoges Ritual für den Laien voraussetzt. Die Vorschrift, daß der Priester 'nach seinem Reinwerden' 7 Tage zählen und dann bei seinem erneuten Dienstantritt ein Sündopfer darbringen soll, läßt aber eine Vorschrift dieser Art vermuten" (Zimmerli, *Ezechiel*, 1136).

kiel 44 borrowed locutions from Lev 15:13, 28 and reversed them in accordance with Seidel's law:[211]

ואחרי טהרתו שבעת ימים יספרו לו

and after his cleansing they shall count seven days for him (Ezek 44:26).

וספר לו שבעת ימים לטהרתו

and he shall count for himself seven days for his cleansing (Lev 15:13).

וספרה לה שבעת ימים ואחר תטהר

and she shall count for herself seven days, and afterward she will be clean (Lev 15:28).

The effect of this application of Seidel's law is curious, because it creates a two-stage purification for the corpse-impure priest. The *zab* and the *zabah* must wait seven day after their discharge at which point they may approach the sanctuary with their offering (15:14–15, 29–30). The priest must be purified, and then wait a further seven days before he may enter the inner court to resume his service.

2.2.6 The Relationship between the Instructions in Ezekiel 44 and Leviticus 10 and 21

The careful analysis of the individual instructions that I have undertaken presents what appears on first sight to be a set of contradictory data. Some of Ezekiel's rules appear to presuppose the rules in Leviticus and move beyond them. The instructions concerning mourning in Lev 10:6; 21:5–6, 10 are well integrated into the concerns of the Holiness Code. Ezekiel's instructions concerning hair appear to be a development of those earlier instructions. The mourning context has entirely disappeared so that we have a rule about how priests are to keep their hair. This rule presents a *via media* where hair must be kept neatly trimmed. Some of Ezekiel's rules appear to reflect legislation found elsewhere in the Pentateuch. Permitting the priest to marry a widow may reflect Deut 25:5–6, the judicial responsibilities described in Ezek 44:23 likely depend on Deut 17:8–13, and the instruction concerning purification from corpse impurity reflects the purity laws in Leviticus 11–15. On the other hand, Ezekiel frequently has an earlier text with clear evidence that the related instructions in Leviticus have been expanded secondarily. In the alcohol prohibition יין is probably an earlier text than the typical pairing יין ושכר. In the marriage instructions, the orig-

---

211 Konkel, on the other hand, argues that "auch hier nimmt die Vorschrift Ez 44,26 f offensichtlich eine allgemeine kultische Tradition auf" (Konkel, *Architektonik*, 124).

inal rule corresponds to Ezek 44:22a, bα with the notable exception that מעמיו is an earlier reading than מזרע בית ישראל. Ezekiel's instructions concerning dead bodies preserves the more original text than Leviticus 21, which has various expansions including הבתולה הקרובה אליו, לשארו הקרב אליו and אשר לא היתה לאיש.

On the basis of this evidence it is readily apparent how different scholars have reached contradictory conclusions. Arguments can be adduced for the position that Ezekiel 44 utilized Leviticus 10 and 21, and for the position that Leviticus 10 and 21 utilized Ezekiel 44. But this can only be done by taking a partial view of the textual evidence. In fact, we cannot explain the present form of Ezekiel 44 as a reuse of the present form of Leviticus 10 and 21. Nor can we explain the present form of Leviticus 10 and 21 as a reuse of the present form of Ezekiel 44. Instead, a comparison of the instructions in Leviticus and Ezekiel reveals a common text. This common text is to be found in what we have labelled the instructions proper and a comparison of the instructions in Ezekiel and Leviticus indicates that Ezekiel frequently preserves this common text in a more original form.

It is tempting to conclude with Tuell that there was a third text – no longer preserved – which Ezekiel and Leviticus both utilized independently of the other. We must not overlook, however, the different ways in which the instructions in Ezekiel and Leviticus have developed. In the case of Leviticus 10 and 21 the expansions reflect an assimilation to the diction and themes of the book of Leviticus. In the instructions concerning alcohol, the final clause ולא תמתו (Lev 10:9) is also found in 10:6 and reflects the narrative about the deaths of Nadab and Abihu. In the instructions about marital partners I have demonstrated the degree of internal development that has occurred in Leviticus 21, not least through introducing stipulations concerning the ordinary priests into the requirements on the exalted priest. Both rules are considerably expanded by statements about the sanctity of the priests and by relating this to YHWH's holiness. In the instructions concerning the exalted priest the avoidance of dead bodies is justified because of the anointing oil. The anointing of Aaron and his sons is described in the ordination ceremony of Leviticus 8. In each case the expansion of the rules concerning priestly conduct ensures a greater correspondence with the rest of the book of Leviticus. The same dynamic is also present in the numerous additions to the instructions concerning dead bodies. As Grünwaldt rightly observes the addition of הבתולה הקרובה אליו, לשארו הקרב אליו and אשר לא היתה לאיש reflect the idiom of the Holiness Code. In contrast the changes to Ezekiel's rules rarely touch the instructions proper except for a few occasions where assimilation to the context of the temple vision is required. There are, however, various expansions that reflect a much wider set of textual influences. The instruction concerning teaching roles has been expanded under the influence of Deuteronomy 17 to include judicial roles, whilst the instructions concerning corpse impurity draws on the purity laws of Leviticus 14–15 to specify the process of purification from corpse impurity.

There are at least a couple of ways that we could explain the different profiles of expansion. We could argue that the priestly instructions in Leviticus drew upon Ezekiel 44, which was later developed through *Fortschreibung* with material from elsewhere in the Pentateuch. I have proposed an alternative hypothesis. The composer of Ezekiel 44:20–27 was familiar with the book of Leviticus, but he knew a text that was typologically earlier than that which we now have in the MT. He sought to further clarify and harmonize the instructions with other texts from the Pentateuch, including Leviticus 14–15 and Deuteronomy 17. The text of Leviticus 10 and 21 in our Masoretic Text reflects internal textual growth during its transmission.

The obvious criticism that may be brought against this proposal is that we have no manuscript evidence that the priestly rules in Leviticus existed in an earlier form. Nevertheless, the Masoretic Text, the Septuagint, the Samaritan Pentateuch, and the biblical manuscripts from Qumran give evidence for the existence of multiple versions of biblical texts during the Second Temple period. The hypothesis that the composers of Ezekiel 44.20–27 had to hand a manuscript with an earlier text-type of Leviticus than we now have in the Masoretic Text is a reasonable one. In addition, as I have shown the present form of the instructions concerning marital partners provides evidence of internal textual growth within Leviticus 21.

My proposal also seeks to do justice to three additional features that are difficult to explain if Leviticus and Ezekiel drew on a common source. We have observed two of these already. First, there is some evidence of *textual conflation* in the instructions concerning hair and dead bodies in Ezekiel 44. This is particularly significant in Ezek 44:20, where it is difficult to see how the rules in Leviticus 21 could have been derived from Ezekiel 44, whilst the reverse is readily explicable. Secondly, the specification in Ezek 44:22 that the priests must marry a virgin "from the seed of the house of Israel" appears to reflect the idiom of the Holiness Code. Thirdly, each of the rules in Leviticus 10 and 21 is reflected in Ezekiel 44, such that Ezekiel 44 can be viewed as a compact compendium of the pentateuchal rules concerning priestly conduct. As we have seen the only rule duplicated in Leviticus 10 and 21 is the rule concerning mourning practices, where Ezek 44:20 appears to be a conflation of both texts, On the other hand, if the rules in Leviticus 10 and 21 are derived from Ezekiel 44, the decision of the composers of Leviticus to distribute the rules between Leviticus 10 and 21 is without obvious parallel. Why did the composers of Leviticus 10 and Leviticus 21 leave out certain rules that were present in Ezekiel 44, and why were those that they left out present elsewhere in Leviticus (with the notable exception of the rule about mourning practices)? The distribution of the instructions in Leviticus 10 and 21, and Ezekiel 44 is striking and provides an important clue to the structure and composition of the rules in Ezekiel 44:20 – 27.

2.2.7 The Structure and Composition of the Rules in Ezekiel 44:20 – 27

If we view the rules in Ezekiel 44:20 – 27 as a compendium of rules concerning priestly conduct known from Leviticus 10 and 21, it is apparent that we have a fascinating instance of scriptural re-use, as can be appreciated in the table below.

Rule	Ezekiel 44	Leviticus 10	Leviticus 21
Hair	20	6	5, 10
Alcohol	21	9	
Marital Partners	22		7 – 8, 13 – 15
Teaching and Judicial Roles	23 – 24	10 – 11	
Dead Bodies	25 – 27		1 – 4, 11 – 12

The two sets of instruction from Leviticus have been interwoven moving back and forth between the two precursor texts. Recognizing this pattern allows us to address the question that I posed at the beginning of this chapter: is it possible to account for the order of the rules in vv. 17 – 31? The apparent lack of logical order in vv. 20 – 27 that has often been observed can be explained in a simple and elegant manner as the result of scriptural re-use: the composer of Ezekiel 44 has woven the two sets of priestly laws together. Significantly, we have seen the same technique of scriptural re-use employed earlier in the chapter. In Ezek 44:10 – 15 the precursor texts, Num 18:1 – 7 and Ezek 14:1 – 11, have been interwoven using the same pattern.[212]

---

212 Viewing Ezekiel 44 as the original text from which Leviticus 10 and 21 derive results in significant difficulties. With relatively small alterations, the composers of Leviticus have produced order from a disorderly Ezekiel 44. Christophe Nihan, for example, argues that Leviticus 10 is one of the latest parts of the Pentateuch, and believes that this necessitates its dependence on Ezekiel 44. He seeks to justify this relationship by arguing that "Lev 10 *goes beyond* Ez 44" (Nihan, *Priestly Torah*, 592). He argues that the two rules concerning priestly teaching and prohibiting alcohol "are no longer simply juxtaposed, as in Ez 44, but a logical relation is defined between them, i.e., if priests must abstain from alcohol it is *because* they must be able

This way of interweaving texts, though intricate, is not unattested elsewhere. In Jer 48:29–38 an oracle about Moab has been created by interweaving Isa 15:2–7 and 16:6–12.[213]

Jeremiah 48	Isaiah 16	Isaiah 15
29–33	6–10	
34		4–6
35		
36a	11	
36b		7
37–38		2–3

Two closely related examples are found in a reworked Pentateuch from Qumran, 4QRP[a], and the Samaritan Pentateuch of Exodus 20.[214] 4QRP[a] interweaves Exodus 20 and Deuteronomy 5:

4QRP[a]	Exodus 20	Deuteronomy 5	
frag. 6 1–2		27	
frag. 6 2–4	19b–21		
frag. 6 4–5		28b–29	
frag. 6 6–9			Deut 18:18–22
frag. 7 1–2	12 (?)–17[215]		
frag. 7 3–4		30–31	
frag. 7 5ff.	22 *ff.*		

The Samaritan Pentateuch is almost identical:

---

to separate between sacred and profane and unclean and clean" (Ibid.). But, rather than appeal to serendipity – presumably not only for Leviticus 10, but also for Leviticus 21 – it is more likely that Leviticus 10 and 21 represent the original logic, which was lost when the text was reused in a manner inattentive to that original logic.

213 For recent discussion, see Julie Irene Woods, *Jeremiah 48 as Christian Scripture*, Princeton Theological Monograph Series 149 (Eugene, OR: Pickwick, 2011).

214 I am grateful to Reinhard Kratz for drawing this example to my attention.

215 Segal rightly observes that we cannot be certain whether the entire text of the Decalogue was placed here in 4QRP[a], since the text only begins with the fifth commandment (Michael Segal, "Biblical Exegesis in 4Q158: Techniques and Genre", *Text* 19 [1998]: 58).

SP Exodus 20	MT Exodus 20	Deuteronomy 5
	1–19aα	
1–21a		24–27
	19b–21	
		28b–29
21b		Deut 18:18–22
		30–31
22 ff.	*22 ff.*	

In the case of 4QRP[a] and the Samaritan Pentateuch of Exodus 20 there is no alteration to the texts apart from rearranging them. In the cases of Jeremiah 48 and Ezekiel 44 there appears to have been additional alterations to the text.

In addition to weaving Leviticus 10 and Leviticus 21 together, the rules in Ezekiel 44 blend together various pentateuchal laws on a common theme. The exegetical technique is similar to that employed in the Temple Scroll from Qumran (11QT). In the Temple Scroll commandments on the same subject are merged, and duplicate commandments are harmonized. The relevance of the Temple Scroll for our understanding of the biblical text was recognized by Stephen Kaufman within a few years of the publication of the Temple Scroll.[216] Although the exegetical technique of the Temple Scroll has received more recent analysis, Kaufman's work is a seminal account of biblical interpretation and still offers an elegant summary of the Temple Scroll's use of biblical texts.[217] Kaufman identifies five ways in which the Temple Scroll manipulates pentateuchal laws.

First, Kaufman describes a pattern that he labels "paraphrastic conflation". Because of their paraphrastic nature these also often appear with Late Biblical Hebrew forms and vocabulary, and lack textual tension. Kaufman illustrates with an example first deployed by Yadin: 11QT 51:19–21. This text is a paraphrastic conflation based on Deut 16:21–22 and Lev 26:1, with additional ideas supplied from Deut 12:8 and 12:30–33. A related, though arguably distinguishable, example is found in 11QT 43:12–17, which is a rewording of Deut 14:24–29. Remarkably, almost nothing remains of the original biblical phrasing. Kaufman fur-

---

216 Kaufman, "The Temple Scroll".
217 See, e.g., Dwight D. Swanson, *The Temple Scroll and the Bible: The Methodology of 11QT*, STDJ 14 (Leiden: Brill, 1995); Simone Paganini, *"Nicht darfst du zu diesen Wörtern etwas hinzufügen": Die Rezeption des Deuteronomiums in der Tempelrolle. Sprache, Autoren und Hermeneutik*, BZABR 11 (Wiesbaden: Harrasowitz, 2009).

ther observes that "the only truly biblical idiom in this entire text, דרך שלשית ימים, is actually taken from a totally different, unrelated source (Exod 3:18)".[218] Second, Kaufman identifies a further form of conflation that he labels "fine conflation". This produces texts that are highly biblical in style, but are a patchwork of biblical fragments. In 11QT 59 the curse from Deuteronomy 28 is given additional colour through quotations from non-pentateuchal material. These biblical fragments are never more than four words long. The texts are: Zech 7:13; Jer 11:11; Jer 21:12; Ezek 39:23; Ezek 34:8, 2 Kgs 21:14; Deut 28:29; Judg 2:18 and Jer 15:21. Third, "gross conflation" is the bringing together of different commandments on the same subject. The blending of sources together can often be done quite skillfully. Kaufman observes that in 11QT 45:7–12 an originally Deuteronomic introduction (Deut 23:11–12) has been given something of a priestly style. Fourth, Kaufman examines examples that he calls "modified Torah quotation". A single pentateuchal law is reproduced, but a number of significant changes are made to the text. Fifth, Kaufman identifies the "extended Torah quotation". This is particularly common in the sections that are derived from Deuteronomy.[219]

Examining the use of pentateuchal texts in Ezek 44:20–27 with Kaufman's terminology we have examples of mostly gross conflation and modified Torah quotation. The result is that we can justifiably appropriate Swanson's observation about the Temple Scroll for Ezekiel 44: "there is very little which cannot be traced to a biblical source".[220]

2.2.8 The Missing High Priest

Before we leave the question of the relationship between the rules in Leviticus and Ezekiel, it is necessary to address the principal argument adduced in favour of the priority of Ezekiel 44: the absence of a high priest. Since Ezekiel's vision knows nothing of P's high priest and his cultic competencies, it is claimed that the relative antiquity of Ezekiel's vision is established. As Zimmerli argues, "Da von einem Hohenpriester in Ez 44 noch nicht die Rede ist, würde man nur ungerne tiefer in die nachexilische Zeit hinuntergehen, in der diese Gestalt

---

218 Kaufman, "Temple Scroll", 38.

219 David Carr rightly raises the fact that scholarship on the Temple Scroll has recognized that the Temple Scroll is a compilation of earlier materials and thus we must reckon with the possibility that "different sources of the scroll may have done quite different things with Scripture" (David M. Carr, *The Formation of the Hebrew Bible: A New Reconstruction* [Oxford: Oxford University Press, 2011], 50).

220 Swanson, *Temple Scroll*, 227.

immer deutlicher heraustritt, wie Hag und Sach zeigen".[221] The careful distinction between priest and exalted priest in Leviticus 21, and the absence of this distinction in the similar rules of Ezekiel 44, is of particular significance. If Leviticus 21 is a later version of rules also known from Ezekiel 44, we can argue that Leviticus 21 introduces a distinction that is unknown in Ezekiel's vision. On the other hand, if we were to claim that Ezekiel 44 is a development of the rules in Leviticus 21, it would appear that Ezekiel 44 consciously removed the distinction between priest and high priest. Various reasons have been proposed for why Ezekiel might not have wished to have a high priestly figure in his vision of a new temple: he viewed the prince as the functional equivalent of the high priest; he viewed himself as the high priest; he believed the strictures concerning the high priest should apply to every priest of Zadokite descent, and that every priest should bear the same dignity as the high priest. None of these proposals have proved sufficiently compelling so as to dispel the concerns to which the absence of the high priest have given rise.

Yet if the absence of the high priest from Ezekiel 40–48 is troubling, the view that Leviticus 21 draws on Ezekiel 44 has its own problems. In the present form of the Pentateuch a distinction between priests and Levites is clearly articulated in the book of Numbers, a book that is now recognized as one of the latest components of the Pentateuch.[222] In the books of Exodus and Leviticus the distinction between Levites and priests is rare. The Levites are mentioned in the genealogy of Aaron (Exod 6:14–25), in the sin of the Golden Calf (32:26–29), once in the Tabernacle account (38:21) and in the Jubilee legislation (Lev 25:32–34). In every case there are good grounds for thinking that we have instances of *Fortschreibung* that reflect the later perspective of the book of Numbers.[223] Thus,

---

221 Zimmerli, *Ezechiel*, 1248.

222 For extensive discussion see Achenbach, *Die Vollendung der Tora*.

223 The priestly genealogy in Exod 6:14–25 is widely recognized as an insertion, interrupting the dialogue between yhwh and Moses. The interruption is clearly marked by *Wiederaufnahme* (6:12, 30). The genealogy is indebted to Gen 46:8–11 and Num 3:17–20 (Gertz, *Tradition und Redaktion*, 251–52). The reference to "*all* the sons of Levi" in Exod 32:26 may not yet distinguish between priests and Levites. The story of the Golden Calf should be judged as a post-Priestly composition, already familiar with 1 Kings 12. The reference to the Levites is a secondary addition to the Golden Calf story (see, *inter alia*, Jan Christian Gertz, "Beobachtungen zu Komposition und Redaktion in Exodus 32–34", in *Gottes Volk am Sinai: Untersuchungen zu Ex 32–34 und Dtn 9–10*, ed. Matthias Köckert and Erhard Blum, Veröffentlichungen der Wissenschaftlichen Gesellschaft für Theologie 18 [Gütersloh: Gütersloher Verlagshaus, 2001], 9–40; Hans-Christoph Schmitt, "Die Erzählung vom goldenen Kalb Ex. 32* und das Deuteronomistische Geschichtswerk", in *Rethinking the Foundations: Historiography in the Ancient World and in the Bible. Essays in Honour of John Van Seters*, ed. Steven L McKenzie and Thomas C. Römer, BZAW 294 [Berlin: de

the distinction between Levites and priests is absent from the original Priestly document and the Holiness Code, despite the fact that Leviticus 21 is believed to have utilized Ezekiel 44 where such a distinction is made. In other words, we must chose either the problem of the missing high priest in Ezekiel 44 or the problem of the missing Levites in the Holiness Code.

Can attention to the literary growth of Ezekiel 44 provide some insight into the reasons *why* Ezekiel 44 lacks a reference to an exalted or high priest? It is important to observe that the absence of the high priest at earliest stages in the oracle's compositional history is not troubling: Ezekiel's new temple is served by "sons of Zadok", whose name harks back to the time of the united monarchy and stands in contrast to the "sons of the foreigners". The problem only emerges at the very last stage of the development of the text, when the rules of vv. 20–27 are appended to the oracle. But by this stage the scribal author is already working with a number of constraints imposed by the text. The care of the temple is in the hands of a *group of priests*, who trace their ancestry back to David's *chief priest*. As such it is apparent why a scribal author could have held that they come under both the regulations for the priests *and* the regulations for the exalted priest.

2.3 Priestly Perquisites

Ezekiel's rulings concerning priests reach their conclusion with the instructions about priestly perquisites (vv. 28–31). This final section is clearly distinguished from what precedes it by the words נאם אדני יהוה, "declaration of my lord YHWH",[224] and the shift in subject matter.[225] The new section announces a general principle (v. 28), before the specific provisions are outlined (vv. 29–30). They set out in brief compass what offerings are due to the priests, before concluding with a warning to the priests not to eat any animal carcass that they

---

Gruyter, 2000], 235–50). There is also widespread agreement that Exod 38:21–31 is a late addition to the Tabernacle account. It presupposes the census in Numbers 1 (Harald Samuel, *Von Priestern zum Patriarchen: Levi und die Leviten im Alten Testament*, BZAW 448 [Berlin: de Gruyter, 2014], 294–95). The right of the Levites to buy back their property in Lev 25:32–34 is usually judged a later addition. It presupposes the assignment of Levitical cities. The idea of Levitical cities is unknown to H and P, and found only in the late texts of Num 35:1–8 and Josh 21 (Nihan, *Priestly Torah*, 522).

224 The words נאם אדני יהוה are also found in v. 15 where they marked the conclusion of the original oracle. Their use in v. 27 may have originated as a *Wiederaufnahme* marking the insertion of vv. 16–19 in the first expansion of the oracle.

225 Gese, *Der Verfassungsentwurf*, 62.

might come across (v. 31). The form of this final simple prohibition is uncharacteristic of the other verses in this short section and has more in common with the various prohibitions to be found in vv. 17–27.

In the Pentateuch the only comprehensive enumeration of priestly dues is found in Num 18:8–32. A brief examination of Ezekiel 44 and Numbers 18 shows that both passages overlap to a significant degree. As we have seen the general principle stated in Ezek 44:28 that the priests receive no inheritance because YHWH is their inheritance has a number of parallels in the Hexateuch, including Num 18:20.[226] The priests' rights to the grain offering, purification offering, and reparation offering, are found in similar terms in both Ezek 44:29a and Num 18:9–10. The statement about proscribed dedications is phrased in exactly the same way in Ezek 44:29b and Num 18:14. Finally, the assignment of the first-fruits to the priests is found in both Ezek 44:30 and Num 18:12–13a. Since the two passages overlap to such a degree, some literary relationship must exist between them. The question is: which text is the earlier, and which the later?

Wellhausen's incisive arguments about the significant place of Ezekiel 44 in the history of the priesthood suggest a clear answer. Since Numbers 18 distinguishes sharply between the dues owed to priests and those owed to Levites, it must be a later composition than Ezekiel 44, which, according to Wellhausen, first introduced the distinction between clerical ranks. Many scholars have championed this perspective since Wellhausen's time, most recently Achenbach in his exhaustive redaction-critical analysis of the book of Numbers. In Numbers 18, Achenbach argues, we see the influence of the exiled Zadokite priesthood and its ritual lore. Ezekiel 44 provided the model for the theocratic editor who composed Numbers 18, and we are presumably dealing with the same priestly circle.[227]

Such reconstructions of the compositional history need to be re-examined and, I will argue, the reverse position taken: Ezekiel 44 presupposes and utilizes Numbers 18. To substantiate this argument I will proceed in three steps. First, I will demonstrate that Numbers 18 is a compendium of pentateuchal instructions about priestly and Levitical dues. The composer of Numbers 18 utilizes numerous pentateuchal texts, and other parts of the Pentateuch provide all the necessary textual pieces by which the compendium on priestly dues in Numbers 18 could have been compiled. Second, I will show that Numbers 18 was interpreted in Ezekiel 44, and demonstrate that certain features of Ezek 44:28–31 can only be ex-

---

226 See also Deut 10:9; 18:2; Josh 13:33.
227 Achenbach, *Die Vollendung der Tora*, 141–72. On Ezek 44:29 Achenbach writes, "die wörtlichen und sachlichen Übereinstimmungen zwischen beiden Texten deuten wieder auf den gleichen Traditionskreis" (Ibid., 158).

plained as exegetical reuse of Numbers 18 and other pentateuchal texts. Conversely, I will argue that it is difficult to see how the writer of Numbers 18 could have written what he did on the basis of Ezekiel 44. Third, I will argue that the position advocated by Wellhausen and Achenbach cannot explain why the instructions on priestly dues originated, whilst a reason lies immediately to hand if we recognize that Numbers 18 was the earliest list of priestly emoluments. Fourth, and finally, I will turn to the concluding prohibition against eating an animal carcass (v. 31).

2.3.1 A Pentateuchal Compendium

The main pentateuchal corpora – the Priestly document, the Deuteronomic Code, and the Holiness Code – do not provide any comprehensive enumeration of priestly dues.[228] They touch upon the issue of priestly allocation only tangentially and in relation to a variety of different cultic practices. This should cause us no surprise. The officiating priest need only know what actions were to be followed for the particular sacrifice or donation that the worshipper had brought. A comprehensive account of priestly emoluments was not needed, and there is no reason to think it was an ancient genre. When the textual traditions of the Pentateuch began to be brought together, however, a different set of pressures was introduced. Priestly and Deuteronomistic texts contained a variety of prescriptions specifying what the priest was to receive. These could lead to evident contradictions as when Leviticus assigns the officiating priest the breast and the right thigh, but Deuteronomy, the shoulder, the cheeks and the stomach.[229] More often, it meant there were a number of partially overlapping specifications scattered across the various ritual prescriptions of the Pentateuch. In Numbers 18 an attempt is made to gather them together in one place. The result is a new genre: a compendium of priestly dues.

---

228 Stackert follows Knohl in holding that Numbers 18 is part of the Holiness legislation (Jeffrey Stackert, *Rewriting the Torah: Literary Revision in Deuteronomy and the Holiness Legislation*, FAT 52 [Tübingen: Mohr Siebeck, 2007], 165–208; Israel Knohl, *The Sanctuary of Silence: The Priestly Torah and the Holiness School* [Minneapolis: Fortress, 1995], 53–54, 72–73). My problem with Knohl's analysis is his division of the broader priestly literature of the Pentateuch into just two divisions distinguished primarily by their vocabulary: the Priestly source and the Holiness School. The re-use and re-working of biblical materials by the ancient scribes requires that vocabulary be analysed with the recognition that such intertextual reuse may also have been in play in the composition of parts of the Pentateuch.
229 Lev 7:28–34; Deut 18:3.

The compendium of Numbers 18 is given the barest structure, but one that is crucial for understanding the compendium's purpose and origins. Sacrificial portions and tithes are arranged into a series of speeches according to the recipient.[230] The first assigns the various sacrificial offerings to the Aaronide priests and their families for their priestly service (vv. 8–19). The second part assigns the annual tithe to the Levites for their service (vv. 20–24). The final part requires that the Levites tithe the annual tithe and present it to the priests (vv. 25–32). The structure indicates that a crucial contribution of the compendium is the division of cultic dues amongst priests and Levites.

The list of dues for the Aaronide priests weaves together a number of pentateuchal texts: Leviticus 1–7, 23 and 27, and Deuteronomy 18. The result is not comprehensive for, as Gray observed,

> These sources of priestly income, which are not distinctly specified in the present c[hapter], though some may be covered by its general terms, are the skin of the burnt-offering (Lev. 7[8]), the shewbread (Lev. 24[5–9]), amounts paid in compensation for fraud in cases in which no representative of the defrauded person exists (Nu. 5[8]), certain similar payments (Lev. 5[16] 22[14]), unredeemed fields (Lev. 27[21]), and certain specially large dues for regular offerings in specific cases (e.g. Nu. 6[19f.]).[231]

More exhaustive lists were created in rabbinic literature.[232] In the following pages I will examine each of the biblical texts that contributes to this pentateuchal compendium, and how it does so.

The compendium begins in Num 18:9–11 with the main sacrifices as described in Leviticus 1–7. The same organizing principle that provides the structure of the entire chapter can also be perceived here: the sacrifices are arranged according to their beneficiaries. A distinction is drawn between those eaten by the priests alone (vv. 9–10) and those that are eaten by the priests and their families (v. 11). Those consumed by the priests are designated as קדש הקדשים, "most holy", (v. 9). The offerings that may be consumed by the priestly family are usually understood to be merely קדש, "holy" (v. 19). This distinction can already be found in Lev 21:22, where it is said of even the blemished Aaronide: מקדשי הקדשים ומן-הקדשים יאכל, "he may eat from the most holy and from the holy".

---

230 Each of the speeches is introduced in a similar way:

V. 8: וידבר יהוה אל-אהרן, "now yhwh spoken to Aaron";

V. 20: ויאמר יהוה אל-אהרן, "now yhwh said to Aaron";

V. 25: וידבר יהוה אל-משה לאמר, "now yhwh spoke to Moses saying".

231 George Buchanan Gray, *Numbers*, ICC (Edinburgh: T&T Clark, 1903), 240–41.

232 Jacob Milgrom, *Numbers* במדבר: *The Traditional Hebrew Text with the New JPS Translation*, The JPS Torah Commentary (Philadelphia: Jewish Publication Society of America, 1990), 148–49.

The sacrifices that are described as קדש קדשים, "most holy", are the grain offering, the purification offering and the reparation offering.[233] The association of these sacrifices together could have derived from a careful reading of the sacrificial legislation in Leviticus 1–7. Each of these offerings is identified as a קדש קדשים, "most holy", and the priests consume that which is not burnt on the altar in the holy place (בקדש).[234] The writer of Numbers introduces a complication by creating an exact correlation between the sanctity of the offering and the sanctity of its place of consumption. Thus, according to Num 18:10, and in contrast to Leviticus 1–7, the priestly portions of the קדש קדשים, "most holy", are consumed בקדש קדשים "in the most holy place".[235] It is clear that the Tabernacle court is meant, rather than the Holy of Holies.[236] The restriction of the קדש קדשים, "most holy", to priestly males is also derived from Leviticus 1–7.[237]

The sacrificial legislation in Leviticus 1–7 does allow one sacrifice to be consumed by the priest's family: the well-being offering. It is to this sacrifice that v. 11 turns, though this is not immediately obvious from the opaque expression תרומת מתנם לכל־תנופת בני ישראל, "gift-offering with every elevation offering of the sons of Israel".[238] This is best understood as an allusion to the offering of

---

233 There is, of course, no mention of the burnt offering in Num 18 as either a קדש קדשים or a קדש, because it is consumed by fire on the altar in its entirety (Lev 1).

234 Grain offering (Lev 2:3, 10; 6:10; cf. 10:12); purification offering (6:10, 18, 22; cf. 10:17); reparation offering (6:10; 7:1, 6; cf. 14:13). The Sabbath bread is also said to be קדש קדשים (Lev 24:9), but is not listed in Num 18. It is included in the rabbis enumeration of the קדש קדשים.

235 There have been various attempts to avoid the translation of בקדש קדשים as "in the most holy place" and so to harmonize Num 18 with Lev 1–7. Some understand the preposition as a *beth essentiae*, eat it "as the most holy things" (e.g. NIV, NRSV), but this is unsatisfactory since it results in a tautology. Milgrom offers "in a most sacred state" (Milgrom, *Numbers*, 150). The *beth locale* is to be preferred despite its difficulties (Ernst Jenni, *Die hebräischen Präpositionen. Band 1: Die Präposition Beth* [Stuttgart: Kohlhammer, 1992], 204; Eryl W. Davies, *Numbers*, NCB Commentary [London: Marshall Pickering, 1995], 188; Baruch A. Levine, *Numbers: A New Translation with Introduction and Commentary*, AB 4 [New York: Doubleday, 1993], 1.445).

236 For discussion of קדש קדשים and קדש, see Philip Peter Jenson, *Graded Holiness: A Key to the Priestly Conception of the World*, JSOTSup 106 (Sheffield: JSOT Press, 1992), 89–93.

237 Lev 6:11 (grain offering); 6:29 (purification offering); 7:6 (reparation offering).

238 It is not entirely certain how תרומת מתנם לכל־תנופת בני ישראל should be translated. The difficulty is the preposition ל. Jenni classifies this instance of ל as a *lamed revaluationis*. It is a "repräsentierende Reidentifikation einer Kollektivgröße", which suggests a translation "das heißt alle..." (Ernst Jenni, *Die hebräischen Präpositionen. Band 3: Die Präposition Lamed* [Stuttgart: Kohlhammer, 2000], 45–46). In this way תנופה can be thought of as a particular instance of the more general תרומה. This is already apparent in H, for Lev 22:12 uses תרומה of all the offerings that may be consumed by the priestly family. Thus, on analogy with כל־קרבנם לכל־מנחתם ולכל־חטאתם ולכל־אשמם (v. 9), תרומת מתנם לכל־תנופת (v. 11) could be understood with תרומת מתנם as the overarching category of sacrifices and לכל־תנופת as one set of particular instances

well-being as described in Lev 7:28 – 34.[239] In the offering of well-being as Leviticus 7 describes it the breast is elevated (תנופה; vv. 30, 34) and the right thigh is presented (תרומה; v. 34).[240]

The appearance of מתן, "gift",[241] is best explained as due to the requirement that, after the offerings are ritually presented, they are to be *given* to the priest (נתן; vv. 32, 34, 36). Deuteronomy 18:3 likewise uses the verb נתן for the transfer of some of the sacrifice to the officiating priest, but the parts of the animal are different. Leviticus 7 specifies the breast and the right thigh, whilst Deuteronomy 18 requires the shoulder, the jowls and the stomach. Numbers 18 simply avoids the contradiction by declining to specify the meat joints, referring to them rather generically as "these things are also yours" (זה לך; v. 11).

Budd observes that in Leviticus 7 "no indication was given as to whether these were for males alone or for families as a whole".[242] Despite lacking explicit guidance on the subject in the sacrificial legislation of Leviticus, the author of Num 18 would have had good exegetical reasons for understanding the offering of well-being to be permissible for the entire priestly family. First, the priestly sacrificial legislation in Leviticus 3 and 7:11– 21, 28 – 36 does not specify the offering of well-being as קדש הקדשים, "most holy", nor does it restrict consumption

---

(cf. vv. 8, 19). Alternatively, the preposition ל could be understood as a *lamed ascriptionis*. Since the expression תרומה can be used in Num 18 of the tithe, the words לכל־תנופת provide further specification. It is those gift offerings which have an elevation offering.

239 See Gray, *Numbers*, 223; Levine, *Numbers*, 446; Davies, *Numbers*, 188. In an early study Milgrom appears to regard v. 11 as a heading that covers all the "holy offerings". He asks, "Are all the items in this list (Num 18:9 – 19) subject to the tĕnûpâ?" He rightly observes that this cannot be the case with the first-born or the proscribed items (Jacob Milgrom, "Hattĕnûpâ", in *Studies in Cultic Theology and Terminology*, SJLA 36 [Leiden: Brill, 1983], 143 n. 18. Others understanding v. 11 as a heading include Timothy R. Ashley, *The Book of Numbers*, NICOT [Grand Rapids: Eerdmans, 1993], 348). It is most natural to conclude that v. 11 does not function as a heading, but should be understood as a specific sacrifice.

240 The two terms תנופה and תרומה appear together on numerous occasions, most especially in the offering of well-being. The rabbis sought to understand their interrelationship as two distinct but similar motions. The תנופה had a horizontal motion, whilst the תרומה had a vertical motion. This distinction gave rise to the terminology "wave offering" and "heave offering" (Milgrom, *Leviticus 1– 16*, 461). Milgrom makes the important observation that the תנופה is always done "before YHWH", whilst תרומה is done "to YHWH". On the basis of this and other exegetical and philological arguments, Milgrom argues that תנופה "refers to an actual or symbolic elevation rite in the sanctuary whereby an offering is dedicated to the Lord" (Ibid., 473), whilst תרומה is "the dedication of things to the Lord" (Ibid., 474).

241 The expression מתן only occurs on one other occasion in the Pentateuch: in Gen 34:12, a non-cultic context. The cultic term מתנה is found very occasionally in the priestly tradition (Exod 28:38; Lev 23:38; Num 18:6, 29).

242 Philip J. Budd, *Numbers*, WBC 5 (Waco, TX: Word Books, 1984), 202– 03.

to the priests within the Tabernacle courtyard. Secondly, if the offering of well-being was קדש הקדשים, "most holy", and so restricted to priests alone, we should expect it to have been mentioned alongside the other most holy offerings in Lev 6:10. Leviticus 6:10 appears to provide an exhaustive list of קדש הקדשים, "most holy", restricting this category to the grain offering, the purification offering and the reparation offering. Thirdly, Lev 10:12–15 distinguishes between the "most holy" which are to be eaten in the holy place, and the priestly share of the offerings of well-being, which is for consumption by the priestly family in a clean place. This last requirement appears to be reflected in Num 18:11, though it insists not that the location be clean (במקום טהור), but rather the participants (כל טהור בביתך).

In Num 18:12–13 we have a first glimpse of the exegetical manoeuvrings that have to be undertaken in compiling the different textual traditions on priestly dues. In v. 12 the ראשית of the oil, wine and grain is the priestly portion, but according to v. 13 so also are the בכורים of the land. Scholars have struggled to express the difference between the two. First, some suggest that the two terms, ראשית and בכורים, are simply synonymous.[243] Similarly, E. Davies finds the cultic terminology in Numbers 18 rather loose in comparison with other priestly texts, and argues that it is not prudent to distinguish between the terms.[244] Such suggestions do not explain, however, why the legislation is repetitious. Second, Gray distinguished between those items given directly to the priest, and those that need a ceremony. Milgrom bolsters this suggestion by observing that different verbs are used in each case. The ראשית are given (נתן), whilst the בכורים are brought (הביא). Thus, the former can take place outside the temple, whilst the latter verb implies that the firstfruits were brought into the sanctuary area.[245] As Milgrom observes the distinction is rabbinic and, whilst derived from the biblical text, is not clearly articulated anywhere in the Hebrew Bible. We should be cautious about attributing this logic to the author of Numbers 18. Third, Milgrom seeks to distinguish between the first processed produce (ראשית) and the first ripe fruit (בכורים).[246] Neither Lev 23:10 nor the use of דגן in Num 18:12 would appear to support Milgrom's suggestion. Both texts describe the offering of unprocessed grain as a ראשית.

An explanation is best sought on the level of intertextual reuse. The combination of two different textual traditions explains both the redundancy and the two different expressions. The first verse is a citation of Deut 18:4:

---

243 Ashley, *Numbers*, 349; Budd, *Numbers*, 206.
244 Davies, *Numbers*, 188.
245 Milgrom, *Numbers*, 151.
246 Ibid., 427–28.

ראשית דגנך תירשך ויצהרך וראשית גז צאנך תתן לו

The firstfruits of your grain, your wine, and your oil, and the firstfruits of the fleece of your sheep, you shall give to them (Deut 18:4).

כל חלב יצהר וכל חלב תירוש ודגן ראשיתם אשר יתנו ליהוה לך נתתים

All the best of your oil and all the best of your wine and grain, their firstfruits that they give to YHWH, I have given them to you (Num 18:12).

This is as clear an instance of Seidel's law as one is likely to find: shared terms in reverse order indicating textual reuse. The list of three crops is a distinctive Deuteronomic expression,[247] and Num 18:12 is the only occasion in the Hebrew Bible that the terms are reversed.[248] The inverted order indicates that Num 18:12 is the intertextual reuse. In Deut 18:4 the Israelites are instructed to "give", נתן, the firstfruits to the Levitical priests. In Numbers 18 this is understood to mean that the firstfruits are to be given to the priests, but not to the rest of the Levitical tribe. The inspiration for the following verse concerning the בכורים is probably the instructions about the Feast of Weeks in Leviticus 23. During the festival two loaves of bread were "brought...to YHWH" (תביאו...ליהוה) as בכורים (v. 17), and they are explicitly numbered amongst the priestly perquisites and designated as "holy", קדש (v. 20).[249]

The bifurcation of firstfruits into ראשית and בכורים is not a novelty in Numbers 18. It had already been made in the festival legislation of the Holiness Code. Leviticus 23 relates two festivals of firstfruits. The first is the day when the first sheaf is offered. This is identified as a ראשית that is given to the priest (v. 10). Seven weeks later the feast of weeks is celebrated, in which the two loaves of bread were brought as בכורים (v. 17). The Holiness writer innovatively associates the Deuteronomic ceremony for offering the first harvest (Deut 26:1–11) and the harvest festival in the Covenant Code (Exod 23:16). The differences are harmonized by generating an additional festive celebration of firstfruits with the two occasions separated by the seven-week period prescribed in Deuteronomy 16. The Holiness writer exploits the terminological difference between Deuteronomy 26 and Exodus 23 to distinguish the two occasions: the elevation of the sheaf is a ראשית-offering (Lev 23:10) and the elevation of the loaves fifty days later is a

---

247 Deut 7:13; 11:14; 12:17; 14:23; 18:4; 28:51.
248 Achenbach, *Die Vollendung der Tora*, 159.
249 At an early stage v. 17 was probably followed by v. 20b. Verses 18–20 are usually judged to be overloaded and are a result of scribal harmonization inspired by Num 28:27–30. For a recent discussion of the issues and possible solutions see Nihan, *Priestly Torah*, 506–07.

בכורים-offering (23:20). In this way the originally independent synonyms, ראשית and בכורים, were related to each other.[250]

The last major text that we see utilized in the list of priestly dues is Leviticus 27. This chapter has long been recognized as a rather loose appendix to the Holiness Code added at a later stage. It legislates for the redemption of persons, animals, property and objects that have been vowed to the sanctuary.[251] Its relevance for the subject of priestly dues arises from its assignment of some consecrated items to the priests (v. 21) and the identification of some of them as "holy", קדש (vv. 9, 10, 23, 30, 32, 33) and even "most holy", קדש־קדשים (v. 28). The author of Numbers 18 is particularly interested in Lev 27:26–29, which describe those items that cannot be redeemed: firstlings and proscribed items. These remain the inviolable possession of the sanctuary, that is, the priests.

The author of Number 18 takes up the case of proscribed items first. According to Lev 27:28, "every proscribed item is most holy to YHWH", כל־חרם קדש־קדשים הוא ליהוה. A few verses earlier the proscribed field and the priest's property are brought into close association, perhaps even equated: "when the field is released in the Jubilee, it shall be holy to YHWH *as* a proscribed field (קדש ליהוה כשדה החרם); it will become the priest's property" (v. 21). From this the author of Numbers 18 has presumably deduced that other proscribed items are given to the priests for their use. Leviticus 27:28 is skillfully reworded to reflect this understanding: "every proscribed dedication in Israel will be yours", כל חרם בישראל לך יהיה (Num 18:14).

The rules on firstlings in Leviticus 27 describe how redemption relates to them. Sacrificial firstlings belong to YHWH; they cannot be consecrated or redeemed. Unclean animals may be redeemed or they will be sold. The general principle that all firstlings are the property of YHWH and at his disposal is assumed, though never stated. Presumably the instructions about firstlings in Exodus 13 are presupposed: all first offspring of every womb belongs to YHWH, whether animal or human (Exod 13:2). Since humans and donkeys cannot be sacrificed, they must be redeemed. If the donkey is not redeemed, its neck is to be broken (Exod 13:13).

---

250 At some stage the two expressions were aggregated to produce the tautologous ראשית בכורים, "the choicest of firstfruits" (Exod 23:19 // 34:26). Although now attached to the end of the Covenant Code, Exod 23:19 is clearly a later addition. Van Seters rightly observes that Exod 23:19 is "beset with a number of curiosities and problems". He draws attention to the redundancy in using two terms for firstfruits as well as the Deuteronomic expression "YHWH your God" (John Van Seters, *A Law Book for the Diaspora: Revision in the Study of the Covenant Code* [Oxford: Oxford University Press, 2003], 169–70).
251 See Nihan, *Priestly Torah*, 94.

The author of Numbers 18 skillfully weaves together Leviticus 27 and Exodus 13. The general principle that all first offspring belong to the priests is established through a creative citation of Exodus 13.

כל פטר רחם לכל בשר אשר יקריבו ליהוה באדם ובבהמה יהיה לך

The first off-spring of the womb of all creatures which is offered to YHWH – man or beast – will be yours (Num 18:15a).

כל בכור פטר כל רחם בבני ישראל באדם ובבהמה לי הוא

Every firstborn, the first off-spring of every womb, among the sons of Israel – man or beast – is mine (Exod 13:2).

The insistence that human offspring and unclean animals must be redeemed in Num 18:15b, "only you must redeem the first-born of humans and the first-born of unclean beasts you must redeem", אך פדה תפדה את בכור האדם ואת בכור הבהמה הטמאה תפדה, is the result of blending Exod 13:13 and Lev 27:27. A tell-tale sign of reuse is evident in the uncomfortable use of the second person for both the priests in Num 18:15a ("it shall be yours") and the Israelites in 18:15b ("you shall redeem").

In Exodus 13 the redemption of the first-born boys is central to the story. They are threatened by the angel who passes through Egypt. This emphasis on the first-born boys is carried over into Numbers 18 for their redemption is described in v. 16. The price of their redemption is calculated according to the redemption of vows in Lev 27:6, though this verse had nothing to do with the redemption of firstlings. The author of Numbers 18 omits to say anything about how the redemption of unclean animals is to be calculated, though Lev 27:11–13 could have provided guidance on the matter.

Moving straight from first-born boys to clean animals, the author of Numbers 18 again reveals his indebtedness to his source text. The insistence that "you may not redeem the firstlings of cattle, sheep or goats; they are holy" (v. 17) betrays a perspective that has nothing to do with priestly perquisites, but is focussed around questions of redemption as Leviticus 27 is. For the question of redemption of firstlings, the author of Numbers 18 again reaches for the instructions about the redemption of vows. According to Leviticus 27 the sacrificial animal that is vowed is "holy", קדש (v. 9). This statement provides for the author of Numbers 18 a significant clue as to how the sacrifice of the animal must be treated: it is an offering of well-being. The instructions for their sacrifice in Num 18:17–18 are drawn directly from Leviticus 3.

The second and third parts of the compendium deal with the dues of the Levites. The author of Numbers 18 is mostly reliant upon a single text that describes provision for the Levites: Deut 14:22–29. The Deuteronomic tithe law does not concern clerical dues. Instead, it describes how the annual tithe of grain, wine and oil is to be used. Every two years in three the tithe and the firstlings are to be taken to the central sanctuary and consumed in a communal feast. The Levite is possibly included in this annual feast, for the legislator exhorts the Israelite landowner not to neglect the Levite (14:27). In the third year the tithe is collected in the locality and eaten by the marginalized: the resident alien, the widow, the orphan and the Levite. In this law the Levites are not servants within the sanctuary as they are in the book of Numbers and Chronicles, but a landless, marginalized group dependent on the generosity of others.[252]

Although the beneficiaries of the Deuteronomic tithe include a number of different groups, the author of Numbers 18 ignores the other marginalized groups and assigns the tithe to just the Levites, whom he understands as cultic servants. Similarly, the oscillation between a sanctuary feast and a local repast for the poor is abandoned; the entire tithe is provided to the Levites who may eat it wherever they wish.[253] In this way the author of Numbers 18 adds an additional layer to his hierarchy of priestly dues. At the highest level are the "most holy" which can only be consumed by the priests in the sanctuary. The level below are the "holy" which may be consumed by the priestly family in a clean place. At the lowest level is the Levitical tithe, which is not sacred, and may be consumed by the Levites anywhere.

The theological justification for supporting the Levites is also drawn from Deuteronomy. But it is important to notice a significant development in how this theological justification is applied. To do this we need first to appreciate the two texts from Deuteronomy that the author of Numbers 18 had before him. The first is, of course, the Deuteronomic tithe legislation, which motivates the Israelite landholder to share the tithe with the Levite by observing that the Levites have no allotted portion (חלק ונחלה) amongst the Israelites (Deut 14:27, 29). In this text and many others in Deuteronomy the Levites are merely a disenfranchised group who are dependent on the landowner's largesse. They are not a group of cultic servants. This is quite different from the perspective of the second text that the writer of Numbers 18 knew. In Deuteronomy 18 the Levitical priests are also said to have no allotted portion (חלק ונחלה) amongst the Israelites. Their portion is said to be YHWH's offerings (Deut 18:1).[254] In Deuteronomy 18 no dis-

---

252 For the complex presentation of the Levites in Deuteronomy, see esp. Dahmen, *Leviten und Priester*.

253 For the subtle interpretative dynamics of בכל־מקום in Num 18:31, see Stackert, *Rewriting the Torah*, 177–78.

254 Deut 18:2 is usually regarded as a later extension: the portion of the Levitical priests is not just the offerings, but also YHWH himself (see Dahmen, *Leviten und Priester*, 272–77).

tinction is made between the priests and the Levites: they are one and the same group. As a result a novelty is introduced in which Levitical landlessness is attributed to the priests.[255]

The composer of Numbers 18 takes this novelty a step further, by exploiting the hendiadys חלק ונחלה. The full expression חלק ונחלה is applied to the priests (v. 20), but only the second term נחלה is used of the Levites (vv. 21, 23, 24, 26).[256] It is possible that the inspiration for this distinction was exegetical. In Lev 6:10 the most holy offerings are said to be the priests' portion (חלקם), consequently the composer of Numbers 18 refused to apply the term to the Levites. In this way the hierarchy of priests and Levites is expressed and given an exegetical dimension. The priests receive a חלק ונחלה and the Levites merely a נחלה. The older statement about Levitical landlessness has been taken over and made to be most true of the priests, and only partially true of the Levites. The pre-eminence of the priests is also expressed in the appropriation of the statement in Deuteronomy 18 that "YHWH is his allocation" (יהוה הוא נחלתו).[257] This is applied to the priests alone: "I am your share and your allocation" (אני חלקך ונחלתך). Nothing comparable is said of the Levites.

A surprising feature about the statement concerning the landlessness of the priests is its location in v. 20. The difficulties are apparent when we consider the Masoretic paragraphing. The Masoretes placed a *setuma* at the end of v. 20, though the divine speech clearly ends at v. 19.[258] They understandably felt that the subject matter of v. 20, the inheritance of the priests, belonged with the

---

255 Dahmen rightly finds in Deut 18:1 the origin of the idea of priestly landlessness (Ibid., 266).

256 Stackert, *Rewriting the Torah*, 181, 188–90.

257 There is some uncertainty about whether the text of Deuteronomy 18 that was utilized by the author of Numbers 18 contained v. 2. In its present form Deut 18:2 refers back to Num 18:20 with the words "as he said to them" (כאשר דבר־לו). Was Deut 18:2 added to Deut 18:1, 3 in two stages with the cross-reference a later addition (cf. Carl Steuernagel, *Deuteronomium*, HAT 3/1 [Göttingen: Vandenhoeck & Ruprecht, 1900], 67) or was the entire verse added in light of Numbers 18 (Udo Rüterswörden, *Von der politischen Gemeinschaft zur Gemeinde: Studien zu Dt 16,18–18,22*, BBB 65 [Frankfurt-am-Main: Athenäum, 1987], 70–71)? One piece of evidence is the use of נחלה in Deut 18:2 and נחלה וחלק in Num 18:20. In light of the principle that texts usually grow, I lean to the view that Deut 18:2 is the older text, but the evidence is far from conclusive.

258 Amongst recent commentators only Seebass has given this issue the attention it deserves. "Ich folge hier dem Setuma-Intervall und ziehe 20 zum Vorhergehenden (vgl. BBaentsch 557): Wenn man 20 zu 21–24 zieht (z. B. ADillmann 102), wäre Aaron Repräsentant des ganzen Hauses Levim, so daß 20 die Überschrift über 21–24 bilden müßte. An seiner Stelle kann 20 daher nur Abschluß der Zuweisungen an die Priester sein, soll aber als solcher Abschluß auch zum Folgenden überleiten. Die neue Worteinführung erhöht nur das Gewicht der Deklaration zu 8–19 einerseits, 21–24 andererseits." (Horst Seebass, *Numeri 10,11–22,1*, BKAT IV/2 [Neukirchen-Vluyn: Neukirchener Verlag, 2003], 218)

list of priestly dues in vv. 8–19 and not with the Levitical tithe in vv. 21–24. The divine speeches, however, reflect the reception of earlier biblical texts, and vv. 20–24 are an exegetical appropriation and re-orientation of the statements in Deuteronomy about Levitical landlessness. The discrepancy highlights the fact that a statement originally about the Levites has been taken over to refer to the priests.

The tithe in Numbers 18 includes an innovation that finds no parallel in Deuteronomy. Not only must the Israelites give their tithe to the Levites, but also the Levites' tithe must itself be tithed and given to the priests (vv. 25–32). As Noth observed this places the Levites in an intermediary position between the Israelites and the priests.[259] They receive cultic dues, but are themselves subject to pay them.

This novel understanding of the tithe may be the result of an interpretation of Lev 27:30–31. According to Leviticus 27 the tithe belongs to YHWH and is holy: "all the tithe of the land, whether the seed of the land or fruit of the tree, belongs to YHWH. It is holy to YHWH" (וכל מעשר הארץ מזרע הארץ מפרי העץ ליהוה הוא קדש ליהוה). The natural reading of מזרע הארץ מפרי העץ is to understand the twofold מן to be providing a specification of כל מעשר: the tithe includes grains and fruit. It seems likely that the author of Numbers 18 read the מן with a partitive sense: "all the tithe of the land *out of* the seed of the land". In other words, Leviticus 27 was understood to be speaking about a tithe of a portion of the land's produce. In the reckoning of the author of Numbers 18 this fraction of the land's produce that was itself subject to a tithe could only be the Levitical tithe. The tithe was itself tithed, and this percentile of the crops was designated in Lev 27:30 as holy, which meant it must be a priestly perquisite. Consequently the author of Numbers 18 insists that the tithe of the tithe needs to be set to one side for it is consecrated (מקדשו; v. 29).

Ostensibly the list of priestly dues in Numbers 18 is nothing more than a compendium of material from the developing Pentateuch. Various texts have been drawn upon to create a comprehensive and consistent list of dues. As the chapter develops, however, it becomes more and more apparent that the author of Numbers 18 has a revolutionary agenda. He establishes a clear hierarchy between priests and Levites expressed through the dues that each receives. But even as the interpretations become more radical, the nevertheless remain *interpretations*. The author of Numbers 18 rarely ventures a position that cannot be established on the basis of exegesis. For our purposes it is important to observe

---

259 Martin Noth, *Das Vierte Buch Mose: Numeri*, 4th ed., ATD 7 (Göttingen: Vandenhoeck & Ruprecht, 1982), 121.

that Numbers 18 is derived entirely from existing authoritative texts that we have preserved in the Pentateuch. There is no need to posit the existence of any other source, textual or otherwise.

2.3.2 A Précis of Priestly Income

If Numbers 18 should be viewed as a compendium of priestly and Levitical emoluments, Ezek 44:28–30 can be understood as a précis of priestly income. It reproduces most parts of the instructions on priestly dues from Num 18:9–20 in a remarkably succinct manner.

The précis opens with a statement of general principle. "They will have no inheritance; I am their inheritance. No possession shall be given them in Israel; I am their possession" (v. 28). As I have already argued, v. 28 is to be regarded as the continuation of the original oracle and marked the transition to Ezekiel 45. It is dependent on Deut 18:1 and like Deuteronomy 18 attributes landlessness to the "Levitical priests". As we have already seen, the same principle was also developed in Num 18:20 to attribute landlessness to the priests. Its appearance in Num 18:20 presumably provided the inspiration to insert the précis of Numbers 18 in Ezek 44.29–30a.

The list of priestly dues in Ezekiel 44 begins with the three most holy offerings: the grain offering, the purification offering and the reparation offering (v. 29a). Ezekiel 44 follows Numbers 18 not only by beginning with these offerings, but insisting that the priests may eat them.[260] But what comes next departs from Numbers 18. Ezekiel 44 skips the offering of well-being and the firstfruits and mentions the proscribed objects citing Numbers 18 almost verbatim (v. 29b).[261] This alteration may have been inspired by a couple of factors. First, according to Lev 27:28 "every proscribed object is *most holy* to YHWH" (כל־חרם קדש־קדשים הוא ליהוה). The reordering of the priestly dues in Ezekiel 44 brings all the "most holy" dues together. Second, in Ezekiel 44 all the first-fruit and firstling offerings are dealt with together, rather than treating them in two separate places as occurs in Numbers 18. In both cases we can observe a progression from Numbers 18 to Ezekiel 44. In Numbers 18 the priestly dues are arranged according to the textual sources. Ezekiel 44 offers not only a summary, but rearranges the dues according to a logical principle.

---

260 In Numbers 18 consumption of the dues is mentioned in relation to the most holy offerings (v. 10), the offering of well-being (v. 11) and the firstfruits (v. 13). Only the most holy offerings are restricted to the priests alone.

261 וכל־חרם בישראל להם יהיה (Ezek 44:29b); כל־חרם בישראל לך יהיה (Num 18:14).

The summarizing instinct is strongly in evidence in v. 30 and can be seen in the repeated use of "all" (כל). The result is not entirely felicitous, for the resulting text is almost opaque. The difficulties are apparent if the Greek and Hebrew texts are compared. The Masoretes understood the verse as a couple of torturous construct chains: "the firstfruits of all the firstlings of everything and every offering of everything from all your offerings" (וראשית כל־בכורי כל וכל־תרומת כל מכל תרומותיכם). The Greek text distinguishes between two different types of first-fruit: ἀπαρχαὶ πάντων καὶ τὰ πρωτότοκα πάντων. This translation suggests the translator had a Hebrew text that read – or understood the Hebrew text as though it read – וראשית כל ובכורי כל, "first-thing of everything and the firstfruits of everything". If the Greek translation correctly understands the consonantal Hebrew text, this expression would appear to be a summary of Num 18:12–13 where both ראשית and בכורים are mentioned.

What follows וראשית כל ובכורי כל is even more opaque. What is meant by וכל־תרומת כל מכל תרומותיכם, "every offering of everything from all your offerings"? This seems scarcely comprehensible unless we recognize a reference to the tithe of the Levitical tithe.[262]

וכל־תרומת כל מכל תרומותיכם לכהנים יהיה
Every offering of everything from all your offerings shall belong to the priests (Ezek 44:30).

מכל מתנתיכם תרימו את כל־תרומת יהוה
From all of your gifts you shall present every offering of YHWH (Num 18:29).

In Numbers 18 a distinction is drawn between the gifts, מתנה, and the offerings, תרומה. The choice of vocabulary reflects the different perspectives of the donor and the recipient. From the perspective of the Israelites the tithe is an offering that is presented (תרומה; Num 18:24). Similarly, from the perspective of the Levites the tithe of a tithe is an offering that is presented (תרומה; Num 18:26–28). But from the perspective of the Levites the tithe that they receive from the Israelites is a gift (מתנה; Num 18:29). This lexicographical distinction is absent from Ezekiel 44 because only the tithe of the tithe is described, and this is viewed from the perspective of the Israelites. Thus, it is correctly described as an "offering from the offerings" (תרומת מתרמות).

---

262 This suggestion was already made by Gese who also deduced the significance for a relative dating of the texts. "Die hier vorliegende Terminologie steht in Zusammenhang mit derjenigen in Nu 18, 25–32 (vgl. insbesondere v 29), ja scheint von dieser Stelle abhängig zu sein; und Ez 44,30 würde sich damit als sehr spät erweisen" (Gese, *Der Verfassungsentwurf*, 63). Rudnig, however, whilst noting Gese's identification with the tithe of the tithe finds the expression "nicht nachvollziehbar" (Rudnig, *Heilig und Profan*, 284).

The last priestly due in Ezekiel's précis is the first of your dough, ראשית
ערסותיכם. Logically we should expect this first-thing to have been included in
the comprehensive term of v. 30, כל ראשית. Besides this apparent superfluity
we also have the repetitious לכהן. It is probably best to regard v. 30b as an example of *Fortschreibung* inspired by Numbers 15 and added by a scribe out of a desire for completeness. Unique to Ezekiel is the incentive: "so that a blessing may
rest on your house" (Ezek 44:30bβ).

2.3.3 Giving Each Its Due

I have proposed that we see Numbers 18 as a compendium of priestly and Levitical dues, which draws on earlier texts still extant in Exodus, Leviticus and
Deuteronomy. At one level, the author of the chapter does no more than collate
various instructions on clerical dues. At another level, he introduces a sharp distinction between priests and Levites, which is expressed in numerous different
ways. The author of Ezek 44:29–30a is familiar with Numbers 18 and assumes
the pre-eminence of the priests. He provides a pithy summary of priestly dues
in which he takes various steps to create a more logical structure.

The relationship between Numbers 18 and Ezekiel 44 has often been understood in a different way. Achenbach, for example, regards Ezekiel 44 as a piece
of traditional priestly instruction derived from exiled Zadokite circles. Almost
every part has been taken up in Numbers 18 and supplemented with similar material from elsewhere in the Pentateuch. The great advantage of this proposal is
that it accords with the frequently observed tendency for texts to grow: Ezek
44:29–30a is considerably smaller than Numbers 18.

Though texts usually expand as they are supplemented with additional material, textual summaries are not unknown either. Indeed, we have something of
a parallel to what I am proposing occurred in Ezek 44:28–30 in Nehemiah 10.
The Jerusalemites of Nehemiah's day take an oath to keep God's law. This includes the provision of offerings for the temple.

> [We agree] to bring the firstfruits of our soil and the firstfruits of every fruit of every tree to
> YHWH's house every year. And we will bring the firstborn of our sons and our beasts as it is
> written in the law and the firstborn of our cattle and our sheep to the house of our God to
> the priests that minister in the house of our God. And we will bring the first of our dough
> and the fruit of every vine and olive tree to the priests, to the chambers of the house of our
> God. And the tithe of our soil for the Levites, for it is the Levites who collect the tithe in all
> our agricultural towns (Neh 10:36–38).

This list of offerings is not as succinct as Ezek 44:28–30 and the descriptions of the individual offerings are often expanded. Nevertheless, within the space of three verses many of the priestly and Levitical dues from Numbers 18 are covered: firstfruits (v. 12), firstborn (v. 15), and Levitical tithe (vv. 21–24). That we have here a summary drawn from Numbers 18 is clear from the words "as it is written in the law" (ככתוב בתורה).

It is clearly not enough to adduce a parallel to the textual development we have outlined. It is also necessary to submit the alternative position to detailed criticism. For this purpose I shall use Achenbach's analysis, since it is an excellent presentation of the argument that Ezekiel 44 influenced Numbers 18. I will take up my criticism in two ways. First, I shall demonstrate that Ezek 44:28–30 is not needed to explain the text of Num 18:8–19. Second, I will show that Achenbach's proposal results in a number of incongruences. Third, I will question whether Achenbach's proposal can explain how this collection of Zadokite *torot* arose.

First, Achenbach identifies considerable textual reuse in Numbers 18 and describes in detail how other texts were reused in the composition of the chapter. Consequently, his perception of the chapter is very similar to what I have offered above. The principal point of difference is his argument that the author of Numbers 18 utilized the Zadokite legislation that we know from Ezekiel 44 in addition to his other sources.

My criticism of Achenbach's understanding of Numbers 18 is simply an application of Ockham's razor. There is no need to have recourse to Ezekiel 44 to explain the text of Numbers 18, since Pentaeuchal texts supplied all the material necessary. A clear example of this is Achenbach's suggestion that Num 18:9b utilizes Ezek 44:29a to identify the three "most holy" offerings as קרבן.[263] But an appeal to Ezekiel 44 at this point is unnecessary. Achenbach has already demonstrated that Num 18:8 reflects Lev 7:35–36, and thus we can be sure that the author of Numbers 18 was aware of the offering legislation in Leviticus 1–7. It is there and not in Ezekiel 44 that we find the grain offering, the purification offering and the reparation offering identified as "most holy", and it is there and not in Ezekiel 44 that they are identified as קרבן. Appeal to Ezekiel 44:29 cannot explain every feature of the text of Numbers 18, but Leviticus 1–7 can.

The issue is different in the case of proscribed items. Achenbach argues that Num 18:14 is a citation of Ezek 44:29b. He excludes Leviticus 27 as a possible source for Numbers 18 on the grounds that it is a late addition to the Pentateuch.

---

263 Achenbach, *Die Vollendung der Tora*, 158.

Certainly, there is no dispute that Leviticus 27 is a late appendix to the Holiness Code. But at issue is its relative date to Numbers 18.

As we have observed Num 18:14 is not the only text in Numbers 18 that has some connection to Leviticus 27. The redemption of "unclean beasts" (הבהמה הטמאה) is mentioned explicitly in Lev 27:27 (cf. Num 18:15b) and the price for redemption is calculated on the basis of Lev 27:6 (cf. Num 18:16). There are various incongruities in Numbers 18 which all evaporate when we recognize the presence of textual reuse. There is the use of the second person for the priests and the Israelites in v. 15; the third person suffix of פדויו in v. 16 referring to the redemption of men; the digression concerning the sanctuary shekel and redemption of clean animals in v. 16. Most important is the concern with *redemption*, which is about restoring dedicated objects to secular use, and not about what offerings are priestly dues. This interest in redemption is taken over from Leviticus 27. This all suggests that Numbers 18 was familiar with Leviticus 27 and that Num 18:14–16 is best understood as a reappropriation of Leviticus 27. There is no need to appeal to Ezekiel 44.

Finally, the principle of priestly landlessness in Num 18:20 can be explained by appeal to Deut 18:1, and there is no need to have recourse to Ezek 44:28. In addition, Achenbach's arguments cannot explain how it is that a Zadokite *torah* applies an original Levitical landlessness *to the priests*. I have argued that in Ezekiel 44 the principle of landlessness was originally attributed to the "Levitical priests" (vv. 6–7*, 9*, 15*, 28) and only later displaced and attributed to the priests alone under the influence of Numbers 18. In Numbers 18, on the other hand, I have demonstrated how landlessness was attributed to the priests and justified their receipt of all the offerings apart from the tithe.

In conclusion, there is no instance where appeal to Ezek 44:28–30 is necessary to explain the composition of Numbers 18. In many cases we can demonstrate that the author of Numbers 18 had the other Pentateuchal texts to hand because he makes use of them elsewhere in the compendium of priestly and Levitical dues. These Pentateuchal texts together with Second Temple patterns of exegesis are sufficient to explain all the features of Numbers 18.

I will turn, secondly, to the features that Achenbach cannot explain and the resulting incongruences of his position. We may observe three. First, Achenbach's analysis does not explain why it is that אחזה is present in Ezek 44:28, but has been replaced in Num 18:20 with חלק. Second, the reference to the tithe of the tithe in Ezek 44:30 is so opaque that it cannot be understood without recourse to Num 18:20–32. What could Ezek 44:30 have meant as part of a putative Zadokite *torah*? Third, giving the tithe of the tithe to the priest assumes already that the tithe is allocated to the Levites, who are not themselves priests. This idea is not expressed in Ezekiel 44:29–30a, but assumed. But how could this be, if the distinction between Levites and priests is no earlier than Ezekiel 44? Fourth, as we have seen בכורים and ראשית were applied to separate offerings before they were first brought in conjunction with one another in the Holiness Code's festival legislation (Lev 23). Only in a few late texts are they mentioned together. How is it that this is already to be found in a Zadokite *torah* from the exilic period?

Third, I want to consider how such compendiums of priestly dues might have originated. As we have already seen, it is noticeable that no list of priestly dues is to be found in the Priestly, Holiness or Deuteronomic Codes. A compendium like we find in Numbers 18 or Ezekiel 44 is not entirely without precedent for we find a truncated list in Deuteronomy 18.

> This shall be the custom of the priests from the people, those offering a sacrifice, whether ox or sheep: he shall give the priest the shoulder, the jowls and the stomach. The best of your grain, your wine, and your oil, and the best fleece you shall give him (vv. 3–4).

The reason why such compendiums are lacking is that they do not serve any function. What we do have, for example, are instructions for the conduct of sacrificial rituals. The assignment of a portion to the priest was a necessary act within the sacrificial ritual. Priest and offerer did not need a compendium of priestly dues. They needed only to know what the priest was to receive for the specific sacrifice that was being offered.

Why, then, was such a compendium compiled? The answer lies immediately to hand if we examine Numbers 18. A compendium was necessary because the cultic dues were being divided between *two* parties: the priests and the Levites. When priests and Levites had not been distinguished such a compendium was unnecessary. This reasoning would explain why the lists of priestly dues are found in Numbers 18 and Ezekiel 44, where Levites and priests are distinguished. However, it is important to observe that only Numbers 18 lists the perquisites of priests *and* Levites; Ezek 44:28–30 is concerned only with priests. This would suggest that Numbers 18, rather than Ezekiel 44, is the original text, for it is only here that cultic dues are assigned to priests and Levites. Ezekiel 44 cannot be the original form, because it does not make the critical distinction between dues for the priests and those for the Levites.

2.3.4 The Prohibition Against Consuming Animal Carcasses

The instructions to the priests concludes with a final prohibition: "The priests shall not eat anything, whether bird or animal which died of itself or was torn by animals" (v. 31). Its formulation with an object followed by לא and a *yiqtol* verbal form clearly associates it with the instructions about priestly conduct in vv. 20 – 27 and distinguishes it from the instructions about priestly perquisites in vv. 29 – 30a. This is confirmed when we observe that its closest textual parallel is to be found in the Holiness Code's instructions about priestly conduct (Lev 21:1 – 22:16):

כל־<u>נבלה וטרפה</u> מן־העוף ומן־הבהמה <u>לא יאכלו</u> הכהנים

The priests <u>shall not eat anything</u>, whether bird or animal <u>which died of itself or was torn by animals</u> (Ezek 44:31).

<u>נבלה וטרפה לא יאכל</u> לטמאה־בה

He shall not eat that <u>which died of itself or was torn by animals</u> becoming unclean by it (Lev 22:8).

The two texts are almost identical, and although נבלה וטרפה is an attested word-pair,[264] we should probably reckon with some sort of relationship between the two texts. The addition of מן־העוף ומן־הבהמה in Ezek 44:31 is a possible indicator that it may be the dependent text.[265]

Rudnig finds the location of this prohibition inexplicable: "Das Speisegebot, nach dem die Priester weder Aas noch Zerrissenes essen dürfen (V. 31; vgl. Lev 22,8), das aber grundsätzlich für alle Israeliten gilt (vgl. Ex 22,30; Lev 7,24), ist sicherlich ein Anhängsel. Es wirkt in seinem Kontext unmotiviert und wäre hinter V. 22 zu erwarten".[266] Not only is it unclear to me why it would be better placed after v. 22, but Rudnig has also overlooked the fact that the priestly perquisites are edible items: meat, grain, dough. The generous provision of the most holy, the proscribed dedications and the firstfruits (vv. 28 – 30) means that no priest should need to consume animals that have died of natural causes or been killed by another animal (v. 31). It is possibly from the same hand that inserted the rules in vv. 20 – 27.

2.4 The Composition of Ezekiel 44:6 – 31

We are now in the position to summarize our findings on the composition of Ezekiel 44.17 – 31, which we can integrate with our analysis of vv. 6 – 16. I have argued that the chapter developed in three main stages. The first level of indenta-

---

264 See also Lev 7:24; 17:15; and Ezek 4:14.
265 Grünwaldt believes that Lev 22:8 is dependent on Ezek 44:31, but offers no supporting evidence (Grünwaldt, *Das Heiligkeitsgesetz*, 271).
266 Rudnig, *Heilig und Profan*, 284.

tion marks the expansion to the original oracle, and the second level of indention marks the subsequent expansion. Glosses and scribal expansions that cannot be attributed to the three main stages are set in square brackets.

> Original oracle
> > First expansion
> > > Second expansion

⁶Thus says YHWH: Enough of all your abominations, House of Israel, ⁷in your admitting foreigners uncircumcised in heart and flesh to be in my sanctuary to profane it, [my house]
> in your offering my food, fat and blood

and they have broken my covenant in addition to all your abominations.

> ⁸And you did not keep the charge of my holy things, but you set them as keepers of my charge in my sanctuary.

⁹Thus says YHWH: No foreigner uncircumcised in heart and flesh shall enter my sanctuary [of all the foreigners that are in the midst of the Israelites.]

> ¹⁰But the Levites who went far from me when Israel went astray in that they went astray from me after the idols. They will bear their sin. ¹¹They shall be ministers in my sanctuary, responsible for the gates of the temple and ministering in the temple. They will slaughter the burnt offering and the sacrifice for the people. They will stand before them and serve them. ¹²Because they ministered to them before their idols and made the house of Israel stumble into iniquity. Therefore, I have lifted my hand concerning them, says YHWH, they will bear their sin. ¹³They will not come to me to act as priests for me. They will not come near to any of my sacred things, the most sacred things, and they will bear their shame and the abominations that they did. ¹⁴I will appoint them to keep the charge of the temple, all its service and all that is done in it.

¹⁵But the Levitical priests,
> the sons of Zadok that kept charge of my sanctuary when the sons of Israel went astray from me. They

will come near to me to minister to me and they will stand before me to offer to me fat and blood – declaration of Lord YHWH.

> ¹⁶They will enter my sanctuary, and they will approach my table to serve me, and they will keep my charge. ¹⁷When they enter the gates of the inner court, they shall put on linen garments. They shall not put on wool while they minister in the gates of the inner court and in the house. ¹⁸They shall have linen turbans on their heads, and linen undergarments on their loins. They shall not bind themselves with anything that causes sweat. ¹⁹When they go out into the outer court to the people they shall remove their garments in which they have been ministering. They will lay them down in the holy rooms.
> > ²⁰They shall not shave their heads, and they shall not let their locks grow out. They must trim their head. ²¹None of the priests shall drink wine when they enter the inner court. ²²They shall not take a widow or a divorcee as a wife, but only a virgin from the seed of the house of Israel or a widow who is the widow of a priest. ²³They shall teach my people the difference between holy and common, and instruct them on the difference between unclean and clean.

²⁴In a dispute they shall stand to judge. By my judgements they will judge it. They will keep my teaching and my statutes concerning all my festivals, and sanctify my Sabbaths. ²⁵He shall not go to a dead person to defile himself, but only for father, mother, son, brother, and unmarried sister they may defile themselves. ²⁶After his purification, they shall count seven days for him. ²⁷On the day that he enters the holy place, into the inner court, to minister in the holy place, he shall offer his purification offering

– declaration of Lord YHWH.

²⁸There will not be an inheritance for them; I am their inheritance. You shall give them no holding in Israel; I am their holding.

²⁹They shall eat the grain offering, the purification offering, and the reparation offering. Every devoted thing in Israel will be theirs. ³⁰The first-thing of everything and the firstfruits of everything and every offering of everything from all your offerings shall belong to the priests. [You shall also give to the priests the first of your dough in order that a blessing may rest on your house.]

³¹The priests shall not eat anything, whether bird or animal which died of itself or was torn by animals.

The original oracle in 44.6 – 7*, 9*, 15* was composed as a response to the oracle in Isaiah 56, which was understood as a programme to consecrate foreigners as priests. The idea is unequivocally rejected with pentateuchal texts from Genesis and Deuteronomy providing the authoritative grounds. The admission of foreigners would break the covenant, and only Levitical priests are to offer sacrifices. This oracle was integrated into Ezekiel's temple vision by means of v. 5 and v. 28. The first expansion of the oracle drew upon Numbers 18 and Ezekiel 14 to insist upon the pentateuchal ordering of the temple clergy. Levites have a subordinate role that is distinguished from that of the priests (Num 18:1–6). The original oracle's tone of rebuke is taken over and applied to the Levites, whose lower status is attributed to sin. The oracle's perspective on the priests, on the other hand, is also expanded under the influence of Numbers 18. The priests have a special role within the sanctuary (44:16–19; cf. Num 18:7) and receive sacrificial portions as a reward for their role (44:29–30a; cf. Num 18:8–20). Finally, the oracle was expanded once more, this time under the influence of Leviticus 10 and 21–22. It transforms the second part of the oracle into a book of rules for the priests.

3 Zadok and the Sons of Zadok in Second Temple Judaism

The argument that Ezekiel 44:6–31 is not only a relative latecomer to Ezekiel's temple vision, but are also later than Isaiah 56, requires that we date the origin of the oracle well into the Second Temple period, perhaps even into the Hellenistic period. It raises significant questions about whether this argument can be coordinated with other evidence from the Second Temple period. The indebtedness of the oracle to scriptural precedents has raised doubts about whether the "sons of Zadok" are a historically identifiable group from that period. Rather, as others before have suggested, it is a biblically-inspired moniker for the priestly ideals that it is imagined will serve in Ezekiel's eschatological temple. Yet others have argued that there was a priestly sept known as the Zadokites that played a significant role in Second Temple Judaism. It is claimed that they were the dominant priestly clan during the Second Temple period prior to the rise of the Hasmoneans, and that they included among their numbers the high priestly line.[267]

The existence of a powerful priestly grouping whose members were identified or identified themselves as Zadokites might be expected to have left its imprint on the literature of the late Second Temple period, especially if it included the high priestly line. In this chapter I will examine the explicit references to Zadok and the sons of Zadok from the Second Temple period. How well does the evidence align with the theory of a ruling Zadokite family or with our proposal that Ezekiel 44 was a relatively late composition? I will begin by turning to the appearance of Zadok in the late biblical composition of Chronicles before examining the appearance of the sons of Zadok in the scrolls from the Qumran community, in Ben Sira and in Josephus. Our discussion of Josephus leads us to consider the Sadducees, one of the Jewish parties that Josephus identifies. Also known from the writings of the New Testament and Rabbinic literature, the Sadducees' name in Hebrew, צדוקים, has often been thought to suggest an association with the Zadokite clan. For the sake of clarity throughout this chapter I will distinguish between the terms "sons of Zadok" and "Zadokites". The former refers to the textual references to the "sons of Zadok", whilst the latter concerns

---

267 E.g. Rooke, *Zadok's Heirs*; Frank Moore Cross, *The Ancient Library of Qumrân and Modern Biblical Studies*, 1st ed. (Garden City, NY: Doubleday, 1958); James C. VanderKam, *From Joshua to Caiaphas: High Priests after the Exile* (Minneapolis: Fortress, 2004); Heinz-Josef Fabry, "Zadokiden und Aaroniden in Qumran", in *Das Manna fällt auch heute noch: Beiträge zur Geschichte und Theologie des Alten, Ersten Testaments: Festschrift für Erich Zenger*, ed. Frank-Lothar Hossfeld and Ludger Schwienhorst-Schönberger (Freiburg im Breisgau: Herder, 2004), 201–17.

the theory that there existed in the Second Temple period a powerful priestly sept that bore the name of Zadok.

3.1 Zadok and his Family in the Book of Chronicles

In the book of Chronicles the Israelite and Judahite history that is known from the books of Samuel and Kings is retold from a Second Temple perspective. This perspective is especially apparent in the attention the book devotes to the establishment of the Jerusalem Temple and its cult in the reigns of David and Solomon. No less than 28 chapters are devoted to these two reigns alone. David prepares for the building of the temple and organizes the priests and Levites, whilst Solomon builds the temple. A considerably more complicated temple bureaucracy is envisaged than that which is found in the book of Kings. It presumably reflects to some degree the organization of the temple with which the composers of Chronicles were familiar.

At first blush the presentation of Zadok in Chronicles has almost no overlap with that found in 2 Samuel and 1 Kings. In the earlier history Zadok comes to particular prominence only in the story of Absalom's rebellion (2Sam 15–19), when he and his fellow priest Abiathar remain loyal to David, and in the account of Solomon's ascent to the throne (1Kgs 1–2), when the two priests sided with different aspirants to the Israelite kingship. Otherwise Zadok is only mentioned in the lists of officials for David and Solomon (2Sam 8:17; 20:25; 1Kgs 4:2, 4). In addition to these explicit references to Zadok, there is also the important promise in 1 Samuel 2 that Eli's house will come to an end, and in its place the house of a faithful priest will be established. The prophecy is viewed as fulfilled when Abiathar is banished from Jerusalem (1Kgs 2:25–27), leaving no doubt that the promised "faithful priest" is Zadok. The book of Chronicles passes over the attempts by Absalom and Adonijah to seize the throne and presents instead a smooth and orderly transition of power from David to Solomon. The prophecy concerning Zadok's house and its fulfilment at the beginning of Solomon's reign is also absent from Chronicles. Thus, the only reference to Zadok in Samuel–Kings that has an exact parallel in Chronicles is the list of officials (2Sam 8:15–18; 1Chr 18:14–17) where the description of Zadok is unchanged.[268] The remaining references to Zadok belong to texts that are unique to Chronicles (the so-called *Sondergut*).

---

[268] 1 Chronicles does, however, avoid the idea that Benaiah ben Jedoiada, the Cherethites, the Pelethites and David's sons were priests during David's reign. Benaiah is placed in charge of the Cherethies and Pelethites (cf. 2Sam 20:23), whilst David's sons are said to be chief officials or firstborn sons of David (for discussion of הראשנים, see Gary N. Knoppers, *I Chronicles 10–29:*

Despite these significant divergences from Samuel-Kings, the Chronicler's presentation of Zadok has been subtly and decisively influenced by the history in Samuel and Kings. Various details of the Chronicler's Zadok probably result from exegetical deductions, and the contrasting fortunes of the families of Zadok and Abiathar are represented, albeit in a muted form. Although the stories of fraternal struggles within the royal family have been omitted, Solomon's reign begins with Zadok holding the office of priest uncontested despite sharing the office during David's reign. Abiathar and his family simply fade out of the story without fanfare.

In Chronicles Zadok is introduced earlier in the career of David than in Samuel.[269] Zadok is amongst those who gathered to David at Hebron to make him king over Israel and Judah (1Chr 12:24, 29; cf. 2Sam 5:1). The Chronicler underlines the premature appearance in two ways. First, Zadok is introduced as a "young warrior" (נער גבור חיל) (1Chr 12:29), which appears to emphasize his relative immaturity. Second, whilst Zadok leads a band of officers from his own ancestral house, he is not presented as the leader (נגיד) of the family of Aaron. That position is held by an individual named Jehoiada (12:28).[270]

The advanced introduction of Zadok allows the Chronicler to profile Zadok's steady rise from being a young officer to acting as the sole priest and leader of the Aaronides. After the mustering at Hebron, the next mention of Zadok is found in 1Chr 15:11 where Zadok is listed alongside Abiathar as David's priest. Abiathar quietly disappears from the scene, and is replaced by his son Ahimelech who himself forms a pair with Zadok in 1Chr 18:6; 24:3, 6, 31.[271] In 1Chr

---

A New Translation with Introduction and Commentary, AB 12A [New York: Doubleday, 2004], 706).

269 Ralph W. Klein, *1 Chronicles: A Commentary*, Herm (Minneapolis: Fortress, 2006), 323.

270 Rooke argues that vv. 27–29 list the clerical families in reverse order of precedence. "Levites mentioned first as the most numerous and least exalted class, the "prince" (נָגִיד, *nāgîd*) Jehoiada of the house of Aaron mentioned next with fewer personnel, and finally Zadok, shown as the most exalted person, obviously from a house of commanders, and accompanied only by commanders" (Rooke, *Zadok's Heirs*, 67). In contrast, Olyan argues that "Zadok is only a subordinate of Jehoiada, and not himself the leader of the Aaronid group" (Saul M. Olyan, "Zadok's Origins and the Tribal Politics of David", *JBL* 101 [1982]: 188). Rooke rightly objects to Olyan understanding נער as an indicator that Zadok is a subordinate to Jehoiada, and is likewise correct to see the order of vv. 27–29 as an indication of the "Chronistic schematization of the priesthood" (Rooke, *Zadok's Heirs*, 67). The order, however, need not point to precedence, but merely the nesting effect of the genealogical ordering of the clerical families. The wider group, the family of Levi, is mentioned first, which includes within it the Aaronides, which itself includes within it the house of Zadok (cf. Knoppers, *I Chronicles 10–29*, 568).

271 The Chronicler's approach appears to have stemmed from his appropriation of the list of Davidic officials in 2 Samuel 8, the only mention of Zadok from 2 Samuel that was copied across

27:17 it is Zadok and not Jehoiada that is named as the leader (נגיד; v. 16) or prince (שר; v. 22) of the Aaronides, and by the time of Solomon's anointing Ahimelech has also disappeared from the scene as his father had before him. Zadok is anointed alongside Solomon: the one to be priest, the other king. This final vignette of Zadok has puzzled interpreters. Apart from in the account of the consecration of the Tabernacle in Exodus and Leviticus, the priests are not described as anointed. There are various possible solutions. We may have here an assimilation to the pentateuchal presentation. Or, it may be that Chronicles reflects post-exilic ideas of a diarchy with both priest and king sharing in the leadership.[272] Alternatively, the anointing may be the way that Chronicles reflects Zadok's final, peerless status in 1 Kings 2.[273]

The steady rise of Zadok and the unheralded disappearance of Abiathar and his family contrasts with the picture in 1–2 Samuel where Abiathar's fall from grace stems from his support of Adonijah, Solomon's rival to the throne. The book of Chronicles reaches the same destination, but without highlighting the rivalries within the royal family that marred David's latter years in 2 Samuel. At the same time the prophecy-fulfilment dynamic is absent, and as a result there is no emphasis on Zadok establishing a house. The authors of Chronicles do not appear to be seeking to suppress any evidence of a rivalry between Zadok and the Elides; their purpose seems to be rather to construct the reigns of David and Solomon as an ideal period for the monarchy.

Where Chronicles departs most radically from its source text in 2 Samuel is in its provision of Zadok with a genealogy. In 1 Chronicles 5–6 Zadok's lineage is traced back to Aaron and Levi in two separate genealogies. In the first a descent is traced from Levi through Aaron and Zadok to Jehozadak who was exiled to Babylon by Nebuchadnezzar (5:27–41). The genealogy begins as a segmented ge-

---

to Chronicles without alteration. The list of officials in 2 Samuel 8 lists Ahimelech son of Abiathar as priest alongside Zadok. It is usually assumed that the text in 2 Samuel is corrupt, since Abiathar is elsewhere described as the son of Ahimelech, and Abiathar appears to have remained priest alongside Zadok throughout David's reign in 2 Samuel. (The simplest explanation of the corruption is that a careless scribe accidentally transposed the names Abiathar and Ahimelech. Because Zadok's father is said to be Ahitub and Ahimelech's father is identified as Ahitub [1Sam 22:9, 11, 20], some interpreters have regarded the textual corruption to be more complicated and that the text originally gave Ahitub as Abiathar's grandfather and Ahimelech as his father.) In Chronicles this corrupt reading has been fully assimilated so that Abiathar is replaced by Ahimelech part way through David's reign. (Following various Hebrew mss which have אחימלך at 1Chr 18:16 – see also the versions – rather than MT which reads אבימלך).
272 See, e. g., William M. Schniedewind, "King and Priest in the Book of Chronicles and the Duality of Qumran Messianism", *JJS* 94 (1994): 71–78.
273 Klein, *1 Chronicles*, 541.

nealogy (vv. 27–29), before focussing on the line of Eleazer (vv. 30–41). In the second genealogy a descent is traced from Aaron to Zadok's son Ahimaaz (6:34–38).

The importance of these genealogies to critical scholarship stems from Wellhausen's observation that Zadok appears in 2 Samuel as a *homo novus*. He is simply introduced as the son of Ahitub (2Sam 8:17). Whilst this has given rise to fairly speculative arguments about Zadok's pedigree, the lack of genealogical interest is not unusual in Samuel and Kings. Patronyms are fairly common, but more extensive genealogies are only provided for Elkanah (1Sam 1:1), Kish (1Sam 9:1) and Ahijah (1Sam 14:3). To make much of Zadok as a *homo novus* is to argue from silence, and a silence that is by no means out of place.

In contrast to the book of Samuel's disinterest in genealogy, in the book of Chronicles Zadok has been provided with an Aaronic pedigree that he did not possess earlier. In this way the Zadok of Samuel–Kings has been assimilated to the norms of the priestly literature, which insists that all priests stem from Aaron. The provision of Zadok with a genealogy has frequently been correlated with theories of rival priestly families and seen as evidence of a legitimization of the Zadokite sept or its subordination within the Aaronide or Levitical sept.[274] Such theories go beyond what the textual evidence itself will bear. First, the two priestly genealogies place no particular emphasis on Zadok.[275] Like the other genealogies in 1 Chronicles 1–9, they show an interest in the period of

---

[274] Joseph Blenkinsopp, "The Judaean Priesthood during the Neo-Babylonian and Achaemenid Periods: A Hypothetical Reconstruction", *CBQ* 60 (1998): 25–43 views Chronicles as an accommodation of Zadokite and Aaronide perspectives.

[275] The same is true of Ezra's genealogy in Ezra 7:1–5, which is concerned to trace Ezra's line back to Aaron who is described as הכהן הראש (v. 5). The similarities between the genealogy in Ezra and Chronicles suggests some literary relationship between the two. The genealogy in Ezra is clearly redactional, as is indicated by the awkward resumptive הוא עזרא in v. 6. Apparently on this basis Williamson holds that Ezra has borrowed from Chronicles or a common source (Hugh G. M. Williamson, *Ezra, Nehemiah*, WBC 16 [Waco, TX: Word Books, 1985], 92–93). The omission of six names between Azariah and Meraioth may well have occurred accidentally, a plausible thesis given the repetitions in the Chronicles' genealogy. The omissions would include Zadok, David's priest, which hardly suggest that *Zadokite* descent was particularly important to the redactor who added the genealogy to the book of Ezra (cf. Neh 11:10–12). Alternatively, others have argued that Chronicles is dependent on Ezra's genealogy. Of the six names added by the Chronicler to the genealogy (Amariah, Ahitub, Zadok, Ahimaaz, Azariah, Johanan), four are priests known from 2 Samuel–1 Kings (Sara Japhet, *I & II Chronicles: A Commentary*, OTL [Louisville: Westminster John Knox, 1993], 151–52; J. R. Bartlett, "Zadok and His Successors at Jerusalem", *JTS* 19 [1968]: 1–6). Thus, priestly figures from Israel's history are given an Aaronide descent, as required by the priestly literature, but there is nothing to suggest that Zadok is given any prominence.

the United Monarchy and in the returnees from exile. In the first genealogy two individuals are highlighted: Azariah, the priest who served in Solomon's Temple,[276] and Jehozadak, who was exiled by Nebuchadnezzar.[277] In the second genealogy, the line of descent ends with Ahimaaz and not with Zadok (6:38).[278] Secondly, it is not just Zadok that the book of Chronicles provides with a respectable and ancient pedigree: Ahimelech's descent is said to trace back to Ithamar, Aaron's second son (1Chr 24:3), whilst Samuel is made to be a Kohathite (6:7–13). Zadok's more exalted genealogy is worth emphasising, but the genealogies may have been constructed so as to reflect the received narrative about the priesthood in the United Monarchy. Zadok will be the preferred priest and so his genealogy must be the most august. Thirdly, each of the tribal genealogies in 1 Chronicles stretches back to the patriarchal age and begins with the tribe's eponymous ancestor. The genealogies of Levi's family are no different. Thus, the fact that the priestly genealogy begins with Levi and his son cannot be taken as an attempt to subordinate the Zadokite family by Levitical partisans, or at least not without further supporting evidence. The first part of the genealogy would appear to have been drawn from Exod 6:16–25. The location of Zadok within the family of Aaron clearly reflects the perspective of the priestly literature that only Aaron's descendants can be priests. Thus, Aaronic descent in 1Chr

---

276 It is often suggested that the Azariah of v. 35 and the Azariah of v. 36 have become confused during textual transmission. The remark "it was he that served as priest in the house that Solomon built in Jerusalem" should have been attached to Azariah ben Ahimaaz ben Zadok. It is reasonable chronologically to envisage Zadok's grandson officiating in the Jerusalem Temple at its completion.

277 Knoppers has argued that Zadok is the central figure in a chiastic structure (Gary N. Knoppers, *I Chronicles 1–9: A New Translation with Introduction and Commentary*, AB 12 [New York: Doubleday, 2003], 257–58). Knoppers rearranges the text graphically to demonstrate Zadok's central position within the putative chiastic arrangement, but as Sparks has convincingly demonstrated the text lacks any indicators that the genealogy is chiastically arranged. "The varying levels do not build upon one another, nor do they lead to an understandable climax in the centre. They are, in effect, a mere list of names" (James T. Sparks, *The Chronicler's Genealogies: Towards an Understanding of 1 Chronicles 1–9*, AcBib 28 [Atlanta: Society of Biblical Literature, 2008], 116). Additionally, Sparks observes that Knoppers has omitted Levi and the figures in 5:27–29 who do not belong to the direct lineage of Jehozadak. The remarks about Azariah in v. 35 and Jehozadak in v. 41 are the only textual guide we have to the significance of the genealogy for the book of Chronicles. Two key events are highlighted: the building of the temple and the fall of Judah and Jerusalem.

278 The suggestion that 5:27–41 is a list of high priests has been convincingly rejected by Knoppers, *I Chronicles 1–9*, 412–15; Sparks, *The Chronicler's Genealogies*, 66, 107–15. The text of Chronicles makes no such claim for this genealogical list in contrast to Josephus' lists of high-priests in *Ant.* 20.224–31.

5:27–41 and 6:35–38 demonstrates no more than that the Chronicler has harmonized the portrayals of the priesthood in the Pentateuch and the book of Samuel.

There are grounds for thinking that many of the references to Zadok and other priests have been added to the text of Chronicles secondarily.[279] In the earlier version of Chronicles there is a strong focus on the Levites, and we might reasonably surmise that the original book was composed by someone who would have identified himself as a Levite.[280] To say that the original composition is pro-Levite, is not to insist that it was anti-priest or opposed to any particular priestly clan, such as the Aaronides. This would be to assert more than the evidence itself demands. The book does not envisage the Levites assuming roles that are elsewhere granted exclusively to the Israelite priests. Rather, it is concerned to outline the variegated roles that the Levites undertake within the temple cult. It might be better to say that the original book has a strong interest in the Levites, rather than describing it as "pro-Levite", if "pro-Levite" implies opposition to other clerical groups.

The subsequent redaction of the book shows that for one scribe who transmitted the book of Chronicles adequate account of the role of the priesthood in the First Temple had not been given. Various additions provided a correction, adding priests to the picture of the cult during the United Monarchy. Again, al-

---

279 Hugh G.M. Williamson, "The Origins of the Twenty-Four Priestly Courses: A Study of 1 Chronicles XXIII–XXVII", in *Studies in the Historical Books of the Old Testament*, ed. John A. Emerton, VTSup 30 (Leiden: Brill, 1979), 251–68. The first genealogy appears to have been added through resumptive repetition (5:27; 6:1), whilst the second lacks a connection to the preceding Levitical genealogies (Knoppers, *I Chronicles 1–9*, 425). In the mustering at Hebron Jehoiada and Zadok are the only individuals named and loosely attached with a connective *waw* (1Chr 12:28–29). Although Zadok and Abiathar are summoned together with the Levites in 15:11, it is only the Levites who are addressed in v. 12. The placing of Zadok and other cultic functionaries at the shrine of Gibeon in 16:39–42 could also be a redactional addition, somewhat clumsily added to the list of cultic functionaries serving before the ark in Jerusalem (vv. 37–38). Japhet notes that "the matter is presented abruptly, rather like an addendum to the main issue, introduced before its conclusion" (Japhet, *I & II Chronicles*, 320). The list of twenty-four courses in 24:1–19 is intrusive in a context that is focussed on the Levites, and vv. 20–31 are closely linked (see Williamson, "Twenty-Four Priestly Courses", 258–60). In 27:17 not only is Aaron's inclusion amongst the tribes unusual, but also the fathers of the other leaders are named (the only exception being Elihu who is named as David's brother). In the anointing of Zadok in 29:22 we would not expect the object of מֹשׁח to be introduced with לְ, and the focus of the pericope is otherwise entirely on Solomon.

280 For a comprehensive discussion of the Levites in Chronicles and a review of earlier scholarship, see Antje Labahn, *Levitischer Herrschaftsanspruch zwischen Ausübung und Konstruktion: Studien zum multi-funktionalen Levitenbild der Chronik und seiner Identitätsbildung in der Zeit des Zweiten Tempels*, WMANT 131 (Neukirchen-Vluyn: Neukirchener Verlag, 2012).

though we might label this perspective as pro-priestly, to do so is not to imply it is also anti-Levite.[281] This redaction draws upon the final perspective of the Pentateuch, which distinguishes between the roles of priests and Levites in the care of the cult. The pro-priestly redactor adds what he perceives to have been omitted, rather than setting out to restrict or diminish the Levites.

Despite its inclusion of priestly genealogies that mention Zadok, this later redaction of Chronicles cannot be aligned with the perspective of Ezekiel 44. Even if Zadok represents the senior Aaronide line of Eleazer, Abiathar and other Aaronides still act as priests in the Jerusalem Temple and do so without censure or criticism. In terms of cultic service the Zadok of David's time is *primus inter pares*. The redactor of Chronicles views Zadok positively apparently taking his cues from the narrative of Samuel and Kings. Nevertheless, Zadok and his descendants are not the only reliable, authentic priests as Ezekiel 44 imagines them to be.[282] The redactor of Chronicles neither stridently rejects the view of the priesthood in Ezekiel 44, nor does he advocate it. It would be reasonable to conclude that he has no knowledge of it.[283] There is no basis for understanding Chronicles as an accommodation between conflicting Aaronides and Zadokites, or Zadokites seeking to legitimate their line. Undoubtedly, the different roles of the Levites are well developed, but in many other respects Chronicles is an assimilation of the narratives about the First Temple to the perspective of the priestly literature.

---

281 *Contra* Rooke who writes about the "later reviser who felt it necessary to raise the priestly profile for more polemical purposes" (Rooke, *Zadok's Heirs*, 204). Certainly the profile of the priests is being raised, but it is unclear to me what its polemical purposes were. The addition of a thematic element to a text that previously lacked it may not always be best described with the term "polemical".

282 Steven Schweitzer, *Reading Utopia in Chronicles*, LHBOTS 442 (London: Bloomsbury T&T Clark International, 2009), 134.

283 Since the book of Ezekiel appears to have had little impact upon the book of Chronicles, this conclusion may not seem too dramatic. (For the relation of the major prophets to Chronicles see, *inter alia*, Christopher T. Begg, "The Non-Mention of Ezekiel in the Deuteronomistic History, the Book of Jeremiah and the Chronistic History", in *Ezekiel and His Book: Textual and Literary Criticism and Their Interrelation*, ed. J. Lust, BETL 74 [Leuven: Peeters, 1986], 340–43; William M. Schniedewind, *The Word of God in Transition: From Prophet to Exegete in the Second Temple Period*, JSOTSup 197 [Sheffield: Sheffield Academic, 1995]).

3.2 The Sons of Zadok at Qumran and in the Damascus Document

Amongst Second Temple texts, the expression "the sons of Zadok" occurs with the greatest frequency in the finds from the caves near Khirbet Qumran. It has consequently played a prominent role in the reconstructions of the Qumran sect's history. Two of the earliest texts published from Cave 1 were the *Community Rule* or *Serekh ha-Yaḥad* (1QS) and the *Habakkuk Pesher* (1QpHab). 1QS mandates the sons of Zadok with a central role in the community's organization, whilst the *Habakkuk Pesher* apparently traces the origins of the sect to a conflict between two priests, the Teacher of Righteousness and the Wicked Priest.[284] These two texts allowed scholars to hypothesize about the sect's origins and original composition, and to coordinate these theories with what was already known about late Second Temple history from non-sectarian sources. In the 1950s Milik, Vermes and Cross developed a compelling account of the sect's origins.[285] The early sect was composed of Hasidim who opposed the usurpation of the high priesthood by the non-Zadokite Hasmoneans. This resistance to the new dynasty eventually led to conflict and the exclusion of the Hasidim and their Zadokite leaders from the Jerusalem cult. At Damascus and then at Qumran the Hasidim formed their own community, which remained true to the principle of hereditary Zadokite leadership.

With the publication of the entire corpus of the Dead Sea scrolls there has been a reassessment of the importance of Zadokite pedigree and high priestly succession for the Qumran sect. Whilst the earliest published scrolls suggested that the sons of Zadok had a central role in the community, it can now be seen that early accounts of the sect's origins exaggerated the importance of Zadokite descent for the Qumran community. Altogether there are twelve references to the sons of Zadok in the finds from Qumran and the Cairo Damascus document, and all but one of these had been published by 1969.[286] But, as Charlotte Hempel has observed, with the publication of the entire corpus it can now be

---

284 Although the designation of the founder of the Qumran sect does not focus on his priestly role, the identification of the Teacher of Righteousness as a priest is made in 1QpHab II, 8 and 4Q171 III, 15.

285 J. T. Milik, *Ten Years of Discovery in the Wilderness of Judaea*, SBT 26 (London: SCM, 1959); Geza Vermes, *Les manuscrits du Désert du Juda*, 2nd ed. (Paris: Desclée, 1954); Cross, *The Ancient Library*. The major difference between Milik, Vermes and Cross is their identification of the Wicked Priest. Whilst Cross identifies Simon III as the Wicked Priest, Milik and Vermes argued instead for Jonathan.

286 1QS V, 2, 9; IX, 14; 1QSa I, 2, 24–25; II, 3; 1QSb III, 22; 4Q163 22, 3; 4Q174 1 I, 17; CD III, 12–IV, 1; IV, 3; 4Q266 5 Ib, 16.

seen that references to the sons of Aaron outnumber those to the sons of Zadok.[287] Further, the publication of manuscripts from Cave 4 included additional copies of the *Community Rule*, which did not feature the sons of Zadok.

In a detailed redaction-critical analysis of the *Community Rule* Sarianna Metso has argued that 1QS is a revision of an earlier text that is known from Cave 4 manuscripts. At various points the cave 4 versions of the *Community Rule* have a shorter text than 1QS and, most importantly, 4QS[b] and 4QS[d] lack the references to the sons of Zadok that are attested in column 5 of 1QS.[288] The relevant section of column 5 of 1QS is set out below, where the "sons of Zadok" is mentioned twice (lines 2 and 9), together with the parallel texts from 4QS[b] and 4QS[d]. In the text of 1QS the underlined words are not paralleled in 4QS[b, d].

4QS[b] IX, 2–8 // 4QS[d] I, 2–7 // 1QS V, 1–10

2 ולהבד[ל] מעדת א[נשי העול ולהיות יחד בתורה ובהון ומשובים] 3 על פי הרבים לכול דבר לתורה] ולהון
לעשות ענוה וצדקה ומשפט ואהבת] 4 חסד והצנע לכת בכול דרכיהמה אשר[לוא ילך איש בשרירות לבו
לתעות] 5 כי אם ליסד מסד אמת לישראל ליחד לכול] המתנדב לקודש באהרן ובית] 6 אמת לישראל והנלוים
עליהם ליחד וכול הבא [לעצת היחד יקים על נפשו] 7 באסר לשוב אל תורת משה בכול לב ו[בכול נפש כול
הנגלה מן התורה על פי] 8 עצת אנשי היחד

2...and to keep apa[rt] from the congregation of the m[en of injustice and to constitute a community in law and property and acquiesce] 3 to the authority of the many with regard to all matters of law [and property to achieve humility, and righteousness and justice and compassionate] 4 love and seemly behaviour in all their ways so that [no one shall walk in the stubbornness of their heart in order to go astray] 5 but rather establish a foundation of truth for Israel, for the community, for all [those who freely volunteer for holiness in Aaron and the house of] 6 truth for Israel and the ones joining them for the community. And everyone entering [the council of the community shall take upon himself] 7 by binding to return to the law of Moses with whole heart and [whole soul all that has been revealed from the law by the authority] 8 of the council of the men of the community (4QS[b] IX, 2–8).

2 ולבדל מעדת אנשי העול להיות י[ח]ד בתו[ר]ה] ובהון ומשובים על פי הרבים לכל דבר 3 לתורה ולהון ולעשות
ענוה וצדקה ומשפט ואהבת] חסד וה]צנע לכת בכל דרכיהם 4 [אשר]לא ילך איש בשרירות לבו לתעות כי אם
ליסד] מוסד]אמת לישראל ליחד לכל 5 המתנדב לקדש באהרן ובית אמת לישראל והנלוי[ם] על[יה]ם ליחד וכל

---

287 Charlotte Hempel, "Do the Scrolls Suggest Rivalry Between the Sons of Aaron and the Sons of Zadok and If So Was It Mutual?", *RevQ* 24 (2009): 135–53; Charlotte Hempel, "The Sons of Aaron in the Dead Sea Scrolls", in *Flores Florentino: Dead Sea Scrolls and Other Early Jewish Studies in Honour of Florentino García Martínez*, ed. T. Hilhorst, Emile Puech, and Eibert J. C. Tigchelaar, JSJSup 122 (Leiden: Brill, 2007), 207–24; Charlotte Hempel, "אַהֲרוֹן ʾaharôn", *ThWQ* 1: 76–81.
288 Sarianna Metso, *The Textual Development of the Qumran Community Rule*, STDJ 21 (Leiden: Brill, 1997).

הבא לעצת 6 [ה]י[ח]ד יק[י]ם על נפשו באסר ל[שוב א]ל [ת]ורת מש[ה] בכל לב ובכל נפש כול הנגלה מן 7 הת
[ורה ע]ל[ל] פי] עצת אנש[י]היחד

2...and to keep apart from the congregation of the men of injustice in order to constitute a co[mmu]nity in la[w] and property and acquiesce to the authority of the many with regard to all matters 3 of law and property to achieve humility, and righteousness and justice and [compassionate] love [and se]emly behaviour in all their ways 4 [so that] no one shall walk in the stubbornness of their heart in order to go astray but rather establish [a foundation of] truth for Israel, for the community, 5 for all those who freely volunteer for holiness in Aaron and the house of truth for Israel and the ones joini[ng] th[e]m for the community. And everyone entering the council of 6 [the] com[mu]nity shall t[ak]e upon himself by binding to [return t]o the [l]aw of Mos[es] with whole heart and whole soul all that has been revealed from 7 the l[aw b]y [the authority] of the council of the me[n] of the community (4QS^d I, 2−7).

1 להבדל מעדת 2 אנשי העול להיות ליחד בתורה ובהון ומשובים על פי בני צדוק הכוהנים שומרי הברית ועל פי
רוב אנשי 3 היחד המחזקים בברית על פיהם יצא תכן הגרול לכול דבר לתורה ולהון ולמשפט לעשות אמת יחד
וענוה 4 צדקה ומשפט ואהבת חסד והצנע לכת בכול דרכיהם אשר לוא ילך איש בשרירות לבו לתעות אחר
לבבו 5 ועיניהו ומחשבת יצרו (כ)יאם למול ביחד עורלת יצר ועורף קשה ליסד מוסד אמת לישראל ליחד ברית
6 עולם לכפר לכול המתנדבים לקודש באהרון ולבית האמת בישראל והנלוים עליהם ליחד ולריב ולמשפט 7
להרשיע כול עוברי חוק ואלה תכן דרכיהם על כול החוקים האלה בהאספם ליחד כול הבא לעצת היחד 8 יבוא
בברית אל לעיני כול המתנדבים ויקם על נפשו בשבועת אסר לשוב אל תורת מושה ככול אשר צוה בכול 9 לב
ובכול נפש לכול הנגלה ממנה לבני צדוק הכוהנים שומרי הברית ודורשי רצונו ולרוב אנשי בריתם 10
המתנדבים יחד לאמתו ולהתלך ברצונו

1...to keep apart from the congregation of 2 the men of injustice in order to become as a community in law and property and acquiesce to the authority of the sons of Zadok, the priests who keep the covenant and the multitude of the men of 3 the community who hold fast the covenant. By their authority decision by lot shall go forth with regard to all matters of law, property and custom, to achieve together truth and humility, 4 righteousness and justice, compassionate love and seemly behaviour in all their ways so that no one shall walk in the stubbornness of their heart in order to go astray after his heart 5 and his eyes and the thoughts of his inclination, but rather he should circumcise in the community the foreskin of his inclination and stiff neck in order to establish a foundation of truth for Israel, for the community of the eternal 6 covenant to atone for all those who freely volunteer for holiness in Aaron and the house of truth in Israel and the ones joining them for the community, lawsuit and judgement 7 to proclaim guilty all who transgress the statute. These are the regulations of their way concerning all these statutes when they join the community. And everyone entering the council of the community 8 enters the covenant of God in the eyes of all who freely volunteer. He shall take upon himself with a binding oath to return to the law of Moses according to all that he commanded with whole 9 heart and with whole soul, according to all that has been revealed of it to the sons of Zadok, the priests who keep the covenant and seek out his pleasure and the multitude of the men of their covenant 10 who freely volunteer together for his truth and to walk according to his will (1QS V, 1−10).

The priority of the 4QS$^{b, d}$ text has been made on a couple of grounds. First, the texts of 4QS$^{b, d}$ are considerably shorter than 1QS, and the shorter text is to be preferred on the text-critical principle of *lectio brevior*. When 4QS$^{b, d}$ are viewed

as the earlier text, it is apparent that the text has been expanded with additions
at a number of different points to produce the text in 1QS. It is easy to see how
the text of 4QS[b, d] has been expanded with short explanatory comments and longer alterations. Conversely it is difficult to imagine how the same texts could
have been cut from 1QS without producing some grammatical and logical inconsistencies. The selection from the fifth column of 1QS and the parallels in 4QS[b, d]
reproduced above provide a representative sample of the differences. 1QS V is
noticeably longer. Secondly, the longer text in 1QS includes theologically significant additions in comparison to 4QS[b, d], and increased scriptural allusions and
idioms. A comparison of the fifth column of 1QS and the parallels in 4QS[b, d] fur-
nishes a number of examples of these changes besides the references to the
"sons of Zadok". Amongst the theologically significant additions we can number
the references to "covenant" (1QS V, 2, 3, 8, 9) and "eternal covenant" (1QS V,
5–6) as well as the "inclination" (1QS V, 5). The reference to a "stiff neck"
(1QS V, 5) is probably an allusion to the story of the Golden Calf (Exod 32;
Deut 9–10), whilst an example of a scriptural idiom is "according to all that
he commanded" in 1QS V, 8. It is difficult to explain why a scribe would have
removed theologically significant ideas or scriptural allusions and idioms.

As well as the references in 1QS V, there is an additional reference to the
"sons of Zadok" in 1QS IX, 14. It seems likely that this reference has come
about under the influence of the earlier occurrences in column 5. According to
1QS IX, 14 amongst the duties assigned to the "instructor", משכיל, is that "he
should separate and weigh the sons of Zadok according to their spirits"
(להבדיל ולשקול בני הצדוק לפי רוחום). In contrast, 4QS[e] III, 10 requires that the instructor "should separate and weigh the sons of righteousness according to
their spirits" (להבדיל ֯ל֯ לשקול בני הצדק לפי ר֯[ו]חמה).[289] The reading in 4QS[e] is to
be preferred, for the textual development has left a tell-tale sign in the anomalous definite article before the proper name Zadok.

Hempel has argued that a similar redactional process to what Metso observed in relation to 1QS also took place in the *Rule of the Congregation* where
we also find three references to the sons of Zadok (1QSa I, 2, 24–25; II, 3).[290]
The Qumran finds provide no divergent textual tradition as we have with the
Community Rule. Nevertheless, the *Rule of the Congregation* does show evidence
of redactional growth and Hempel's suggestion of an eschatologically-orientated

---

289 For "the sons of righteousness" elsewhere in the Dead Sea Scrolls see 1QS III, 20, 22; 4Q286
1 II, 7; 4Q424 3 10; 4Q503 48–50 8.
290 Charlotte Hempel, "The Earthly Essene Nucleus of 1QSa", *DSD* 3 (1996): 253–69.

redaction does resolve a number of textual difficulties.[291] Hempel argues that the same hand was probably responsible for both the redaction of the *Community Rule* and the *Rule of the Congregation*.[292] This is more uncertain. Stephen Pfann has argued that the *Rule of the Congregation* manuscripts in cryptic script from cave 4 have a text that appears to be substantially the same as 1QSa.[293] In addition there is no evidence for the *Community Rule* amongst the cryptic scrolls, which suggests that the *Community Rule* and the *Rule of the Congregation* were not circulating together when the cryptic manuscripts were written. Consequently, the redaction that Hempel proposes for 1QSa appears to have been undertaken prior to 1QS and 1QSa being joined together on a single scroll. It appears we must reckon either with the compositions that make up 1Q28 being brought together because of their shared subject matter, or the redaction of 1QS having been influenced by 1QSa when they were written on a common scroll.

If Metso's and Hempel's analyses of the Serekh tradition are correct, the Zadokites cannot have enjoyed a central role in the structure of the community from its beginnings and the hypothesis that the Qumran community originated in a dispute about priestly descent must be re-examined. Although Vermes had shaped the original consensus, he was one of the first to appreciate the importance of the Cave 4 variations in the Serekh tradition. Vermes offered as an

---

291 The first reference to the sons of Zadok (I, 2) occurs in an introduction to the *Rule of the Congregation* (I, 1–5). The appearance of two similar headings (וזה הסרך לכול...) in I, 1 and I, 6 strongly suggests redactional activity. Hempel observes that the eschatological perspective of I, 1–5 is not replicated elsewhere in the *Rule of the Congregation*. The appearance of the sons of Zadok in I, 24 is clearly redundant. The authority of the priests and the clan heads I, 24– 25 has already been asserted in I, 23, although there the priests are identified as the sons of Aaron. In II, 3 we have an appendix to a regulation which defines the community's council. It repeats significant parts of I, 27 and subordinates the council under the sons of Zadok. Like I, 24–25 it appears somewhat redundant, except for the emphasis on the Zadokites.
292 "Now if whoever was responsible for 1QS 5 was reworking the Community Rule in favour of the 'sons of Zadok' tradition, it is quite likely that the same person inserted references to that tradition into 1QSa on the same scroll" (Hempel, "The Earthly Essene Nucleus of 1QSa", 259).
293 In particular, Stephen Pfann's analysis of the *Rule of the Congregation* manuscripts in cryptic script from cave 4 suggests that the sons of Zadok were probably present in 4QSE[e] and 4QSE[g]. These manuscripts date to the second century BCE, which is earlier than any of the extant manuscripts of the *Community Rule*. In addition, there are no fragments of the *Community Rule* among 4Q249 or 4Q250, which implies that the *Rule of the Congregation* was circulating at this point without the *Community Rule* (Stephen J. Pfann, "Cryptic Texts", in *Qumran Cave 4. XXVI Cryptic Texts and Miscellanea, Part I*, by Stephen J. Pfann et al., DJD 36 [Oxford: Clarendon, 2000], 515– 74). Pfann's analysis must be treated with some caution. The fragments that constitute 4Q249 and 4Q250 are very small, making it difficult to draw far-reaching conclusions about the development of the rule traditions.

alternative historical reconstruction an original community with a democratic character with Aaronides offering legal and doctrinal expertise. At some point the community was taken over by Zadokites who effectively displaced the Aaronides. Vermes compares this event to the founding of the temple at Leontopolis by Onias IV, the last of the Oniads who was ousted from Jerusalem.[294] Hempel develops Vermes' observations about the late appearance of the Zadokites, but avoids co-ordinating the scrolls with the demise of the Oniads. She argues that the references to the sons of Aaron in the scrolls are ideologically neutral. The sons of Aaron perform typical priestly duties, and the expression is simply another designation for a priest. The references to the sons of Zadok, by contrast, reflect the Zadokites' aspirations to lead the community.[295]

Metso's redaction-critical analysis of the *Community Rule* has not gone uncontested. A significant problem is the palaeographical dating of the Serekh manuscripts. Cross dates 1QS to 100–75 BCE,[296] but he dates 4QS[b, d] to 30–1 BCE.[297] Even allowing for some uncertainty in palaeographical dating, Metso's ordering on redactional grounds is the reverse of the dates of the extant manuscripts. Philip Alexander has been the most vociferous in insisting that the order of composition should be assumed to reflect the palaeographical dating. For whilst younger manuscripts can preserve older texts, in the case of the *Community Rule* "we are dealing...with an important official document passed down within a small, closely knit, hierarchical and highly localised religious sect,

---

294 Geza Vermes, "The Leadership of the Qumran Community: Sons of Zadok-Priests-Congregation", in *Geschichte-Tradition-Reflexion: Festschrift für Martin Hengel zum 70. Geburtstag. Vol. 1, Judentum* (Tübingen: Mohr Siebeck, 1996), 375–84.

295 Hempel, "Rivalry". Fabry also finds Vermes' suggestion of a late Zadokite incursion into the community attractive. He argues that there was a rivalry between the Aaronide and Zadokite priesthoods, which may lie behind the prominence of the priestly traditions of Levi and Melchizedek (Fabry, "Zadokiden und Aaroniden in Qumran"; Heinz-Josef Fabry, "Priests at Qumran: A Reassessment", in *Dead Sea Scrolls: Texts and Context*, ed. Charlotte Hempel, STDJ 90 [Leiden: Brill, 2010], 243–62).

296 Cross classifies the script as "semi-formal Hasmonean" (Frank Moore Cross, "The Development of the Jewish Scripts", in *The Bible and the Ancient Near East: Essays in Honor of William Foxwell Albright*, ed. George Ernest Wright [Garden City, NY: Doubleday, 1961], 198 n. 116). The same scribe wrote a number of other scrolls, including 4QSam[c] (Eugene Charles Ulrich, "4QSam[c]: A Fragmentary Manuscript of 2 Samuel 14–15 from the Scribe of the *Serek Hay-Yahad* (1QS)", *BASOR* 235 [1979]: 1–25).

297 Cross describes the writing as "typical early Herodian formal script" (Cross in James H. Charlesworth, *Rule of the Community and Related Documents*, The Dead Sea Scrolls 1 [Louisville: Westminster John Knox, 1994], 57).

characterised by a strong reverence for the written word".[298] Alexander's arguments require that the *Community Rule* was abbreviated at various points and, in particular, the references to the sons of Zadok removed. Alexander speculates that the Qumran community may have been founded by a disenfranchised group of Zadokites, but their power had waned by the time that 4QS[b, d] were produced. Since the Zadokites were possibly a small group of closely-related individuals, they were vulnerable to the line dying out, especially in a sect that valued celibacy.[299]

Despite incisive observations about the palaeographical dating, Alexander's arguments are not able to overturn Metso's redaction-criticism. Alexander does not address the provision of scriptural proofs in 1QS that are not present in 4QS[b, d], or the addition of theologically significant language in 1QS, such as ברית. Whilst Alexander rightly observes that many redaction-critical arguments can be reversed, this is not the case in every instance nor may the alternatives be equally compelling. Thus, in the case of 1QS and 4QS[b, d] it is difficult to understand why a scribe abbreviating 1QS would remove scriptural evidences or theological language that was significant to the community.[300] In addition, Alexander's understanding of the relationship between the texts cannot explain the anomalous definite article in בני הצדוק of 1QS IX, 14 in a convincing manner.[301] Nevertheless, Alexander's case suggests that it is necessary to reconsider our conception of the Qumran sect or how textual diversity in authoritative texts such as the *Community Rule* was handled. In other words, do all the sectarian manuscripts reflect, as Alexander suggests, "a small, closely knit, hierarchical and highly localised religious sect" or, again, does "strong reverence for the writ-

---

298 Philip S. Alexander, "The Redaction History of *Serekh Ha-Yaḥad*: A Proposal", *RevQ* 17 (1996): 448.

299 Alexander, "Redaction History".

300 As Metso observes, "adding theologically significant words to the text is a natural thing to do, but finding any reasons for omitting them is very difficult" (Metso, *Textual Development*, 79). Lucas rejects the argument about theological language by drawing a comparison with Josephus' *Jewish Antiquities* where Israel's historical traditions are retold with much less emphasis on election or covenant (Alec J. Lucas, "Scripture Citations as an Internal Redactional Control: 1QS 5:1– 20a and Its 4Q Parallels", *DSD* 17 [2010]: 30 – 52). This is not an apt example, since the vocabulary like ברית and כפר which Metso highlights was central to the self-conception of the Qumran community, whereas it is possible to think of socio-political reasons why Josephus would have played down Israel's election and covenant traditions when writing with a Roman audience in mind.

301 The text in 1QS IX, 14 is sometimes emended, not least because of the difficulties of accommodating the subordination of the Zadokites to the משכיל with theories of Zadokite supremacy at Qumran. (For arguments against emendation, see Robert A. Kugler, "A Note on 1QS 9:14: The Sons of Righteousness or the Sons of Zadok?", *DSD* 3 (1996): 315 – 20).

ten word" imply a single, authoritative recension of a text? In her recent work Alison Schofield attempts to reconsider the first of these assumptions by arguing that the different recensions of the *Serekh* tradition reflect a textual development within the larger Essene group at more than one location.[302]

Why, though, did the *Serekh* tradition undergo the redactional development that Metso proposes? As we have seen, a number of scholars like Vermes believe this points to a change in the composition of the community, such as a takeover by Zadokites expelled from Jerusalem. But the differences between 1QS and the cave 4 manuscripts has led some scholars to a more fundamental questioning of the older consensus about the origins of the Qumran sect. Should the redactional evidence be understood not as an indication of the Qumran leadership's genealogical descent, but as a claim to spiritual authority based on biblical precedents?[303] Metso herself has argued that the addition of the sons of Zadok is part of a more extensive redactional activity that sought to "provide a Scriptural legitimation for the regulations of the community and to reinforce the community's self-understanding".[304]

I will argue that a careful examination of the references to the sons of Zadok in the texts from Qumran suggests that there existed within the sect a *pesher*-like interpretation of Ezekiel 44.[305] To uncover this we may begin with the two ap-

---

302 Alison Schofield, *From Qumran to the Yaḥad: A New Paradigm of Textual Development for the Community Rule*, STDJ 77 (Leiden: Brill, 2009).

303 "The appeal to 'sons of Zadok' in the Scrolls is primarily a claim of spiritual superiority rather than genealogical legitimacy" (John Joseph Collins, *Beyond the Qumran Community: The Sectarian Movement of the Dead Sea Scrolls* [Grand Rapids: Eerdmans, 2010], 98). Baumgarten sees the later inclusion of Zadokites in the Serekh tradition as an attempt to control charismatic excess within the early Qumran community. He leaves open whether Zadokite descent was real or imaginary (Albert I. Baumgarten, "The Zadokite Priests at Qumran: A Reconsideration", *DSD* 4 [1997]: 137–56). Kugler observed how the redactional history spoke against the earlier consensus and cautions against the tendency to find evidence of "social realities when the literature more often seems to convey imagined realities instead" (Robert A. Kugler, "Priesthood at Qumran", in *The Dead Sea Scrolls after Fifty Years: A Comprehensive Assessment*, ed. Peter W. Flint and James C. VanderKam, vol. 2 [Leiden: Brill, 1998], esp. 114 n. 69; Robert A. Kugler, "Priests", *EDSS* 2: 688–93). Grossman is likewise cautious in using statements about Zadokites to reconstruct the history of the sect. She shows how the texts are patient of a number of quite different historical reconstructions (Maxine L. Grossman, *Reading for History in the Damascus Document*, STDJ 45 [Leiden: Brill, 2002], 162–209).

304 Metso, *Textual Development*, 105.

305 For the reconstruction of *pesher*-style interpretations outside the *pesharim*, see Menahem Kister, "Biblical Phrases and Hidden Biblical Interpretations and *Pesharim*", in *The Dead Sea Scrolls: Forty Years of Research*, ed. Deborah Dimant and Uriel Rappaport, STDJ 10 (Leiden: Brill, 1992), 27–39.

pearances of the sons of Zadok in 1QS V. In 1QS the sons of Zadok and the men of the community replace the entire community as the locus of authority. This is probably not intended as a substantial change to the community's self-organization for 4QS[b, d] had already distinguished between the community and its priestly leadership. The priestly leadership are "all who freely volunteer for holiness in Aaron and the house of truth in Israel", לכל המתנדב לקדש באהרון ובית אמת לישראל, whilst the lay members are "the ones joining them for the community", והנלוים עליהם ליחד (4QS[b] IX, 5–6 // 4QS[d] I, 4–5). In 1QS the community and leadership and described in different terms, the re-interpretation being placed before (1QS V, 2–3) and after (1QS V, 9–10) the original description which is preserved in 1 QS V, 5–6.

The community is originally described as "the ones joining them for the community", והנלוים עליהם ליחד (4QS[b] IX, 5–6 // 4QS[d] I, 4–5). The use of the *niphal* participle of the relatively rare verb לוה with a definite article is reminiscent of Isaiah 56, where והנלוים occurs twice of the eunuchs and foreigners who join themselves to YHWH (vv. 3, 6).[306] It is the same individuals who are described in Isaiah 56 as "holding fast to the covenant" (ומחזיקים בבריתי) (vv. 4, 6). In 1QS this language is taken up to describe the men of the community (המחזקים בברית; 1QS V, 2).[307]

The priestly leadership, on the other hand, are depicted in 4QS[b, d] as "all who freely volunteer for holiness in Aaron and the house of truth in Israel", לכל המתנדב לקדש באהרון ובית אמת לישראל. The expression "the house of truth" (בית אמת) does not occur in the Hebrew Bible. The juxtaposition of "the house of truth" with Israel's first priest, however, does bring to mind the divine promise in 1Sam 2:35 that God will establish "a sure house" (בית נאמן) for Zadok's family. An allusion to Zadok was certainly how an early redactor understood this passage. In 1QS V the priestly leadership are now identified as "the sons of Zadok" and those who "keep the covenant" (שומרי הברית). This characterization of the sons of Zadok blends two expressions drawn from Ezekiel 44: in v. 15 the sons of Zadok are commended as those "who kept the charge of my sanctuary" (אשר שמרו את־משמרת מקדשי), and this behaviour contrasts with the Israelites who in v. 7 are said to have "broken my covenant" (ויפרו את־בריתי). The association of the community's priestly leadership with Zadok would have been confirmed by the original contrast of the community with those who go astray (לתעות; 4QS[d] I,

---

306 The *niphal* participle of לוה only otherwise occurs at Esth 9:27.
307 The opponents of the community are also described with terms drawn from the Hebrew Bible (1QS V, 11–13). In the text of 1QS V unparalleled in 4QS[b, d] Metso notes allusions to Zeph 1:6, Deut 29:28, Num 15:30, Ezek 24:8, and Deut 29:21 (Metso, *Textual Development*, 80).

4), language that is used on three occasions in Ezekiel 40–48 to describe what the sons of Zadok did not do (44:10, 15; 48:11).

Our examination of the redaction of the *Community Rule* suggests that the original description of the community and its priestly leadership was reinterpreted in light of both Isaiah 56 and Ezekiel 44. This fact suggests not only that the mention of the "sons of Zadok" in the *Community Rule* was exegetically inspired, but also that the composer of these descriptions in 1QS V was conscious at some level of the close relationship that existed between the two biblical passages.

The exegetical tradition of reading Ezekiel 44 and Isaiah 56 together was clearly well established amongst the sectarians, because we find it represented in two other compositions from Qumran: the *Rule of Blessings* and the *Damascus Document*. The *Rule of Blessings* (1QSb) is found on the same scroll as the *Community Rule* (1QS), and the shared interest in the sons of Zadok may have been one of the reasons for the inclusion of both texts on a single scroll. The *Rule of Blessings* prescribes the blessings to be recited in the community. Whilst the *Community Rule* envisages a binary division of the community into priestly leaders and laity, the *Rule of Blessings* imagines a threefold division of the community into those who fear God, the sons of Zadok and the prince of the congregation (נשיא העדה). The addition of the prince to the structure of the Messianic community clearly reflects Ezekiel's temple vision (Ezekiel 40–48). The blessing over the sons of Zadok describes the priests in a variety of ways, and the first of these echoes Isaiah 56 when it describes the sons of Zadok as "those whom God has chosen to strengthen his covenant", אשר בחר בם אל לחזק בריתו (1QSb III, 23).

The *Damascus Document* presents more challenges to the interpreter. The only reference to the sons of Zadok in the manuscripts of the *Damascus Document* from the Qumran caves is in a rather fragmentary context. Nevertheless, in the text that has been preserved we have an echo of Isaiah 56, "those who remained ste]adfast to his ho[ly name" (המחזי[קים בשם קו־]שו) (4QD[a] 5 Ib, 9), occurring in close proximity with a reference to "the s]ons of Zadok, the priests" (ב[ני] צדוק הכהנים) (4QD[a] 5 Ib, 16).[308]

To make further progress on understanding the fragmentary text of the *Damascus Document* from Qumran, it is necessary to have recourse to the more fully preserved versions of the *Damascus Document* from the Cairo Genizah, in particular the third and fourth columns of the Cairo Damascus document a (CDa).[309]

---

308 Wernberg-Møller observed already in 1953 that 1QS V and CD III–IV had similar interpretations of Ezekiel 44 (Preben Wernberg-Møller, "צדק, צדיק and צדוק in the Zadokite Fragments (CDC), The Manual of Discipline (DSD) and the Habakkuk-Commentary (DSH)", *VT* 3 [1953]: 310–15).
309 Hempel, "Rivalry".

Nevertheless, we must exhibit caution; CDa is not identical with the Damascus Document from Qumran. In particular, it has had a more lengthy history of textual transmission. Despite these caveats, there are important similarities between how the Damascus document develops its understanding of the sons of Zadok and what we see in the texts from Qumran. In the Cairo Damascus document a *pesher*-style interpretation of Ezek 44:15 is developed in which priests, Levites and sons of Zadok delineate three stages in the Damascus group's existence.[310] The final, climactic stage is represented by the sons of Zadok who stand and serve "at the end of days" (באחרית הימים) (CDa IV, 4). The sons of Zadok do not correspond to a priestly hierarchy within the Damascus group, but to the group itself at some stage in its history. Since the group imagined itself to be living in the latter days, they probably identified themselves with the sons of Zadok.

The designation "the sons of Zadok" has been chosen to describe the eschatological community because of its associations with faithfulness amid widespread apostasy. Immediately prior to the citation of Ezek 44:15 in CDa there is an allusion to 1Sam 2:35 where God promises to build a "faithful house" (בית נאמן) to replace the family of Eli (CDa III, 19).[311] This promise is judged not to have been fully fulfilled in the past, but is now being realized in the eschatological age. The righteous will be characterized by their loyalty to it. This commitment is described with vocabulary that draws on Isaiah 56: those who remain steadfast to the house of Zadok (המחזיקים בו) will attain eternal life and the glory of Adam (CDa III, 20). The righteous are envisaged as a minority, to whom has been revealed the hidden ways in which the rest of Israel has

---

310 Philip R. Davies, *The Damascus Covenant*, JSOTSup 25 (Sheffield: JSOT Press, 1983), 91–92; Ben Zion Wachholder, *The New Damascus Document: The Midrash on the Eschatological Torah of the Dead Sea Scrolls: Reconstruction, Translation and Commentary*, STDJ 56 (Leiden: Brill, 2007), 182. The alternative position is that the three terms correspond to three categories of membership in the Qumran community (most recently, Christian Metzenthin, *Jesaja-Auslegung in Qumran*, ATANT 98 [Zurich: Theologischer Verlag, 2010], 132). The strongest argument against this proposal is the reference to the "priests" in the past, but the sons of Zadok "at the end of days". Dimant's interpretation offers a combination of the two perspectives: "According to the CD author, then, the various groups within the community are identical to the faithful Levite priests who will officiate in the future temple, as in the vision shown to Ezekiel" (Deborah Dimant, "The Apocalyptic Interpretation of Ezekiel at Qumran", in *Messiah and Christos: Studies in the Jewish Origins of Christianity. Presented to David Flusser on the Occasion of His Seventy-Fifth Birthday*, ed. Ithamar Gruenwald, Shaul Shaked, and Gedaliahu G. Strousma, TSAJ 32 [Tübingen: Mohr Siebeck, 1992], 37).
311 Davies, *Damascus Covenant*, 90.

"gone astray" (תעה; III, 13–14).[312] Thus, the apostates are described with an allusion to Isaiah 56 just as the faithful in the community were in 1QS V, 11 and the language of "straying" appears to be a further allusion to Ezekiel 44.

Our examination of the *Damascus Document* has demonstrated not only that the language of Isaiah 56 is being employed to explicate Ezekiel 44, but also that the promise concerning Zadok's house in 1 Samuel 2 is woven into the web of scriptural proofs. The significance of the "faithful house" in the immediate context of the citation of Ezek 44:15 increases confidence that the reference to "the house of truth" in the *Community Rule* is to be understood as an allusion to 1 Samuel 2.

The eschatological interpretation of the sons of Zadok in the Cairo Damascus document is similar to what we find in the *Rule of the Congregation* (1QSa): "this is the rule of the entire congregation of Israel at the end of days (באחרית הימים)". The *Rule of the Congregation* has the same binary community structure as that found in the *Community Rule*. The laity and their priestly leaders are distinguished: the latter are the sons of Zadok and the former, the men of their covenant. The community's distinctive and sectarian stance is expressed in the *Rule of the Congregation* in a similar way to the *Damascus Document*. The lay members of the congregation are described as "having tur[ned away from walking in] the way of the nation (סר]ו מלכת ב[דרך העם)" (1QSa I, 2–3), a clear allusion to Isa 8:11.

The sense of alienation from the path chosen by the rest of the nation is also expressed in 4Q174. Better known as 4QFlorilegium, 4Q174 includes amongst its exegetical reflections a "midrash" (מדרש) on Psalm 1.[313] The composer of the midrash has collected together a number of biblical texts that are concerned with what is taken to be the psalm's principal theme, "turning from the way [of the wicked]" ([סרי מדרך [הרשעים) (4Q174 I, 14). The introduction of additional biblical texts is achieved via individual words from Psalm 1. Thus, the link-word "way" (דרך) from Ps 1:1 inspires a citation of Isa 8:11,[314] which is understood to relate to "the end [of] days (לאחרית ה]ימים)": "and it happened that with a strong [hand he turned me aside from walking in the way of] this people", ויהי כחזקת] היד ויסרני מלכת בדרך] העם הזה. This is immediately followed by a citation of Ezek 37:23: "they shall not defile themselves again with any of their idols" לו[א]

312 Davies notes that "the word 'strayed' (תעה)…which provides a verbal link with the preceding passage (line 14), is also used in CD to describe the situation of the Jewish people outside the community in the post-exilic period" (Ibid., 91). The accusation of "straying" recurs throughout CDa I–V: I, 15; II, 13; III, 1, 4, 14; V, 20.

313 Only Ps 1:1aα is cited, but it is usually recognized that it is used as an incipit.

314 George J. Brooke, *Exegesis at Qumran: 4QFlorilegium in Its Jewish Context*, JSOTSup 29 (Sheffield: JSOT Press, 1985), 147–48.

יטמאו.³¹⁵ עוד בכול ג[ל]ו[ל]יהמה Neither the citation of Psalm 1 nor Ezekiel 37 includes the word that inspired the association, but it would appear that the link-word "seat" (מושב) has been the means of association. The mention of avoiding idols (גלולים) permits the composer of 4Q174 to spring to another text: the conduct of the sons of Zadok and their opponents in Ezek 44:10 (4Q174 I, 16–17). This verse is not cited, but does provide the identification that is key to the community's interpretation: "these are the sons of Zadok and the men of their council". Thus through a catena of biblical texts, the individuals of which Psalm 1 spoke are identified; they are the ones who have turned away from the wickedness that characterizes those in Israel who do not follow the teachings of the Qumran sect.³¹⁶

Our examination of the references to the sons of Zadok in the scrolls from Qumran and the Cairo Damascus document has shown that each one of them reflects what appears to be a common tradition of interpretation. Texts from 1 Samuel 2, Isaiah 8, 56, Ezekiel 44, and Psalm 1 are interpreted in light of one another. In them the Qumran community saw itself and its opponents portrayed. A number of the documents from Qumran interpret these scriptural texts as eschatological; they concern the "latter days". Since Ezekiel's temple vision had not been realized in the Second Temple period, it is clear why the sectarians adopted this interpretative perspective for Ezekiel 44. In the *Community Rule*, however, the community appears to be regulating conduct in the present. It might not be wise to press this distinction, since for the community saw itself as living in the latter days. A further distinction may be drawn between those community documents that apply the sobriquet "sons of Zadok" to the entire community,

---

315 4Q174 is very broken at this point and the citation was originally identified as Ezek 44:10. The text is correctly identified as Ezek 37:23, see George J. Brooke, "Ezekiel in Some Qumran and New Testament Texts", in *The Madrid Qumran Congress: Proceedings of the International Congress on the Dead Sea Scrolls Madrid 18–21 March, 1991*, ed. Julio C. Trebolle Barrera and Luis Vegas Montaner, vol. 1, STDJ 11 (Leiden: Brill, 1992), 326–27. Oddly, Florentino García Martínez and Eibert J. C. Tigchelaar, eds., *The Dead Sea Scrolls Study Edition* (Leiden: Brill, 2000), 355. correctly restore Ezek 37:23, but then erroneously identify the citation as Ezek 44:10.

316 It is possible that the same exegetical instinct lie behind the appearance of "the sons of Zadok" in 4Q163, a *pesher* on Isaiah. It contains a reference to the "sons of Zadok" (4Q163 22 3), but the text is very fragmentary. In the following line Isa 30:23 appears to have been cited: "bread, the pro[duce of the earth...]", and frag. 23 contains a citation of Isa 30:19–21. Possibly frag. 22 offers an interpretation of Isa 30:20–21, which reads, "YHWH will give you bread of adversary and water of oppression. Your teacher will hide himself no longer and your eyes will see your teacher. Your ears will hear a word behind you, 'This is the way; walk in it', when your walk to the left or to the right". In common with Isa 8:11, Isa 30:20–21 may have been understood to be promising a guiding hand which will help the community walk in "the way" (הדרך).

and those that distinguished between the leadership and the rest of the community.

The different referents, the consistently exegetical use of "the sons of Zadok", and the eschatological nature of many of the allusions raises significant questions for the theory that a Zadokite sept played a role in the history of the Qumran sect. The issue is not that biblical exegesis and eschatological imaginations cannot reflect communal realities. They can and do. The problem is that if there were a Zadokite sept, why are there not references to them that *do not* draw upon Ezekiel 44 and other biblical texts for inspiration? This is what we would expect were such a family to have been prominent in the Qumran community.

Rather than postulating the existence of a Zadokite coterie at Qumran, the evidence suggests that we view the "sons of Zadok" as yet another biblically-inspired sobriquet that the Qumran community coined to describe itself, its leaders or its opponents. These include, "the builders of the wall", "the seekers after smooth things", "the sons of Belial", "Ephraim", "the house of Peleg", "the penitents of Israel" and so on.[317] It is not difficult to see the attraction of Ezekiel 44's expression "sons of Zadok" for a community that saw itself as embodying cultic faithfulness in the context of widespread apostasy.

3.3 The Sons of Zadok in Ben Sira

In all but one of the extant manuscripts of Ben Sira there are no references to the "sons of Zadok". The exception is a single Hebrew manuscript (B) from the Cairo Genizah, which has an extensive psalmic addition in the final chapter of the book at 51:12a–o. The psalm is clearly modelled after the biblical Psalm 136 with its principal theme being the praise of YHWH's name. It consists of fifteen lines, and all but the last conclude with the refrain "for his fidelity endures forever" (כי לעולם חסדו). The ninth line of the psalm reads, "praise to the one who chose the sons of Zadok to serve as priests, for his fidelity endures forever" (הודו לבוחר בבני צדוק לכהן כי לעולם חסדו) (51:12i).

The absence of the psalm on the names of God from the Greek, the Old Latin and Syriac traditions raises questions about whether the psalm belonged to Ben Sira's original composition.[318] Arguments have been arraigned for and against its

---

317 For recent discussions of the sobriquets from Qumran, see Deborah Dimant, "The Vocabulary of the Qumran Sectarian Texts", in *History, Ideology and Bible Interpretation in the Dead Sea Scrolls*, FAT 90 (Tübingen: Mohr Siebeck, 2014), 57–100; Matthew A. Collins, *The Use of Sobriquets in the Qumran Dead Sea Scrolls*, LSTS 67 (London: Bloomsbury T&T Clark, 2012).
318 Sirach 51 is not extant in the other Hebrew manuscripts.

authenticity. Its appearance in a Hebrew text convinced earlier scholars that the psalm was original, but most scholars since the middle of the twentieth century have viewed it as an addition.[319] It is difficult to see why the psalm would have been omitted if it were part of Ben Sira's original work. Conversely, the insertion of the psalm on the names of God at this point was probably inspired by the concluding verse of the preceding thanksgiving psalm in 51:1–12, which reads:

> He has redeemed me from every evil,
>   and delivered me in the day of distress;
> Therefore, I give thanks (הודיתי) and offer praise,
>   and I bless the name of YHWH (שם יהוה) (v. 12).

In the Greek, Old Latin and Syriac the thanksgiving psalm is followed in vv. 13–30 by an alphabetic acrostic poem about wisdom, modelled on Prov 31:10–31. It is easy to see how reading the concluding lines of the thanksgiving psalm in which Ben Sira promises to give thanks and praise the name of YHWH, but which he does not obviously fulfil in the following poem, could have inspired the insertion of the psalm on the names of God.

The psalm on the names of God has a noticeably biblical style. Di Lella only overstates the matter slightly when he argues that "the psalm is completely biblical in its phrasing, orientation and theology".[320] Some of the verses are simply citations from the Old Testament psalms,[321] and many of the divine names are found in the Old Testament.[322] Those names that do not have an exact biblical parallel have clearly been inspired by biblical diction.[323] Almost at the centre of the psalm is the statement about the sons of Zadok twinned by a statement about the Messiah: "Give thanks to him who makes a horn to sprout for the

---

319 For bibliography on the text-critical discussion see Alexander A. Di Lella, *The Hebrew Text of Sirach: A Text-Critical and Historical Study* (Berlin: de Gruyter, 1966), 101–105; Françoise Mies, "Le Psaume de Ben Sira 51,12a–o Hébreu: L'Hymne aux Noms divins. Deuxième partie", *RB* 116 (2009): 498–99. Both Mies and Di Lella agree that the evidence does not permit a decisive answer to be given, though both tend to the view that the psalm on the names of God is an addition (Mies very cautiously).

320 Patrick W. Skehan and Alexander A. Di Lella, *The Wisdom of Ben Sira: A New Translation with Notes*, AB 39 (Garden City, NY: Doubleday, 1987), 571. For a detailed discussion, see Françoise Mies, "Le Psaume de Ben Sira 51,12a–o Hébreu: L'Hymne aux Noms divins. Première partie", *RB* 116 (2009): 343–55.

321 Sir 51:12a = Ps 136:1; Sir 51:12o = Ps 148:14.

322 Sir 51:12c, cf. Ps 121:4; Sir 51:12d, cf. Jer 10:16; 51:19; Sir 51:12e, cf. Isa 49:7; Sir 51:12f, cf. Isa 56:8; Sir 51:12j, cf. Gen 15:1; Sir 51:12l, cf. Gen 49:24; Sir 51:12m, cf. Ps 132:13.

323 Sir 51:12b, cf. Pss 63:4; 147:12 etc.; Sir 51:12k, cf. Gen 49:24; Deut 32 etc.; Sir 51:12n, cf. Deut 10:17.

house of David" (51:12h). Amongst the balanced lines of the psalm, these two lengthy lines stand out.[324] They highlight the two central authorities for the ideal Jerusalem: the Davidic messiah and the sons of Zadok. Biblical diction is just as strong here as elsewhere in the psalm. The statement about David reproduces Ps 132:17a with only a slight alteration.[325] The statement about the sons of Zadok reflects the language of Ezekiel 40 – 48 and combines it with the language of election, which is used elsewhere in the Hebrew Bible with priests.[326]

The emphasis on a messianic figure and the priests descended from Zadok is not characteristic of the rest of Ben Sira. Whilst Sir 47:11 and 47:22 can be interpreted as evidence that he hoped for a Davidic restoration, royal messianism is, at best, muted in Ben Sira. The tone of the rest of the book is quite different from the explicit messianism of the psalm.[327] The sons of Zadok do not appear elsewhere in Ben Sira, though the sage is an enthusiastic supporter of the Jerusalem priesthood. In Sirach 7, for example, Ben Sira reformulates the love commandment from Deut 6:5 so as to instil respect for the priesthood.

> With all your soul fear God,[328]
> and revere his priests.
> With all your strength love your maker
> and do not neglect his ministers.
> Honour God and respect the priesthood
> and give their portion just as you were commanded. (7:29 – 31).

For Ben Sira the treatment of the priests is a mirror of how highly God is esteemed. They are, after all, *his* priests and ministers, and the provision of the

---

324 This could suggest that these lines were composed later than the rest of the psalm. The first part of the bicolon in all the other lines has three or four accents, whilst 51:12h, i have five accents. Without 51:12h – i the psalm has lines with four accents at the beginning and the end of the psalm, and lines with four accents right at the centre (51:12f – g). The remaining lines have three accents. The centre of the psalm would then emphasize the return of the people to the city and sanctuary.

325 Ben Sira reads "the house of David" for "David". The expression בית דוד/דויד is found twenty-five times in the Hebrew Bible.

326 See Deut 21:5; Ps 105:26; cf. Num 16:20 [17:5]; Deut 18:5; 1Chr 15:2; 2Chr 29:11.

327 There is some debate about the presence of messianism within Ben Sira. Corley provides a bibliography of recent discussion, whilst making use of the distinction between priestly and royal messianism (Jeremy Corley, "Seeds of Messianism in Hebrew Ben Sira and Greek Sirach", in *The Septuagint and Messianism*, ed. Michael Anthony Knibb, BETL 195 [Leuven: Peeters, 2006], 301– 12).

328 Heb. ms A reads "heart". As a result of parablepsis vv. 27– 28 were omitted.

priesthood is stipulated in *his* commandments.[329] Ben Sira's own esteem for the priesthood is especially evident in the Praise of the Fathers (Sir 44–50). Considerable space is given to the praise of Aaron, describing in detail his priestly vestments and functions (45:6–22). Phinehas too has a prominent place with particular emphasis on the granting of a "high priesthood forever" (45:24).[330] The literary exaltation of Aaron and Phinehas anticipates the exuberant climax of the praise of the fathers: the panegyric on Simon II (50:1–24).

Ben Sira's muted messianism and his emphasis on the Aaronic priesthood provide further ground for attributing the psalm on the names of God in Sirach 51 to a secondary hand. But it also raises the question of how we are to evaluate the relationship between these two perspectives on the priesthood. Olyan attributes the divergence to differing priestly ideologies. Ben Sira is the proponent of a pan-Aaronid ideology. He engages in a "subtle polemic" against those who hold that only Zadokites may be priests: "all Aaronids, not only Zadokite Aaronids, are legitimate temple priests".[331] Against those who wish to assert the priestly rights of the Levites, Ben Sira pursues a different approach. He refuses "to recognize the existence of the Levites as a group. He opposes their claims and uses silence for his polemic".[332] The addition of the psalm on the divine names in Sirach 51 reflects the activities of Zadokites who continued to assert their claim to an exclusive priesthood.

The weakness in Olyan's proposals is readily apparent. His arguments are based upon the silence of the text, a particularly troubling form of argumentation, even more so when tied to the idea of *polemic*. Olyan is on firmer ground when he observes that Ben Sira's understanding of the priesthood has been decisively shaped by priestly texts in the Pentateuch. Since the Pentateuch's final redactors accorded priestly texts a determinative role in the shape of the Pentateuch, Olyan's observation does no more than demonstrate Ben Sira's indebtedness to the Pentateuch in much the same form as we now have it. His indebtedness is illustrated by his loyalty to the priesthood. There is no reason to attribute any polemical sharpness to this reliance on a scriptural precursor. Turning to the

---

329 According to Olyan, "It is not overstating the case to argue that Ben Sira all but equates the individual's relationship with God to the same individual's relationship to the priesthood" (Saul M. Olyan, "Ben Sira's Relationship to the Priesthood", *HTR* 80 [1987]: 263).
330 As Olyan rightly observes Ben Sira goes beyond Numbers 25 by insisting that Phinehas was granted the *high* priesthood forever. This would appear to be a logical deduction from the Pentateuch. Since Aaron and his descendants have been granted the priesthood, it is natural to ask what novelty the promise in Numbers 25 introduces. Ben Sira deduces that it was the "high priesthood" that was promised in perpetuity to Phinehas' family.
331 Olyan, "Ben Sira's Relationship", 276.
332 Ibid., 279.

psalm on the divine names we find a similar indebtedness to the Jewish scriptures. The paralleling of the sons of Zadok with the Davidic messiah suggests an eschatological hope inspired by scriptural texts, and need not refer to a group of priests contemporary with the redactor.

The appearance of the "sons of Zadok" in the psalm on the divine names and in the Dead Sea scrolls has frequently been the basis for positing a relationship between the composer of the psalm and the Qumran community. Thus Di Lella argues that the psalm "could quite plausibly have been written by a member of the Qumrân sect".[333] This proposal is based on the hypothesis that the Qumran community was led at some point in its history by Zadokite partisans. As we have already seen the evidence from Qumran is inadequate to support this hypothesis. The most we can say is that the instinct we saw in the Serekh tradition to increase a text's biblical diction, particularly through appeal to prophetic and eschatological texts, is also evident in the transmission history of Ben Sira. The appeal in two texts to a scripture held in common by many, if not all, Jewish groups at the end of the Second Temple period cannot be used as evidence that both texts stem from the same circle or that they were composed at around the same time.

3.4 Josephus and the Zadokites

The view that the Zadokite descent of the priesthood was important in the late Second Temple period finds no foothold in the great Jewish historian Josephus. As Klawans has recently observed, Josephus is indifferent to the issue of whether or not the high priesthood of his time could claim Zadokite descent.[334]

> Josephus nowhere suggests that sectarian disputes concerned questions about the legitimacy of the high priesthood. To the contrary, the evidence from Josephus suggests quite the opposite: priestly descent never figures among the sectarian disputes that Josephus mentions. When he discusses conflicts concerning the priesthood, Zadokite descent per se is not a concern...when he explicitly discusses changes in priestly descent, conflict does not usually result.[335]

In his rehearsal of the history of the United Monarchy, Josephus rarely departs from the presentation of Zadok that we find in the books of Samuel, Kings,

---

333 Alexander A. Di Lella, "Qumrân and the Geniza Fragments of Sirach", *CBQ* 24 (1962): 265.
334 Jonathan Klawans, *Josephus and the Theologies of Ancient Judaism* (Oxford: Oxford University Press, 2012), 18–23.
335 Ibid., 20.

and Chronicles (*Ant.* 7–8). Josephus does, however, develop the account of Abiathar's expulsion from the Jerusalem priesthood. Weaving together the prophecy about a "sure house" in 1 Samuel 2 and the priestly genealogies in 1 Chronicles 5–6, Josephus sees Zadok's sole possession of the priestly office as the elevation of the house of Phinehas over that of Ithamar (*Ant.* 8.11–12). In a similar way to 1 Chronicles 5:27–41, Josephus provides a continuous line of male descendants from Zadok down to Josadak who was exiled by the Babylonians. The central part of Josephus' genealogy diverges markedly from that in 1 Chronicles 5 with names that have no parallel from biblical sources,[336] and in a further departure from 1 Chronicles Josephus views each of the descendants as a high priest (*Ant.* 10.151–153). At no point in his writings does Josephus allude to Ezekiel's preference for the sons of Zadok and his disqualification of the other Levites.

The rupture of the exile is ended in the post-exilic period and Josephus views the priestly descent continuing down to the time of Onias III (*Ant.* 20.231–235). Although many scholars have seen the end of the Oniads as a major crisis for Jewish political and religious identity, Josephus does not make any claim that the Oniads were Zadokites or that their demise marked the end of the Zadokite line. Zadok is not mentioned in the history of the high priesthood in *Antiquities* 20, and Josephus seems only concerned that the priests lay claim to descent from Aaron. Thus, with other writers of the Second Temple period, including Chronicles, Josephus shares a heightened interest in genealogies and legitimation, but shows no special interest in Zadokites *per se*.

3.4.1 The Sadducees

One of the contemporary Jewish "sects" that Josephus identifies bears the name "Sadducees" (Σαδδουκαῖοι),[337] and many scholars have claimed that this group were Zadokite partisans. According to Geiger's influential theory they bore their name, which in rabbinic texts is צדוקים, because of their staunch allegiance

---

336 1 Chronicles lists Azariah, the grandson of Zadok, as the father of Johanan. The list then follows with another Azariah, then Amariah, Ahitub, Zadok and Shallum. Josephus identifies the great-grandson of Zadok as Joram, who is succeeded by Jos, Axioram, Phideas, Soudaias, Jouel Jotham, Ourias, Nerias, and Odaias, before rejoining the course of the 1 Chronicles' list with Shallum.

337 For the meaning of αἱρέσεις see Anthony J. Saldarini, *Pharisees, Scribes and Sadducees in Palestinian Society* (Edinburgh: T&T Clark, 1988), 123–27. The pre-Christian usage is not negative. Josephus also describes the Pharisees, Sadducees and Essenes as philosophical schools. For further discussion, see Steve Mason, *Flavius Josephus: Translation and Commentary. Vol 1b: Judean War 2* (Leiden: Brill, 2008), 96 n. 734.

to the Zadokite family. They were an aristocratic priestly party, and like the Essenes and Pharisees took their defining shape during the Maccabean crisis.[338] With the discovery of the Dead Sea Scrolls and their apparent emphasis on the "sons of Zadok", it was claimed that both the Sadducees and the Qumran community stemmed from the ousting of the Oniads from the high priesthood.[339]

In recent years various scholars have counselled caution.[340] The sources of our knowledge about the Sadducees' beliefs are not only meagre, but also written by those who were openly hostile to the Sadducees: Josephus, the New Testament writers, and the Rabbis.[341] The partisan nature of our sources means that

---

338 Abraham Geiger, *Judaism and Its History*, vol. 1 (New York: Thalmessinger & Cahn, 1866), 168–78.

339 The exact relationship between the Qumran community and the Sadducees has long been a matter of discussion and debate. Already with the publication of the "Zadokite fragments", Schechter raised the issue, observing that "the term Zadokites naturally suggests the Sadducees; the present state of knowledge of the latter's doctrines and practices does not offer enough points of resemblance to justify the identification of them with our Sect" (Solomon Schechter, *Documents of Jewish Sectaries* [Cambridge: Cambridge University Press, 1910], xxi). Charles was rather less nuanced, describing the fragments as the work of "reformed Sadduceeism" (Robert Henry Charles, *The Apocrypha and Pseudepigrapha of the Old Testament in English. Vol 2: Pseudepigrapha* [Oxford: Clarendon, 1913], 790). A relationship with the Sadducees is often postulated by those dissatisfied with the theory of Essene origins for the Qumran sect. Proponents can point especially to similarities between Qumranic halakhah in 4QMMT and positions attributed to the Sadducees in the rabbinic literature (Lawrence H. Schiffman, *Reclaiming the Dead Sea Scrolls*, ABRL [New York: Doubleday, 1995]). Such observations do not diminish the many points of difference between the two groups, and consequently some have suggested a splintering of the Zadokite party as a result of the Hasmonean takeover of the high priesthood. Hultgren, for example, suggests that "there was one group of conservative Zadokite priests who eventually constituted the leadership of the Qumran community. Other Zadokites, perhaps pro-Hellenistic priests, eventually became the party of the 'Sadducees' as usually understood." (Stephen Hultgren, *From the Damascus Covenant to the Covenant of the Community: Literary, Historical, and Theological Studies in the Dead Sea Scrolls*, STDJ 66 [Leiden: Brill, 2007], 253).

340 Martin Goodman, "The Place of the Sadducees in First-Century Judaism", in *Judaism in the Roman World: Collected Studies* (Leiden: Brill, 2007), 123–36; Saldarini, *Pharisees*; Jonathan Klawans, "Sadducees, Zadokites, and the Wisdom of Ben Sira", in *Israel's God and Rebecca's Children: Christology and Community in Early Judaism and Christianity*, ed. David B. Capes et al. (Waco, TX: Baylor University Press, 2007), 261–76; Klawans, *Josephus*. For a more confident reconstruction of a Sadducean party see Hillel Newman, *Proximity to Power and Jewish Sectarian Groups of the Ancient Period: A Review of Lifestyle, Values, and Halakhah in the Pharisees, Sadducees, Essenes, and Qumran*, BRLJ 25 (Leiden: Brill, 2006).

341 Josephus characterizes the Sadducees as "boorish" and harsh in their judgements (*J.W.* 2.164–165; *Ant.* 20.199). Matthew frequently pairs the Sadducees and Pharisees as opponents of Jesus (Matt 16:1–12; 22:23–33; cf. 3:7), and the author of Acts portrays them resisting Peter and John's proclamation of the message of Jesus (Acts 4:1–4; 5:17–18). Rabbinic writings frewe can do little more than provide a negative characterization of the Sadducees: they did not believe in the resurrection and rejected the halakhah of the Pharisees.[342]

We can be no more certain about the historical origins of the Sadducees. Josephus first mentions the Sadducees along with Pharisees and Essenes in the time of Jonathan (160–143 BCE),[343] and the first story about them occurs during the reign of John Hyrcanus (134–104 BCE).[344] This may point to their origins early in the Hasmonean period, but Goodman rightly observes that they made have originated earlier. Unfortunately, our knowledge of Judaism in the third century BCE is extremely poor and establishing a *terminus a quo* for the group's origins is impossible with the limitations of our current knowledge.[345] Uncertainty about

---

quently place the Pharisees and Sadducees in opposition to one another, and as is well-known the rabbis traced their own origins back to the Pharisees. In later rabbinic writings the Sadducees was used as a general expression for heretics (Goodman, "Place of the Sadducees", 125–26. For detailed discussions of the rabbinic portrayal of the Sadducees, see Saldarini, *Pharisees*, 199–237). Klawans makes some incisive observations about negative views about the Sadducees in modern scholarship (Klawans, "Sadducees", 262).

342 Both Josephus, the Synoptics and Acts agree that the Sadducees rejected belief in the resurrection (*J.W.* 2.165; *Ant.* 18.16; Matt 22:23–33; Mark 12:18–27; Luke 20:27–40; Acts 23:6–10). Josephus writes that the "the Pharisees have handed down to the people regulations from the fathers, which are not written in the laws of Moses; and for this reason the Sadducees reject them, and say that we are to accept regulations which are written down, but need not observe those that are derived from the tradition of the fathers" (*Ant.* 13.297). This has often been interpreted as a rejection of any authority apart from the five books of the Torah. Sanders argues, however, that Josephus overstates the matter: "that in fact they rejected the Pharisaic 'traditions of the fathers', as well as, of course, the special Essene revelations. Put another way, they rejected non-biblical traditions of which they did not approve, especially those that *characterized* the other parties" (E. P. Sanders, *Judaism: Practice and Belief 63BCE – 66CE* [London: SCM, 1992], 334; cf. Saldarini, *Pharisees*, 113; Wayne O. McCready, "Sadducees and Ancient Sectarianism", *RelStTh* 12 [1992]: 89–90; Newman, *Proximity to Power*, 75). Rabbinic traditions that may reflect first-century debates portray the Sadducees rejecting aspects of the Pharisees' halakhah.

343 The Jewish parties are mentioned in the context of Hellenistic statecraft: Josephus informs his reader of the Jewish parties immediately after Jonathan's renewal of treaties with the Romans and the Spartans. The mention of the parties may be intended to suggest the similarity between Jewish and Hellenistic polities. Whilst the parties are said to have existed at that point, they are not said to have originated then.

344 Josephus relates how John Hyrcanus was persuaded to shift his allegiance from the Pharisees to the Sadducees (*Ant.* 13.288–98). The lack of further stories about the Sadducees until the reign of Herod the Great led Bammel to suggest that the Sadducees did not originate until Herod's reign (Ernst Bammel, "Sadduzäer und Sadokiden", *ETL* 55 [1979]: 107–15; cf. Günter Stemberger, "The Sadducees: Their History and Doctrines", in *Cambridge History of Judaism Vol. 3, The Early Roman Period* [Cambridge: Cambridge University Press, 1999], 431).

345 Goodman, "Place of the Sadducees", 126.

when the Sadducees originated means we are also ignorant about the reasons the group began.

The association with Zadok, the priest of David and Solomon, is a deeply troubled one. No ancient source makes this connection, and in the Talmud the Sadducees are said to have taken their name from Zadok, a disciple of Antigonus of Soko, who probably lived in the third century BCE.[346] Despite this rabbinic story, it is not even certain that the name Sadducees derived from the name Zadok. The doubled -δδ- in Σαδδουκαῖοι could well suggest a derivation from צַדִּיק,[347] "righteous", though the diphthong -ου- fits more naturally with צָדוֹק.[348] As Goodman observes,

> neither derivation is without philological problems, and both would fit into the rhetoric of Second Temple Jews; the attractions of describing yourself as "righteous" are obvious and the "sons of Zadok" were ascribed a special role by the Dead Sea sectarians, so "Zadok" was evidently a name to conjure with.[349]

In light of this uncertainty, speculations about the support of the Sadducees for a Zadokite priestly sept must be judged as no more than hypothetical, and it would be incautious to assume it in reconstructions of Jewish history during the Hasmonean period.

3.5 Conclusion

When the Dead Sea Scrolls were discovered in the middle part of the twentieth century, the knowledge of the late Second Temple period increased exponentially. The references to the sons of Zadok in the earliest sectarian texts led not only to theories about the role of Zadokite partisans in the origins of the Qumran sect, but also to larger theories about the importance of Zadokites in Second Temple

---

346 Abot R. Nat. 5.

347 The punctuation of צדוקים in manuscripts of rabbinic literature suggests a vocalization Ṣadduqim (Adiel Schremer, "The Name of the Boethusians: A Reconsideration of Suggested Explanations and Another One", *JJS* 48 [1997]: 295 n. 28). Whilst the Masoretic vocalization of צדוק has a qames and no dagesh, the Greek transliteration of the name shows some variation: Σαδδουκ (Ezra, Nehemiah, Ezekiel) and Σαδωκ (Samuel, Kings and Chronicles) (cf. Stemberger, "The Sadducees", 430).

348 For discussion see Robert Grady North, "Qumran 'Sadducees'", *CBQ* 17 (1955): 45–46; J. Le Moyne, *Les Sadducéens* (Paris: Études Bibliques, 1972), 157–63; Schremer, "Name of the Boethusians".

349 Goodman, "Place of the Sadducees", 125–26.

Judaism. In these theories the end of the Oniad dynasty and the triumph of the Hasmoneans was seen as a significant watershed. Prior to the interventions of Antiochus IV, the priesthood had passed down a single family. The self-aggrandisement of Judas Maccabees and his family was a traumatic rupture for many Jews that was never accepted.

The explanatory value of Zadokite theories has been eroded in some recent scholarship and some have abandoned them altogether.[350] Our brief examination of the relevant sources from the Second Temple period demonstrates that the increased scepticism about such theories is warranted. At the beginning of this chapter we introduced a distinction between textual references to the "sons of Zadok" and the existence of a priestly sept that bore the name of Zadok, the "Zadokites". Evidence for "Zadokites" is lacking, but we do have some references to Zadok and the sons of Zadok.

In their retelling of the biblical history, neither Chronicles nor Josephus elevates Zadok beyond what is portrayed in 2 Samuel and 1 Kings. They do not seem to reflect in any way Ezekiel 44's insistence that only the sons of Zadok serve as priests in the temple. Both texts do show a heightened interest in genealogical descent, but in both cases this means a concern with descent from Aaron, and no marked interest in descent from Zadok. Ben Sira demonstrates a similar concern with Aaron and Aaronic descent in his book.

The appearance of the "sons of Zadok" in Sirach 51 and in the sectarian texts from Qumran are extremely interesting, not least because in many cases the references to "the sons of Zadok" have been added by a later hand. As we have shown, the references from Qumran appear to reflect an exegetical tradition that associated a number of texts together in order to characterize the sect and its opponents. Ezekiel's portrayal of the sons of Zadok provided a potent image of cultic faithfulness despite widespread Israelite apostasy. The sectarians saw their own situation reflected in Ezekiel 44. Various other texts brought additional colour to this picture. Drawing on 1 Samuel 2, the sons of Zadok could be seen as the sure house promised by YHWH to Samuel. The intertextual links with Isaiah 56 allowed the Qumran community to portray itself as holding firm to the covenant. Ezekiel's accusation that Israel had "gone astray" provided a linkage to other biblical texts that use the metaphor of a path to describe the righteous and the wicked. These included Psalm 1 and Isaiah 8.

In each of the texts that we have examined from the Dead Sea Scrolls, we encounter the same nexus of biblical texts. The fact that we find no other refer-

---

350 Most vociferously Alice Hunt, *Missing Priests: The Zadokites in Tradition and History*, LHBOTS 452 (New York: T&T Clark, 2006).

ences to the sons of Zadok means that we lack the evidence for the Zadokites of scholarly theory, a distinguishable group of priests that claimed physical descent from Zadok. The Qumran sectarians claimed to be the sons of Zadok, but this was an ideological claim by the sect to represent the same cultic faithfulness as Ezekiel described.

The absence of any reference to the sons of Zadok in earlier texts and its appearance only in later redactional layers of Ben Sira, *The Rule of the Community* and *The Rule of the Congregation* is striking. Do earlier writers and earlier versions of these texts fail to allude to Ezekiel 44 because it did not exist? There are various reasons why a writer in the Second Temple period may not have alluded to Ezekiel 44. Josephus, for example, writing in the first century AD makes no reference to the sons of Zadok from Ezekiel, but his historical interest means he has little to say about any of the canonical prophets.[351] In contrast, the Qumran texts show an interest in eschatological ideas, and consequently the community found prophetic and apocalyptic literature an important resource for its thinking. Various prophetic images were explored in order to try and interpret the community's experience, discern God's will and understand how the future would unfold. Ezekiel 44 is one of a panoply of texts that the community found enlightening. It is tempting to draw a comparison with my arguments for the very late appearance of the sons of Zadok in the book of Ezekiel. Whilst such an argument would go beyond what the evidence can bear, it does raise the interesting possibility that the book of Ezekiel was still undergoing revision at the time that some of the Qumran texts were being composed. What we can say with confidence is that none of the evidence from Second Temple texts contradicts the argument I have made in previous chapters, and it may provide circumstantial evidence in support of it.

---

351 For Josephus and his views on prophecy, see Louis H. Feldman, "Prophets and Prophecy in Josephus", *JTS* 41 (1990): 386–422. Dimant observes that the interest in Ezekiel stands in contrast to its relative neglect in other Second Temple writings (Dimant, "Apocalyptic Interpretation").

Conclusions

1 Text and Historical Reality

This study began with a new appraisal of the relationship between Isaiah 56 and Ezekiel 44. The reigning consensus in scholarship that Isaiah 56 was composed as a response to Ezekiel 44 was shown to rest on unsustainable assumptions, and the evidence pointed in the opposite direction: Ezekiel 44 is a response to Isaiah 56. Remarkably it would appear that the ire of the composers of Ezekiel 44 stemmed from the divine oracle in Isaiah rather than the actual invasion of the sanctuary by foreigners. The scouring of pre-exilic history for foreigners that encroached on the Jerusalem sanctuary proves to be entirely misguided. Of course, we should not imagine that the possibility of foreigners being admitted into the sanctuary was inconceivable. For the time in which he writes, the composer of the original oracle in Ezekiel 44 takes the possibility entirely seriously.

The origins of Ezekiel's accusation against the son of the foreigner challenge typical understandings of the relationship between text and historical reality. Not merely the fact that the text is no simple reflection of historical reality – a problem long understood in Old Testament scholarship; rather, the fact that the text can generate reality. In Second Temple Judaism the reality generated by what is written is no less important than what happens historically. Given the authority invested in certain texts in Second Temple Judaism, especially those claiming to be divine oracles, it is entirely conceivable that the impassioned oracle of Ezekiel 44 is a response to another written oracle. We do not have to have foreigners literally running amok in the temple, only literarily.

2 The End of the Zadokites

Just as illusory as the quest for the foreigners is the quest for the sons of Zadok. In an essay published just over a decade ago, Lester Grabbe posed the question "Were the Pre-Maccabean High Priests 'Zadokites'?" Having reviewed the evidence, he concludes,

> Were the high priests in the Second Temple period thought of as descendants of Zadok? Yes, they probably were, by almost everyone. At the same time, there is no evidence that

the high priestly line (at least, until the Maccabees) was regarded as uniquely Zadokite. Rather, all altar priests were regarded as "sons of Zadok" by some Jews, if not by most.[352]

The critical evidence to which Grabbe appeals is found in 1 Chronicles 5:29–41; 6:35–38; 24:3, 6 and Ezekiel 40:46; 43:19; 44:15; 48:11. First Chronicles places Zadok in the main priestly line descending from Aaron, a line that continued into the Second Temple period. Ezekiel, on the other hand, considered all altar priests as sons of Zadok, though in Grabbe's assessment "it is the only source for several centuries to use that term for priests".[353]

Were the high priests in the Second Temple period thought of as descendants of Zadok? In contrast to Grabbe, my answer is: No, they probably were not, by almost anyone. Labelling the priests as "sons of Zadok" is found in a small fraction of texts: in some of the latest redactions of Ezekiel's temple vision, and in the later developments of the *Serekh* tradition at Qumran, and in one part of the Ben Sira textual tradition. Every other Second Temple source is completely silent on the matter.

Grabbe assumes that the identification of all altar priests as sons of Zadok in Ezekiel 40–48 was known for "several centuries", despite the paucity of textual evidence. The inexplicable silent centuries are eloquent testimony to the problems with the conventional dating of Ezekiel 44 to the neo-Babylonian period. As I have sought to demonstrate a gap of several centuries simply does not exist. The earliest form of Ezekiel 44, which itself does not mention the sons of Zadok, comes from well into the Persian period, perhaps even the Hellenistic period.

The main point of Grabbe's essay is that the pre-Maccabean high priests did not claim exclusive rights to descent from Zadok, and that Zadokite descent was not the issue that led to the rejection of the high priesthoods of Menelaeus and Alcimus. Grabbe's criticism are incisive and part of a wider critique of the Zadokite hypothesis that has taken place within recent Second Temple scholarship. These have included fresh assessments of the Qumran material and Josephus. I concur with the increased suspicion of Zadokite theories. The results from this study provide further support for recent scepticism; they demonstrate that the sons of Zadok were a late innovation in the biblical texts and an intertextual ideal. Before the first revision of Ezekiel 44 was made, no group existed claiming to be the sons of Zadok. It is also helpful to recall that the sons of Zadok are men-

---

352 Lester L. Grabbe, "Were the Pre-Maccabean High Priests 'Zadokites'?", in *Reading from Right to Left: Essays on the Hebrew Bible in Honour of David J. A. Clines*, ed. J. Cheryl Exum and H. G. M. Williamson (London: Sheffield Academic, 2003), 213–214.
353 Ibid, 213.

tioned in a *vision* of the future temple. The only references to them subsequently are in contexts that are clearly exegetical. If the *Serekh* texts from Qumran testify to the existence of a group that identified itself as the sons of Zadok – which is far from certain – this group was inspired by the *textual reference* to the sons of Zadok in Ezekiel. The origins of these sons of Zadok are not to be found in the hoary past, or in genealogical descent; they are the result of textual exegesis. These basic facts about the sons of Zadok should, at very least, give us pause. They should certainly make us reconsider the numerous theories that appeal to Zadokites to account for significant moments in Second Temple religious history, such as the origins of the Pentateuch, the Maccabean crisis, or the origins of the Qumran sect. Discovering the beginnings of the sons of Zadok paradoxically results in bringing the Zadokites of scholarly invention to an end.

3 The Beginnings of the Levites

If the beginnings of the sons of Zadok are to be found in the text of Ezekiel 44, the beginnings of the Levites as minor clergy are not. Wellhausen argued that it was with the prophet Ezekiel that a *de facto* degradation of the Levites was given divine approbation with lasting significance. Since then the debate about whether the division between priests and Levites is found first in Ezekiel 44 or in the priestly literature of the Pentateuch has not abated. The determining factor has often been the date assigned to the priestly literature. Should it be dated to the post-exilic period, or did some or all of it stem from the pre-exilic period?

My argument that the original oracle of Ezekiel 44 can only be viewed as a response to Isaiah 56, and not the reverse, and that the distinction between Levites and priests was only part of the subsequent revision of that original oracle requires us to review the evidence anew. In other words, the relevant texts in Ezekiel stem from much later than was previously thought. My analysis of the relationship between Numbers 18 and Ezekiel 44 suggests that there are reasons to think that Ezekiel 44 is dependent on Numbers 18, rather than the reverse.

As a result the origins of the distinction between priests and Levites should be sought in the Pentateuch, rather than Ezekiel. Recent developments in pentateuchal criticism allow progress to be made where it was not previously possible. A careful reading of the Pentateuch demonstrates that the distinction between priests and Levites is articulated most clearly in the book of Numbers, which is now recognized to be one of the latest parts of the Pentateuch.[354] Other refer-

---

354 Achenbach, *Die Vollendung der Tora*.

ences to the distinction between Levites and priests earlier in the Pentateuch are rare (Exod 32:26 – 29; Lev 25:32 – 33), and a strong case can be made that they are all late interpolations. Without these, one can only be impressed by the fact that the Priestly source speaks only of priests, and makes no reference to Levites, whilst the book of Deuteronomy knows of Levites and Levitical priests. The distinction that the book of Numbers makes between Levites and priests gives the strong impression of being a *via media* between the two main textual corpora that constitute the Pentateuch.

The beginnings of the Levites as minor clergy are, therefore, to be found in the Pentateuch and its emergence as a single, authoritative *Torah*. As was the case with the elevation of the sons of Zadok, the origins of the Levites as minor clergy are textual. In the case of the Levites, an imperative to create a unified Torah required that the different presentations of the priesthood in P and D be harmonized. The result was a distinction between Levites and priests. The distinction did not reflect an extra-textual reality. In time, the extra-textual reality probably imitated the text that had become canonical *Torah*.

4 The Hebrew Bible and the Dead Sea Scrolls

Michael Fishbane described Ezekiel 44 as "an exegetical oracle".[355] As we have seen, Fishbane was correct beyond even what he envisaged. There is almost no part of Ezekiel 44 that does not draw upon another text from elsewhere in the Hebrew Bible: Genesis 17; Leviticus 10, 21 – 22; Numbers 15, 18; Deuteronomy 18; Isaiah 56; Ezekiel 14. The level of intertextuality is almost unparalleled in the Hebrew Bible. In my analysis I compared the exegetical harmonizations and developments with 4QRP[a] and the Temple Scroll. Although an iron curtain often separates scholarship on the Hebrew Bible and Qumran, such comparisons suggest that the boundary between the Hebrew Bible and the texts from Qumran is not so sharp.

The results of this study of Ezekiel 44 indicate that even the language of boundaries may be inappropriate. I have argued that the original oracle of Ezekiel 44 is a relative latecomer to the Hebrew Bible, and the first revision of the oracle, which introduces the sons of Zadok must be later still. As we have seen, the *Rule of the Community* originally lacked any reference to the sons of Zadok. One plausible way of interpreting that data – though not the only way – is that the first revision of Ezekiel's oracle had not yet taken place when the

---

355 Fishbane, *Biblical Interpretation*, 138.

Rule of the Community was composed. If this were the case, the composition of the latest parts of the prophetic corpus of the Hebrew Bible and the composition of some of the sectarian scrolls overlapped chronologically.

★ ★ ★

At the end of this study we are some distance from where we began with the fall of Jerusalem and the collapse of the kingdom of Judah. The chronological adjustment is not the only shift that we have had to make. We have also had to alter the way we think about the groups to which a text makes reference, the relationship between text and historical reality, the way in which texts of the Hebrew Bible relate to one another, and the relationship between the Bible and the Dead Sea Scrolls. Our examination of Ezekiel 44 has been no more than the examination of one chapter of the Hebrew Bible, but it has opened up vistas into larger debates that are continuing to re-shape the way we perceive the sacred text.

Bibliography

Achenbach, Reinhard. *Die Vollendung der Tora: Studien zur Redaktionsgeschichte des Numeribuches im Kontext von Hexateuch und Pentateuch*. BZABR 3. Wiesbaden: Harrassowitz, 2003.
—— "Verunreinigung durch die Berührung Toter: Zum Ursprung einer altisraelitischen Vorstellung". In *Tod und Jenseits im Alten Israel und in seiner Umwelt: Theologische, religionsgeschichtliche, archäologische und ikonographische Aspekte*, edited by Angelika Berlejung and Bernd Janowski, 347–69. FAT 64. Tübingen: Mohr Siebeck, 2009.
Albertz, Rainer. *Israel in Exile: The History and Literature of the Sixth Century B.C.E.* Studies in Biblical Literature 3. Atlanta: Society of Biblical Literature, 2003.
Alexander, Philip S. "The Redaction History of *Serekh Ha-Yaḥad*: A Proposal". *RevQ* 17 (1996): 437–56.
Allen, Leslie C. *Ezekiel 20–48*. WBC 29. Waco, TX: Word Books, 1990.
Ashley, Timothy R. *The Book of Numbers*. NICOT. Grand Rapids: Eerdmans, 1993.
Awabdy, Mark. "YHWH Exegetes Torah: How Ezekiel 44:7–9 Bars Foreigners from the Sanctuary". *JBL* 131 (2012): 685–703.
Bammel, Ernst. "Sadduzäer und Sadokiden". *ETL* 55 (1979): 107–15.
Barstad, Hans M. *The Myth of the Empty Land: A Study in the History and Archaeology of Judah during the "Exilic" Period*. SO Fascicle Supplement 28. Oslo: Scandinavian University Press, 1996.
Bartlett, J. R. "Zadok and His Successors at Jerusalem". *JTS* 19 (1968): 1–18.
Baumgarten, Albert I. "The Zadokite Priests at Qumran: A Reconsideration". *DSD* 4 (1997): 137–56.
Begg, Christopher T. "The Non-Mention of Ezekiel in the Deuteronomistic History, the Book of Jeremiah and the Chronistic History". In *Ezekiel and His Book: Textual and Literary Criticism and Their Interrelation*, edited by J. Lust, 340–43. BETL 74. Leuven: Peeters, 1986.
Berges, Ulrich. *Das Buch Jesaja: Komposition und Endgestalt*. HBS 16. Freiburg im Breisgau: Herder, 1998.
Berner, Christoph. *Die Exoduserzählung: Das literarische Werden einer Ursprungslegende Israels*. FAT 73. Tübingen: Mohr Siebeck, 2010.
Bertholet, Alfred. *Das Buch Hesekiel*. KHC 12. Freiburg im Breisgau: Mohr Siebeck, 1897.
—— *Hesekiel*. HAT I/13. Tübingen: Mohr Siebeck, 1936.
—— *Leviticus*. KHC 3. Tübingen: Mohr Siebeck, 1901.
Betts, Terry J. *Ezekiel the Priest: A Custodian of Tôrâ*. StBibLit 74. New York: Lang, 2005.
Beuken, Willem A. M. *Jesaja IIIA*. POuT. Nijkerk: Callenbach, 1989.
Blenkinsopp, Joseph. *A History of Prophecy in Israel*. 2nd ed. Philadelphia: Westminster, 1996.
—— *Isaiah 40–55: A New Translation with Introduction and Commentary*. AB 19A. New York: Doubleday, 2002.
—— "The Judaean Priesthood during the Neo-Babylonian and Achaemenid Periods: A Hypothetical Reconstruction". *CBQ* 60 (1998): 25–43.
Block, Daniel Isaac. *The Book of Ezekiel*. 2 vols. NICOT. Grand Rapids: Eerdmans, 1997.

Brooke, George J. *Exegesis at Qumran: 4QFlorilegium in Its Jewish Context*. JSOTSup 29.
　　Sheffield: JSOT Press, 1985.
—— "Ezekiel in Some Qumran and New Testament Texts". In *The Madrid Qumran Congress:
　　Proceedings of the International Congress on the Dead Sea Scrolls Madrid 18–21 March,
　　1991*, edited by Julio C. Trebolle Barrera and Luis Vegas Montaner, 1:317–37. STDJ 11.
　　Leiden: Brill, 1992.
Budd, Philip J. *Numbers*. WBC 5. Waco, TX: Word Books, 1984.
Carr, David M. *The Formation of the Hebrew Bible: A New Reconstruction*. Oxford: Oxford
　　University Press, 2011.
—— "Method in Determination of Direction of Dependence: An Empirical Test of Criteria
　　Applied to Exodus 34,11–26 and Its Parallels". In *Gottes Volk am Sinai: Untersuchungen
　　zu Ex 32–34 und Dtn 9–10*, edited by Matthias Köckert and Erhard Blum, 107–40.
　　Veröffentlichungen der Wissenschaftlichen Gesellschaft für Theologie 18. Gütersloh:
　　Gütersloher Verlagshaus, 2001.
—— *Writing on the Tablet of the Heart: Origins of Scripture and Literature*. Oxford: Oxford
　　University Press, 2005.
Charles, Robert Henry. *The Apocrypha and Pseudepigrapha of the Old Testament in English.
　　Vol 2: Pseudepigrapha*. 2 vols. Oxford: Clarendon, 1913.
Charlesworth, James H. *Rule of the Community and Related Documents*. The Dead Sea Scrolls
　　1. Louisville: Westminster John Knox, 1994.
Clements, Ronald Ernest. *Ezekiel*. Westminster Bible Companion. Louisville: Westminster John
　　Knox, 1996.
Collins, John Joseph. *Beyond the Qumran Community: The Sectarian Movement of the Dead
　　Sea Scrolls*. Grand Rapids: Eerdmans, 2010.
Collins, Matthew A. *The Use of Sobriquets in the Qumran Dead Sea Scrolls*. LSTS 67. London:
　　Bloomsbury T&T Clark, 2012.
Colson, Francis Henry. *Philo VII*. LCL 320. Cambridge, MA: Harvard University Press, 1958.
Cooke, G.A. *A Critical and Exegetical Commentary on the Book of Ezekiel*. ICC. Edinburgh: T&T
　　Clark, 1936.
Cook, Stephen L. "Innerbiblical Interpretation in Ezekiel 44 and the History of Israel's
　　Priesthood". *JBL* 114 (1995): 193–208.
Corley, Jeremy. "Seeds of Messianism in Hebrew Ben Sira and Greek Sirach". In *The
　　Septuagint and Messianism*, edited by Michael Anthony Knibb, 301–12. BETL 195.
　　Leuven: Peeters, 2006.
Cross, Frank Moore. *The Ancient Library of Qumrân and Modern Biblical Studies*. 1st ed.
　　Garden City, NY: Doubleday, 1958.
—— "The Development of the Jewish Scripts". In *The Bible and the Ancient Near East: Essays
　　in Honor of William Foxwell Albright*, edited by George Ernest Wright, 133–202. Garden
　　City, NY: Doubleday, 1961.
Dahmen, Ulrich. *Leviten und Priester im Deuteronomium: Literarkritik und
　　redaktionsgeschichtliche Studien*. BBB 110. Bodenheim: Philo, 1996.
Davies, Eryl W. *Numbers*. NCB Commentary. London: Marshall Pickering, 1995.
Davies, Philip R. *The Damascus Covenant*. JSOTSup 25. Sheffield: JSOT Press, 1983.
Di Lella, Alexander A. "Qumrân and the Geniza Fragments of Sirach". *CBQ* 24 (1962):
　　245–67.
—— *The Hebrew Text of Sirach: A Text-Critical and Historical Study*. Berlin: de Gruyter, 1966.

Dimant, Deborah. "The Apocalyptic Interpretation of Ezekiel at Qumran". In *Messiah and Christos: Studies in the Jewish Origins of Christianity. Presented to David Flusser on the Occasion of His Seventy-Fifth Birthday*, edited by Ithamar Gruenwald, Shaul Shaked, and Gedaliahu G. Strousma, 31–51. TSAJ 32. Tübingen: Mohr Siebeck, 1992.

—— "The Vocabulary of the Qumran Sectarian Texts". In *History, Ideology and Bible Interpretation in the Dead Sea Scrolls*, 57–100. FAT 90. Tübingen: Mohr Siebeck, 2014.

Donner, Herbert. "Jesaja lvi 1–7: ein Abrogationsfall innerhalb des Kanons – Implikationen und Konsequenzen". In *Congress Volume: Salamanca 1983*, edited by John A. Emerton, 81–95. VTSup 36. Leiden: Brill, 1985.

Driver, Godfrey R. "Ezekiel: Linguistic and Textual Problems". *Bib* 35 (1954): 145–59, 299–312.

Duguid, Iain M. *Ezekiel and the Leaders of Israel*. VTSup 56. Leiden: Brill, 1994.

—— "Putting Priests in Their Place: Ezekiel's Contribution to the History of the Old Testament Priesthood". In *Ezekiel's Hierarchical World: Wrestling with a Tiered Reality*, edited by Stephen L. Cook and Corrine L. Patton, 43–60. SBL Symposium Series 31. Leiden: Brill, 2004.

Duke, Rodney. "Punishment or Restoration? Another Look at the Levites of Ezekiel 44.6–16". *JSOT* 40 (1988): 61–81.

Ehrlich, A.B. *Randglossen zur Hebräischen Bibel: Textkritisches, sprachliches und sachliches. Zweiter Band: Leviticus, Numeri, Deuteronomium*. Leipzig: Hinrich, 1909.

Eichrodt, Walther. *Ezekiel: A Commentary*. OTL. Philadelphia: Westminster, 1970.

Elliger, Karl. *Leviticus*. HAT 1,4. Tübingen: Mohr Siebeck, 1966.

Engelken, Karen. "שׁרת Šrt". *TDOT* 15: 503–14.

Fabry, Heinz-Josef. "Priests at Qumran: A Reassessment". In *Dead Sea Scrolls: Texts and Context*, edited by Charlotte Hempel, 243–62. STDJ 90. Leiden: Brill, 2010.

—— "Zadokiden und Aaroniden in Qumran". In *Das Manna fällt auch heute noch: Beiträge zur Geschichte und Theologie des Alten, Ersten Testaments: Festschrift für Erich Zenger*, edited by Frank-Lothar Hossfeld and Ludger Schwienhorst-Schönberger, 201–17. Freiburg im Breisgau: Herder, 2004.

Fechter, Friedrich. "Priesthood in Exile according to the Book of Ezekiel". In *Ezekiel's Hierarchical World: Wrestling with a Tiered Reality*, edited by Stephen L. Cook and Corrine L. Patton, 27–42. SBL Symposium Series 31. Leiden: Brill, 2004.

Feldman, Louis H. "Prophets and Prophecy in Josephus". *JTS* 41 (1990): 386–422.

Fishbane, Michael A. *Biblical Interpretation in Ancient Israel*. Oxford: Clarendon, 1985.

Fuhs, Hans Ferdinand. *Ezechiel*. 2nd ed. 2 vols. NEchtB 22. Würzburg: Echter, 1986.

Galambusch, J. "The Northern Voyage of Psammeticus II and Its Implications for Ezekiel 44.7–9". In *The Priests in the Prophets: The Portrayal of Priests, Prophets and Other Religious Specialists in the Latter Prophets*, edited by Lester L. Grabbe and Alice Ogden Bellis, 65–78. JSOTSup 408. London: T&T Clark, 2004.

García Martínez, Florentino, and Eibert J. C. Tigchelaar, eds. *The Dead Sea Scrolls Study Edition*. 2 vols. Leiden: Brill, 2000.

Geiger, Abraham. *Judaism and Its History*. Vol. 1. 2 vols. New York: Thalmessinger & Cahn, 1866.

Gertz, Jan Christian. "Beobachtungen zu Komposition und Redaktion in Exodus 32–34". In *Gottes Volk am Sinai: Untersuchungen zu Ex 32–34 und Dtn 9–10*, edited by Matthias Köckert and Erhard Blum, 9–40. Veröffentlichungen der Wissenschaftlichen Gesellschaft für Theologie 18. Gütersloh: Gütersloher Verlagshaus, 2001.

—— *Tradition und Redaktion in der Exoduserzählung: Untersuchungen zur Endredaktion des Pentateuch*. FRLANT 186. Göttingen: Vandenhoeck & Ruprecht, 2000.

Gese, Hartmut. *Der Verfassungsentwurf des Ezechiel*. BHT 25. Tübingen: Mohr Siebeck, 1957.

Goerwitz, Richard L. "Long Hair or Short Hair in Ezekiel 44:20?". *JAOS* 123 (2003): 371–76.

—— "What Does the Priestly Source Mean by פרע את הראש?". *JQR* 86 (1996): 377–94.

Goodman, Martin. "The Place of the Sadducees in First-Century Judaism". In *Judaism in the Roman World: Collected Studies*, 123–36. Leiden: Brill, 2007.

Grabbe, Lester L., "Were the Pre-Maccabean High Priests 'Zadokites'?". In *Reading from Right to Left: Essays on the Hebrew Bible in Honour of David J. A. Clines*, edited by J. Cheryl Exum and H. G. M. Williamson, 205–215. JSOTSup 373. London: Sheffield Academic, 2003.

—— ed. *Leading Captivity Captive: "The Exile" as History and Ideology*. JSOTSup 278. Sheffield: Sheffield Academic, 1998.

Gray, George Buchanan. *Numbers*. ICC. Edinburgh: T&T Clark, 1903.

Greenberg, Moshe. "The Design and Themes of Ezekiel's Program of Restoration". *Int* 38 (1984): 181–208.

Grossman, Maxine L. *Reading for History in the Damascus Document*. STDJ 45. Leiden: Brill, 2002.

Grünwaldt, Klaus. *Das Heiligkeitsgesetz Leviticus 17–26: Ursprüngliche Gestalt, Tradition und Theologie*. BZAW 271. Berlin: de Gruyter, 1999.

Gunneweg, Antonius H. J. *Leviten und Priester: Hauptlinien der Traditionsbildung und Geschichte des israelitisch-jüdischen Kultpersonals*. FRLANT 89. Göttingen: Vandenhoeck & Ruprecht, 1965.

Hals, Ronald M. *Ezekiel*. FOTL 19. Grand Rapids: Eerdmans, 1989.

Hanson, Paul D. *Isaiah 40–66*. Interpretation. Louisville: John Knox, 1995.

—— *The Dawn of Apocalyptic*. Philadelphia: Fortress, 1975.

Haran, Menahem. "Ezekiel, P, and the Priestly School". *VT* 58 (2008): 211–18.

—— *Temples and Temple-Service in Ancient Israel*. Winona Lake, IN: Eisenbrauns, 1985.

—— "The Gibeonites, the Nethinim and the Sons of Solomon's Servants". *VT* 11 (1961): 159–69.

—— "The Law-Code of Ezekiel XL–XLVIII and Its Relation to the Priestly School". *HUCA* 50 (1979): 45–71.

Hartley, John E. *Leviticus*. WBC 4. Dallas: Word Books, 1992.

Hempel, Charlotte. "Do the Scrolls Suggest Rivalry Between the Sons of Aaron and the Sons of Zadok and If So Was It Mutual?". *RevQ* 24 (2009): 135–53.

—— "The Earthly Essene Nucleus of 1QSa". *DSD* 3 (1996): 253–69.

—— "The Sons of Aaron in the Dead Sea Scrolls". In *Flores Florentino: Dead Sea Scrolls and Other Early Jewish Studies in Honour of Florentino García Martínez*, edited by T. Hilhorst, Emile Puech, and Eibert J. C. Tigchelaar, 207–24. JSJSup 122. Leiden: Brill, 2007.

—— "אַהֲרוֹן 'aharôn'". *ThWQ* 1: 76–81.

Herrmann, Johannes. *Ezechielstudien*. BWAT 2. Leipzig: Hinrichs, 1908.

Hultgren, Stephen. *From the Damascus Covenant to the Covenant of the Community: Literary, Historical, and Theological Studies in the Dead Sea Scrolls*. STDJ 66. Leiden: Brill, 2007.

Hunt, Alice. *Missing Priests: The Zadokites in Tradition and History*. LHBOTS 452. New York: T&T Clark, 2006.

Hurvitz, Avi. *A Linguistic Study of the Relationship between the Priestly Source and the Book of Ezekiel: A New Approach to an Old Problem*. CahRB 20. Paris: Gabalda, 1982.

Japhet, Sara. *I & II Chronicles: A Commentary*. OTL. Louisville: Westminster John Knox, 1993.
Jenni, Ernst. *Die hebräischen Präpositionen. Band 1: Die Präposition Beth*. Stuttgart: Kohlhammer, 1992.
—— *Die hebräischen Präpositionen. Band 3: Die Präposition Lamed*. Stuttgart: Kohlhammer, 2000.
Jenson, Philip Peter. *Graded Holiness: A Key to the Priestly Conception of the World*. JSOTSup 106. Sheffield: JSOT Press, 1992.
Joyce, Paul M. "King and Messiah in Ezekiel". In *King and Messiah in Israel and the Ancient Near East: Proceedings of the Oxford Old Testament Seminar*, edited by John Day, 323–37. JSOTSup 270. Sheffield: Sheffield Academic, 1998.
Kaufman, S. "The Temple Scroll and Higher Criticism". *HUCA* 53 (1982): 29–43.
Kister, Menahem. "Biblical Phrases and Hidden Biblical Interpretations and *Pesharim*". In *The Dead Sea Scrolls: Forty Years of Research*, edited by Deborah Dimant and Uriel Rappaport, 27–39. STDJ 10. Leiden: Brill, 1992.
Klawans, Jonathan. *Josephus and the Theologies of Ancient Judaism*. Oxford: Oxford University Press, 2012.
—— "Sadducees, Zadokites, and the Wisdom of Ben Sira". In *Israel's God and Rebecca's Children: Christology and Community in Early Judaism and Christianity*, edited by David B. Capes et al. 261–76. Waco, TX: Baylor University Press, 2007.
Klein, Anja. "Prophecy Continued: Reflections on Innerbiblical Exegesis in the Book of Ezekiel". *VT* 60 (2010): 571–82.
—— *Schriftauslegung im Ezechielbuch: Redaktionsgeschichtliche Untersuchungen zu Ez 34–39*. BZAW 391. Berlin: de Gruyter, 2008.
Klein, Ralph W. *1 Chronicles: A Commentary*. Herm. Minneapolis: Fortress, 2006.
Knohl, Israel. *The Sanctuary of Silence: The Priestly Torah and the Holiness School*. Minneapolis: Fortress, 1995.
Knoppers, Gary N. *I Chronicles 1–9: A New Translation with Introduction and Commentary*. AB 12. New York: Doubleday, 2003.
—— *I Chronicles 10–29: A New Translation with Introduction and Commentary*. AB 12A. New York: Doubleday, 2004.
Koenen, Klaus. *Ethik und Eschatologie im Tritojesajabuch*. WMANT 62. Neukirchen-Vluyn: Neukirchener Verlag, 1990.
Konkel, Michael Dominik. *Architektonik des Heiligen: Studien zur Zweiten Tempelvision Ezechiels (Ez 40–48)*. BBB 129. Berlin: Philo, 2001.
Koole, Jan Leunis. *Isaiah III.1: Isaiah 40–48*. HCOT. Kampen: Kok Pharos, 1997.
Kratz, Reinhard Gregor. "Innerbiblische Exegese und Redaktionsgeschichte im Lichte empirischer Evidenz". In *Das Judentum im Zeitalter des Zweiten Tempels*, 126–156. FAT 42. Tübingen: Mohr Siebeck, 2004.
Kugler, Robert A. "A Note on 1QS 9:14: The Sons of Righteousness or the Sons of Zadok?". *DSD* 3 (1996): 315–20.
—— "Priesthood at Qumran". In *The Dead Sea Scrolls after Fifty Years: A Comprehensive Assessment*, edited by Peter W. Flint and James C. VanderKam, 2:93–116. Leiden: Brill, 1998.
—— "Priests". *EDSS* 2: 688–93.
Labahn, Antje. *Levitischer Herrschaftsanspruch zwischen Ausübung und Konstruktion: Studien zum multi-funktionalen Levitenbild der Chronik und seiner Identitätsbildung in der Zeit des Zweiten Tempels*. WMANT 131. Neukirchen-Vluyn: Neukirchener Verlag, 2012.

Le Moyne, J. *Les Sadducéens*. Paris: Études Bibliques, 1972.

Leonard, Jeffery M. "Identifying Inner-Biblical Allusions: Psalm 78 as a Test Case". *JBL* 127 (2008): 241–65.

Levenson, Jon Douglas. *Theology of the Program of Restoration of Ezekiel 40–48*. HSM 10. Missoula, MT: Scholars Press, 1976.

Levine, Baruch A. "Later Sources on the Netinim". In *Orient and Occident: Cyrus Gordon Festschrift*, edited by Harry A. Hoffner, 101–7. AOAT 22. Neukirchen-Vluyn: Neukirchener Verlag, 1973.

—— *Numbers: A New Translation with Introduction and Commentary*. 2 vols. AB 4. New York: Doubleday, 1993.

—— "The Netînîm". *JBL* 82 (1963): 207–12.

Levin, M. Z. "חללה". *Beth Mikra* 29 (1984): 180–81.

Levinson, Bernard M. *Legal Revision and Religious Renewal in Ancient Israel*. Cambridge: Cambridge University Press, 2008.

Levitt Kohn, Risa. *A New Heart and a New Soul: Ezekiel, the Exile and the Torah*. JSOTSup 358. London: Sheffield Academic, 2002.

Liss, Hannah. "'Describe the Temple to the House of Israel': Preliminary Remarks on the Temple Vision in the Book of Ezekiel and Question of Fictionality in Priestly Literatures". In *Utopia and Dystopia in Prophetic Literature*, edited by Ehud Ben Zvi, 122–43. Publications of the Finnish Exegetical Society 92. Helsinki: Finnish Exegetical Society, 2006.

Lockshin, Martin I. *Rashbam's Commentary on Leviticus and Numbers: An Annotated Translation*. BJS 330. Providence, RI: Brown Judaic Studies, 2001.

Lucas, Alec J. "Scripture Citations as an Internal Redactional Control: 1QS 5:1–20a and Its 4Q Parallels". *DSD* 17 (2010): 30–52.

Lust, Johan. "For I Lift Up My Hand to Heaven and Swear: Deut 32:40". In *Studies in Deuteronomy: In Honour of C. J. Labuschagne on the Occasion of His 65th Birthday*, edited by F. García Martínez et al., 155–64. VTSup 53. Leiden: Brill, 1994

Lyons, Michael A. *From Law to Prophecy: Ezekiel's Use of the Holiness Code*. LHBOTS 507. New York: T&T Clark, 2009.

—— "Transformation of Law: Ezekiel's Use of the Holiness Code (Leviticus 17–26)". In *Transforming Visions: Transformations of Text, Tradition, and Theology in Ezekiel*, edited by William A. Tooman and Michael A. Lyons, 1–32. Princeton Theological Monograph Series 127. Eugene, OR: Pickwick, 2010.

MacDonald, Nathan. "The Hermeneutics and Genesis of the Red Cow Ritual". *HTR* 105 (2012): 351–71.

Mason, Steve. *Flavius Josephus: Translation and Commentary. Vol 1b: Judean War 2*. Leiden: Brill, 2008.

McConville, J. Gordon. "Priests and Levites in Ezekiel: A Crux in the Interpretation of Israel's History". *TynBul* 34 (1983): 3–31.

McCready, Wayne O. "Sadducees and Ancient Sectarianism". *RelStTh* 12 (1992): 79–97.

Metso, Sarianna. *The Textual Development of the Qumran Community Rule*. STDJ 21. Leiden: Brill, 1997.

Metzenthin, Christian. *Jesaja-Auslegung in Qumran*. ATANT 98. Zurich: Theologischer Verlag, 2010.

Mies, Françoise. "Le Psaume de Ben Sira 51,12a–o Hébreu: L'Hymne aux Noms divins. Deuxième partie". *RB* 116 (2009): 481–504.

—— "Le Psaume de Ben Sira 51,12a–o Hébreu: L'Hymne aux Noms divins. Première partie". *RB* 116 (2009): 336–67.

Milgrom, Jacob. *Ezekiel's Hope: A Commentary on Ezekiel 38–48*. Eugene, OR: Wipf & Stock, 2012.

—— "Hattĕnûpâ". In *Studies in Cultic Theology and Terminology*, 139–58. SJLA 36. Leiden: Brill, 1983.

—— *Leviticus 1–16: A New Translation with Introduction and Commentary*. AB 3. New York: Doubleday, 1991.

—— *Leviticus 17–22: A New Translation with Introduction and Commentary*. AB 3A. New York: Doubleday, 2000.

—— *Numbers* במדבר: *The Traditional Hebrew Text with the New JPS Translation*. The JPS Torah Commentary. Philadelphia: Jewish Publication Society of America, 1990.

—— *Studies in Levitical Terminology: I The Encroacher and the Levite. The Term 'Aboda*. UCPNES 14. Berkeley: University of California Press, 1970.

Milik, J. T. *Ten Years of Discovery in the Wilderness of Judaea*. SBT 26. London: SCM, 1959.

Mulder, M. J. "Die Partikel יַעַן". In *Syntax and Meaning: Studies in Hebrew Syntax and Biblical Exegesis*, edited by C. J. Labuschagne, C. Van Leeuwen, M. J. Mulder, and H. A. Brongers, 49–83. OTS 18. Leiden: Brill, 1973.

Newman, Hillel. *Proximity to Power and Jewish Sectarian Groups of the Ancient Period: A Review of Lifestyle, Values, and Halakhah in the Pharisees, Sadducees, Essenes, and Qumran*. BRLJ 25. Leiden: Brill, 2006.

Nicholson, Ernest. "Once Again Josiah and the Priests of the High Places (II Reg 23,8a.9)". *ZAW* 124 (2012): 356–68.

Niditch, Susan. "Ezekiel 40–48 in a Visionary Context". *CBQ* 48 (1986): 208–24.

Nihan, Christophe. *From Priestly Torah to Pentateuch: A Study in the Composition of the Book of Leviticus*. FAT II/25. Tübingen: Mohr Siebeck, 2007.

North, Robert Grady. "Qumran 'Sadducees'". *CBQ* 17 (1955): 164–88.

Noth, Martin. *Das Vierte Buch Mose: Numeri*. 4th ed. ATD 7. Göttingen: Vandenhoeck & Ruprecht, 1982.

Nurmela, Risto. *The Levites: Their Emergence as a Second-Class Priesthood*. SFSJHJ 193. Atlanta: Scholars Press, 1998.

O'Brien, Julia M. *Priest and Levite in Malachi*. SBLDS 121. Atlanta: Scholars Press, 1990.

Odell, Margaret S. *Ezekiel*. SHBC 16. Macon, GA: Smyth & Helwys, 2005.

O'Hare, Daniel M. *"Have You Seen, Son of Man?": A Study of the Translation and Vorlage of LXX Ezekiel 40–48*. Atlanta: Society of Biblical Literature, 2010.

Olyan, Saul M. "Zadok's Origins and the Tribal Politics of David". *JBL* 101 (1982): 177–93.

—— "Ben Sira's Relationship to the Priesthood". *HTR* 80 (1987): 261–86.

—— *Rites and Rank: Hierarchy in Biblical Representations of Cult*. Princeton: Princeton University Press, 2000.

Oswalt, John. *Isaiah 40–66*. NICOT. Grand Rapids: Eerdmans, 2009.

Paganini, Simone. *"Nicht darfst du zu diesen Wörtern etwas hinzufügen": Die Rezeption des Deuteronomiums in der Tempelrolle. Sprache, Autoren und Hermeneutik*. BZABR 11. Wiesbaden: Harrasowitz, 2009.

Pfann, Stephen J. "Cryptic Texts". In *Qumran Cave 4. XXVI Cryptic Texts and Miscellanea, Part I*, by Stephen J. Pfann, Philip S. Alexander, Magen Broshi, and Esther G. Chazon, 515–701. DJD 36. Oxford: Clarendon, 2000.

Renz, Thomas. *The Rhetorical Function of the Book of Ezekiel*. VTSup 76. Leiden: Brill, 1999.

Riesener, Ingrid. *Der Stamm עבד im Alten Testament: Eine Wortuntersuchung unter Berücksichtigung neuerer sprachwissenschaftlicher Methoden.* BZAW 149. Berlin: de Gruyter, 1979.

Rooke, Deborah W. *Zadok's Heirs: The Role and Development of the High Priesthood in Ancient Israel.* Oxford: Oxford University Press, 2000.

Rooker, Mark F. *Biblical Hebrew in Transition: The Language of the Book of Ezekiel.* JSOTSup 90. Sheffield: JSOT Press, 1990.

Rudnig, Thilo Alexander. *Heilig und Profan: Redaktionskritische Studien zu Ez 40–48.* BZAW 287. Berlin: de Gruyter, 2000.

Rüterswörden, Udo. *Von der politischen Gemeinschaft zur Gemeinde: Studien zu Dt 16,18–18,22.* BBB 65. Frankfurt-am-Main: Athenäum, 1987.

Ruwe, Andreas. *"Heiligkeitsgesetz" und "Priesterschrift": Literaturgeschichtliche und Rechtssystematische Untersuchungen zu Leviticus 17,1–26,2.* FAT 26. Tübingen: Mohr Siebeck, 1999.

Saldarini, Anthony J. *Pharisees, Scribes and Sadducees in Palestinian Society.* Edinburgh: T&T Clark, 1988.

Samuel, Harald. *Von Priestern zum Patriarchen: Levi und die Leviten im Alten Testament.* BZAW 448. Berlin: de Gruyter, 2014.

Sanders, E. P. *Judaism: Practice and Belief 63BCE – 66CE.* London: SCM, 1992.

Schaper, Joachim. *Priester und Leviten im achämenidischen Juda: Studien zur Kult- und Sozialgeschichte Israels in persischer Zeit.* FAT 31. Tübingen: Mohr Siebeck, 2000.

—— "Rereading the Law: Inner-Biblical Exegesis of Divine Oracles in Ezekiel 44 and Isaiah 56". In *Recht und Ethik im Alten Testament: Beiträge des Symposiums "Das Alte Testament und die Kultur der Moderne" anlässlich des 100. Geburtstag Gerhard von Rads (1901–1971), Heidelberg, 18–21 Oktober 2001*, edited by Bernard M. Levinson and Eckart Otto, 125–44. Altes Testament und Moderne 13. Münster: Lit, 2004.

Schechter, Solomon. *Documents of Jewish Sectaries.* Cambridge: Cambridge University Press, 1910.

Schiffman, Lawrence H. *Reclaiming the Dead Sea Scrolls.* ABRL. New York: Doubleday, 1995.

Schmid, Konrad. "Innerbiblische Schriftauslegung: Aspekte der Forschungsgeschichte". In *Schriftauslegung in der Schrift: Festschrift für Odil Hannes Steck zu seinem 65. Geburtstag*, edited by Konrad Schmid, Reinhard Gregor Kratz, and Thomas Krüger, 1–22. BZAW 300. Berlin: de Gruyter, 2000.

Schmitt, Hans-Christoph. "Die Erzählung vom goldenen Kalb Ex. 32* und das Deuteronomistische Geschichtswerk". In *Rethinking the Foundations: Historiography in the Ancient World and in the Bible. Essays in Honour of John Van Seters*, edited by Steven L McKenzie and Thomas C. Römer, 235–50. BZAW 294. Berlin: de Gruyter, 2000.

Schniedewind, William M. "King and Priest in the Book of Chronicles and the Duality of Qumran Messianism". *JJS* 94 (1994): 71–78.

—— *The Word of God in Transition: From Prophet to Exegete in the Second Temple Period.* JSOTSup 197. Sheffield: Sheffield Academic, 1995.

Schofield, Alison. *From Qumran to the Yaḥad: A New Paradigm of Textual Development for the Community Rule.* STDJ 77. Leiden: Brill, 2009.

Schremer, Adiel. "The Name of the Boethusians: A Reconsideration of Suggested Explanations and Another One". *JJS* 48 (1997): 290–99.

Schwartz, Baruch J. "A Priest Out of Place: Reconsidering Ezekiel's Role in the History of the Israelite Priesthood". In *Ezekiel's Hierarchical World: Wrestling with a Tiered Reality,* edited by Stephen L. Cook and Corrine L. Patton, 61–72. SBL Symposium Series 31. Leiden: Brill, 2004.

—— "The Bearing of Sin in Priestly Literature". In *Pomegranates and Golden Bells: Studies in Biblical, Jewish, and Near Eastern Ritual, Law, and Literature in Honor of Jacob Milgrom*, edited by David Pearson Wright, David Noel Freedman, and Avi Hurvitz, 3–21. Winona Lake, IN: Eisenbrauns, 1995.

Schweitzer, Steven. *Reading Utopia in Chronicles.* LHBOTS 442. London: Bloomsbury T&T Clark International, 2009.

Seebass, Horst. *Numeri 10,11–22,1.* BKAT IV/2. Neukirchen-Vluyn: Neukirchener Verlag, 2003.

Segal, Michael. "Biblical Exegesis in 4Q158: Techniques and Genre". *Text* 19 (1998): 45–62.

Skehan, Patrick W., and Alexander A. Di Lella. *The Wisdom of Ben Sira: A New Translation with Notes.* AB 39. Garden City, NY: Doubleday, 1987.

Skinner, John. *The Book of Ezekiel.* The Expositor's Bible. London: Hodder & Stoughton, 1909.

Smith, Paul A. *Rhetoric and Redaction in Trito-Isaiah.* VTSup 62. Leiden: Brill, 1995.

Sommer, Benjamin D. *A Prophet Reads Scripture: Allusion in Isaiah 40–66.* Stanford: Stanford University Press, 1998.

Sparks, James T. *The Chronicler's Genealogies: Towards an Understanding of 1 Chronicles 1–9.* AcBib 28. Atlanta: Society of Biblical Literature, 2008.

Stackert, Jeffrey. *Rewriting the Torah: Literary Revision in Deuteronomy and the Holiness Legislation.* FAT 52. Tübingen: Mohr Siebeck, 2007.

Steck, Odil Hannes. *Studien zu Tritojesaja.* BZAW 203. Berlin: de Gruyter, 1991.

Stemberger, Günter. "The Sadducees: Their History and Doctrines". In *Cambridge History of Judaism Vol. 3, The Early Roman Period*, 428–43. Cambridge: Cambridge University Press, 1999.

Steuernagel, Carl. *Deuteronomium.* HAT 3/1. Göttingen: Vandenhoeck & Ruprecht, 1900.

Stevenson, Kalinda Rose. *The Vision of Transformation: The Territorial Rhetoric of Ezekiel 40–48.* SBLDS 154. Atlanta: Scholars Press, 1996.

Strine, Casey A. *Sworn Enemies: The Divine Oath, the Book of Ezekiel, and the Polemics of Exile.* BZAW 436. Berlin: de Gruyter, 2013.

Stromberg, Jacob. *Isaiah after Exile: The Author of Third Isaiah as Reader and Redactor of the Book.* Oxford Theological Monographs. Oxford: Oxford University Press, 2011.

—— "Observations on Inner-Scriptural Scribal Expansion in MT Ezekiel". *VT* 58 (2008): 68–86.

Swanson, Dwight D. *The Temple Scroll and the Bible: The Methodology of 11QT.* STDJ 14. Leiden: Brill, 1995.

Thackery, H. St J. *Josephus I.* LCL 186. Cambridge, MA: Harvard University Press, 1976.

Tiemeyer, Lena-Sofia. *Priestly Rites and Prophetic Rage.* FAT II/19. Tübingen: Mohr Siebeck, 2006.

Tooman, William A. *Gog of Magog: Reuse of Scripture and Compositional Technique in Ezekiel 38–39.* FAT II/52. Tübingen: Mohr Siebeck, 2011.

Toorn, Karel van der. *Scribal Culture and the Making of the Hebrew Bible.* Cambridge, MA: Harvard University Press, 2007.

Tuell, Steven Shawn. *The Law of the Temple in Ezekiel 40–48.* HSM 49. Atlanta: Scholars Press, 1992.

—— "The Priesthood of the 'Foreigner': Evidence of Competing Politics in Ezekiel 44:1–14 and Isaiah 56:1–8". In *Constituting the Community: Studies on the Polity of Ancient*

Israel, edited by John T. Strong and Steven Shawn Tuell, 183–204. Winona Lake, IN: Eisenbrauns, 2005.

Ulrich, Eugene Charles. "*4QSam^c*: A Fragmentary Manuscript of 2 Samuel 14–15 from the Scribe of the *Serek Hay-Yahad* (1QS)". *BASOR* 235 (1979): 1–25.

VanderKam, James C. *From Joshua to Caiaphas: High Priests after the Exile*. Minneapolis: Fortress, 2004.

Van Seters, John. *A Law Book for the Diaspora: Revision in the Study of the Covenant Code*. Oxford: Oxford University Press, 2003.

—— *The Edited Bible: The Curious History of the "Editor" in Biblical Criticism*. Winona Lake, IN: Eisenbrauns, 2006.

Van Winkle, D. W. "An Inclusive Authoritative Text in Exclusive Communities". In *Writing and Reading the Scroll of Isaiah: Studies of an Interpretive Tradition*, edited by Craig C. Broyles and Craig A. Evans. VTSup 70. Leiden: Brill, 1997.

—— "Isaiah LVI 1–8". *SBLSP* 36 (1997): 234–49.

Vawter, Bruce, and Leslie J. Hoppe. *A New Heart: A Commentary on the Book of Ezekiel*. ITC. Grand Rapids: Eerdmans, 1991.

Vermes, Geza. *Les manuscrits du Désert du Juda*. 2nd ed. Paris: Desclée, 1954.

—— "The Leadership of the Qumran Community: Sons of Zadok-Priests-Congregation". In *Geschichte-Tradition-Reflexion: Festschrift für Martin Hengel zum 70. Geburtstag. Vol. 1, Judentum*, 375–84. Tübingen: Mohr Siebeck, 1996.

Wachholder, Ben Zion. *The New Damascus Document: The Midrash on the Eschatological Torah of the Dead Sea Scrolls: Reconstruction, Translation and Commentary*. STDJ 56. Leiden: Brill, 2007.

Watts, James W. *Leviticus 1–10*. HCOT. Leuven: Peeters, 2013.

Watts, John D. W. *Isaiah 34–66*. WBC 25. Waco, TX: Word Books, 1987.

Weinberg, Joel. "Netînîm und 'Söhne der Sklaven Salomos' im 6.–4. Hj. v. u. Z." *ZAW* 87 (1975): 355–71.

Wellhausen, Julius. *Prolegomena to the History of Israel with a Reprint of the Article Israel from the "Encyclopaedia Britannica"*. Translated by John Sutherland Black and Allan Menzies. Edinburgh: Black, 1885.

Wernberg-Møller, Preben. "צדק, צדיק and צדוק in the Zadokite Fragments (CDC), The Manual of Discipline (DSD) and the Habakkuk-Commentary (DSH)". *VT* 3 (1953): 310–15.

Westermann, Claus. "שרת Šrt". *TLOT* 3: 1405–07.

Wevers, John William. *Ezekiel*. NCB Commentary. Grand Rapids: Eerdmans, 1982.

Whybray, Roger Norman. *Isaiah 40–66*. NCB Commentary. Grand Rapids: Eerdmans, 1975.

Williamson, Hugh G.M. *Ezra, Nehemiah*. WBC 16. Waco, TX: Word Books, 1985.

—— "The Vindication of Redaction Criticism". In *Biblical Interpretation and Method: Essays in Honour of John Barton*, edited by Katherine J. Dell and Paul M. Joyce, 26–36. Oxford: Oxford University Press, 2013.

—— "The Origins of the Twenty-Four Priestly Courses: A Study of 1 Chronicles XXIII–XXVII". In *Studies in the Historical Books of the Old Testament*, edited by John A. Emerton, 251–68. VTSup 30. Leiden: Brill, 1979.

Woods, Julie Irene. *Jeremiah 48 as Christian Scripture*. Princeton Theological Monograph Series 149. Eugene, OR: Pickwick, 2011.

Zimmerli, Walther. *Ezechiel*. 2 vols. BKAT XIII. Neukirchen-Vluyn: Neukirchener Verlag, 1969.

Zipor, Moshe A. "Restrictions on Marriage for Priests (Lev 21:7, 13–14)". *Bib* 68 (1987): 259–67.

Index of Ancient Sources

Hebrew Bible

Apocrypha

New Testament

Qumran and Related Texts

Index of Authors

Index of Subjects